Testimonials

"Excellent for anyone working with youth—I run a youth and family center, and I teach anger management to children, teens, and adults. I am always looking for additional tools to use to share with others. This book is an excellent resource and can be helpful to anyone who reads this. Even if you want help with your own anger. But really understanding adolescents today is key, and this book gives you a clear insight into that. I recommend this book to all! Thanks, Dave, for all you do!"

—**Dr. Carol Carter**, CEO/Cofounder
Sunshine Alternative Education and Prevention Center

"This book illuminates the path—*Peace: The Other Side of Anger* illuminates the path for helping teens cope with frustration and anger. Building upon authentic 'I'm listening to you' communication, Dave Wolffe shows the reader how to encourage young people to WANT to manage their anger; then he shows precisely how to accomplish it. Five stars, Dave!"

—**Dr. James Sutton**, Psychologist and Host,
The Changing Behavior Network

"Dave Wolffe's work with educators to help them understand students' emotions and to learn/practice evidence-based strategies to deal appropriately with de-escalation techniques has evolved to bring us new information for effective violence prevention. Dave's many years as a school counselor and his more recent 'second' career as creator/consultant for his Anger Management Power Program (AMP) meld to bring art and science together with a difficult and sensitive topic: anger. As a guest speaker at our student teaching seminar each semester for many years, he has worked tirelessly to provide practical, updated, and well-researched strategies to our teacher-education graduates at Dominican University, New York (DUNY). His interactive style, humor, and ability to connect with his audience are well-documented, and the inclusion of practical, easy-to-use suggestions for handling conflict are always appreciated by his audiences. We are looking forward to using more powerful and effective strategies presented with his new additions on gun violence, social media influences on behavior, and the impact of the COVID-19 pandemic with his second edition of *Peace: The Other Side of Anger*!"

—**Mike Kelly**, PhD, Director,
Graduate Programs in Education Adolescence
and Special Education Certification Officer,
TPA Coordinator, DASA Trainer Dominican University

Second Edition

PEACE

The Other Side of

ANGER

How to Help Teens Manage Anger

Second Edition

PEACE

The Other Side of

ANGER

How to Help Teens Manage Anger

DAVE WOLFFE

Halo
PUBLISHING
INTERNATIONAL

Halo
PUBLISHING
INTERNATIONAL

Halo Publishing International
7550 W IH-10 #800, PMB 2069
San Antonio, TX 78229

Second Edition, December 2025
ISBN: 978-1-63765-827-7
Library of Congress Control Number: 2025916177

In loving memory of my parents, Morris and Yvette Wolffe;
Frieda Forman, my biological mother; my grandparents;
my brother, Fred; my late wife, Janet; my cousins Jeff, Susie, Dena,
Hal, and Arlene; my niece, Sarah; and all family members
and friends who so greatly contributed to my life.

Foreword

A couple of years ago, I received an email from a gentleman named Dave Wolffe who was interested in some of the things I had written related to anger management. Dave and I struck up a "cyber friendship" and began corresponding about our work. At some point, he mentioned that he was working on a book and wondered if I would be willing to take a look at it. I said, "Of course," and assumed I'd never actually receive the manuscript because people often fail to realize the amount of time and energy it takes to actually write a book. It's easy to talk about—hard to do! Well, Dave Wolffe is a man of his word, and the proof lies in the fact that you are, at this very moment, reading his book.

In *Peace: The Other Side of Anger*, Dave Wolffe provides a very engaging book that is replete with common-sense approaches to helping adolescents manage their anger. Dave's experience as a clinician shines through as he includes many practical tips from years of being "in the trenches" with students. These are not just a collection of ideas he has read in a book. These are practices that Dave has fine-tuned to be used with adolescents.

The book is also filled with interactive sections to help the reader connect to the concepts being explained.

My favorite part of the book was the detailed description of sixty-three [*sic*] techniques to help adolescents manage their anger. Several scenarios require the reader to apply the ideas that follow the explanation of the techniques. Mr. Wolffe understands that people have to practice what they've learned if they hope to ingrain the ideas into their beliefs and behaviors. As a clinician, Dave knows that simply reading the ideas will not get the job done.

This book is far more than just a collection of techniques to be used with angry adolescents. There is [*sic*] a depth and complexity in this work that is often lacking in similar books. Dave gets to the heart of the matter by spending a considerable amount of time discussing relational and developmental issues that are often at the core of anger management problems. Mr. Wolffe recognizes that parents and counselors, social workers, and youth workers have to understand teenagers to help them. There are no shortcuts.

After reading this book, I am confident that you will have a deeper understanding of the issues that confront adolescents on a daily basis. *Peace: The Other Side of Anger* is a well-constructed manual on anger management and adolescent development. Read it and enjoy!

Jerry Wilde, PhD
Author of *Hot Stuff to Help Kids Chill Out:
The Anger Management Book*

Contents

Introduction

E motional reactions occur to different degrees in every setting and relationship. Assisting youngsters in understanding their anger and learning to express it without hurting themselves or others are the goals of *Peace: The Other Side of Anger*. This second edition takes into account the impact of gun violence, social media, and the 2020 pandemic on the lives of teenagers. When the first edition of this book was written, these concerns and influences either did not exist or did not have the impact they now have. The revisions in this version do not alter the original description of the Anger Management Power Program (AMP) or its techniques for teens. They serve as the foundation of both books.

Important to any resource is making it reader friendly by:

- Knowing who may use it

- Looking at factors such as time

- Realizing its possible use as a group experience

- Understanding how the material may be utilized

Any teacher, parent, guardian, family member, counselor, social worker, or agency worker interacting with adolescents knows that three questions immediately come to mind when handling difficult or reactive behavior in adolescents:

Why? What is causing this behavior? Both *obvious* and *obscure* causes are described throughout this book. You may not have an inkling about what goes on in a young person's life. If this is the case, consulting counselors, social workers, staff members, peers, or those working and living in the teen's neighborhood may furnish this information.

How? The reasons for their behavior manifest themselves in different ways—here again, some are obvious; others, less apparent. The chapter on the effects of anger—physical, emotional, and psychological—reveals how it manifests itself or influences a youngster's behavior.

What should you do with this information? Here's where the list of various anger managers comes into play. The "Anger Management Techniques" chapter begins with an inventory of these methods and then provides detailed explanations, precautions, examples, and approaches to help students *de-escalate* their anger and *express* it in *positive* ways. Also, in "Information Boosters" toward the end of the book, you'll find the anger scale and quick tips for keeping peace with teens, along with other helpful tools.

Approaches described in this book rely heavily on my experience with the Anger Management Power Program (AMP). It is a method that adults can utilize in small groups, in classrooms, or on a one-on-one basis with an individual youngster. As a high school counselor, I found analyzing the causes and effects of anger and other strong emotional reactions, then utilizing and gauging the effectiveness of anger managers, extremely beneficial in providing a framework for understanding anger in young people.

More about Anger and Teens

Anger is a feeling, as are love, hate, boredom, excitement, and pride. It is just as important to know how adolescents view this emotion as it is to stress *there is nothing wrong with feeling angry!* It may be a simmering emotion or a hair-trigger response; regardless, we must address how to deal with strong emotional reactions, particularly anger that can spiral out of control and lead to dire consequences like violence and even death. To that end, we'll be discussing ways to help teens both understand their reactions and minimize their negative responses. We'll also be addressing:

- What makes young people so angry
- Why teens explode for no apparent reason
- How to tell when someone is getting angry
- What situations provoke this feeling
- How to defuse the situation before someone "loses it"
- What techniques help adolescents better manage anger
- What methods are effective with teens

Throughout this book, typical adolescent behavior will be described. The shrugging of shoulders, the "Are you crazy?" look, and the often-uttered "I don't know" are examples of how young people frequently respond to adult questions. Their overall attitude toward grown-ups involves not wanting us to know what's going on with them—from their perspective, it's their own private world, we don't have any idea what their world is like, and what we have to say is dumb.

These feelings are common roadblocks to our work with them. But they *are* listening, even if they don't seem to be.

A teen growing up in today's world certainly faces many different challenges—including the effects of the COVID-19 pandemic, the gun-violence epidemic, and the increasingly negative influence of social media—than we ourselves may have encountered in this stage of life. You may not immediately understand their perception of these stressors since you haven't personally experienced them. However, often the behavior of teens is, in effect, a reaction to what they perceive as criticism or an attempt to control them. By communicating your observations in a loud, accusatory tone and expressing a negative view, you may find their anger escalating and becoming more intense. These specific challenges and more will be discussed throughout this book.

If you take a calm and objective approach, however, and show a young person you are really listening to their views, without judgments about their behavior, you increase the chances of having a more productive discussion and forging a closer bond based on trust and respect. In any event, *Peace: The Other Side of Anger* will furnish alternative ideas and approaches for successfully and peacefully dealing with teen anger.

Why I Wrote This Book

What makes me an expert in writing about anger in teens? I was an educator with the New York City Department of Education for over thirty years—a teacher in grades one through nine and a high school guidance counselor during the last thirteen years of my employment. One of my responsibilities was training teens to become peer mediators. This enabled me to observe adolescents involved in conflicts and witness how they tried to resolve issues with the help of their specially trained peers. Because of this program's success, deans and the principal often referred youngsters with anger issues.

As a result of working with teens in this educational environment, I began developing a program aimed at teaching young people how to effectively defuse and deal with strong emotions, specifically anger. This work became the foundation for the Anger Management Power Program (AMP) on which this book is based. This approach can be extremely useful whether you are working with an individual youngster or a group of adolescents. Utilizing different activities and tools, this interactive program focuses on:

- Defining anger management
- Determining the causes of anger, both those that are obvious and those that are less so
- Describing the physical and emotional effects of anger, as well as thoughts related to it
- Providing anger managers (de-escalators) to decrease its intensity and effectively express it

Many of these techniques are described in detail in chapter eleven, but you will find helpful information and suggestions throughout the book.

After retiring, I focused more intensely on AMP, which, at that point, had been presented to over one thousand high school students. With their help, modifications were made. Participating students also received training on developing and facilitating effective workshops for their peers. In addition to all of the students, AMP had been introduced to over six hundred parents and professionals. College students had even been exposed to this curriculum as part of a conflict resolution course. Others had used this training to satisfy their violence-prevention requirement, part of the New York State Department of Education's certification process.

Interactive workshops covering the basic elements of the Anger Management Power Program (AMP) are now available to school staff, parents/guardians, college/university students and staff, and professional organizations. For additional information contact me at peacefulyouth422@yahoo.com.

Much of the material found in *Peace: The Other Side of Anger* is based on observations and discussions with the youth and adults mentioned above, as well as from readings and conferences. It is important to note the material found in this book is only *educational in nature*. It is not therapeutic or a substitute for any form of intervention that may be necessary for individuals with severe emotional and/or social issues. It is a training process to follow, a source for ideas and activities that may be useful to readers in empowering young people to handle their anger in positive ways.

The Anger Management Power Program

The Anger Management Power Program (AMP) is a developmental process created for use with teenagers. It evolved as a result of working with high school students who had difficulty controlling their anger. This method furnishes participants with a means of understanding anger and provides them with ways to maintain control over their reactions to anger-provoking situations. It also provides youngsters the opportunity to help others take control of their anger.

These objectives are met through the presentation of a variety of materials and interactive experiences, including group work and role-playing activities. This training originally took the form of a four-session workshop with teens, and it covered a variety of subjects.

Through a skills-based approach, the program enables the participants to:

- Recognize anger in themselves and in other people
- Express their anger without harming themselves or other people
- Learn how to de-escalate anger—their own and that of others

As a result of the activities and information presented during the Anger Management Power Program, the participants are able to identify:

- Causes and effects of anger
- Anger management—what it is and what it involves
- Positive ways to manage their own anger and deal with the anger of other people in their lives

A month after these workshops were held, a follow-up survey was distributed to students to see if the training they received was useful. Those who had utilized some of the skills they were taught were provided with the opportunity to receive additional training. Those who opted for additional preparation were offered single-period workshops based on their learned skills. Others were taught how to expedite the

mediation process with their peers; this training was provided by guidance counselors and teachers throughout New
York City school districts.

Lessons learned from our AMP student participants can
benefit your work with young people. Hopefully, this will
become apparent as you continue reading through the pages
of this book.

Chapter One

The Anger You See

Our starting point for understanding a teen's anger and how to help them deal with it is to look at the reasons they experience this feeling. The whys of anger take into account many influences and appear in various forms. There are causes that are obvious, and then there are those that are more difficult to detect—the ones that make you wonder, *What's going on with this kid?* All these factors influence how an adolescent is provoked by different people and situations.

In this chapter, we will examine the most apparent causes of anger in young people. To better understand how to deal with a teen's anger, you must view it through their eyes. When you don't take their perceptions of situations into account, wrong conclusions are often drawn. Thanks to over 1,000 youngsters who participated in the Anger Management Power Program (AMP), much valuable information on teen viewpoints was garnered and will be shared with you throughout this book.

The Top-Ten Causes of Anger in Teens

Below is a discussion of the ten most prevalent anger triggers described by AMP participants.

1. Being Lied To

No matter how close the relationship is between an adult and a teen, their bond will suffer serious damage if the grown-up tries to deceive the adolescent. Some of the motives adults give for "stretching the truth" or out-and-out attempts to trick a youngster are: "I wanted to protect my child," or "I have to keep my kid from doing something harmful (or dumb)."

Whatever the reason, a teen wants to be leveled with. If they aren't, their bond is broken, and they will no longer trust the grown-up. The adolescent thinks, *Why listen to that adult? They lied to me before, so why believe what they say now?*

When something happens in the future, the offending adult shouldn't expect the young person to listen to their advice, no matter how helpful it may be. Once an adolescent's trust in a grown-up is shaken, the damage to that relationship is often irreparable.

Being honest with a child, no matter how young they are, pays great dividends. As a youngster's life becomes more pressure filled, their need for guidance from a trustworthy adult becomes greater. If the adult has been honest and has leveled with the child early in their relationship, the adult's influence on how the child thinks and acts is bound to be greater.

In the short run, it sometimes seems easier to skirt the truth. However, over a longer period of time, this is more damaging to the relationship with the young person and, more importantly, to the adolescent's ability to effectively cope with life's challenges.

2. Being Yelled At

This is not to say that when a teen does something wrong, they shouldn't be held responsible for their actions. It is both the manner and location of the scolding that upsets the young person. If they are berated in front of their peers, they may "lose face" or suffer a lowering of self-esteem. Because of this feeling, their response may be more severe than if they had been confronted in private. The most common response from AMP participants to being publicly scolded is "It made me feel like a little kid," which is something they hate.

In most cases, when you discover a teen doing something you wish to correct, it's best to ask them to move to a private place before addressing your concerns or making your point. This accomplishes two things: It gives you a chance to speak privately, and it may allow both of you to calm down before you discuss the situation. Very little is accomplished or learned by shouting.

3. Being Blamed for Something They Didn't Do

Without a doubt, there are many good reasons to think a young person is responsible for something that's gone awry. These infractions may include doors being left unlocked, siblings crying or screaming, classrooms or other places where a teen hangs out being disrupted, property being damaged, or personal property—cars, computers, or clothing—being used without the owner's permission. These are just a few examples; this list can certainly be extended. Adolescents do these types of things frequently.

But suspicions are not conclusive evidence. It is important not to jump to conclusions. To paraphrase a well-known idiom, an ounce of prevention is worth a pound of aggravation for both a teen and an adult.

When allegations are unjustly made, a young person becomes the subject of adult prejudice. This, in turn, creates the impression in a teen's mind that the adult is not being fair. When this happens, an adolescent may feel as if they are being verbally attacked or given the third degree. The response to this accusation will frequently be shouting or shutting down, both of which just compound the situation.

Care should be taken before accusing an adolescent of doing something. The best way of dealing with improper behavior is to only base your conclusion on either your direct observation or the adolescent's admission. Unless you can be sure that the teen is responsible for a particular situation, it is wise not to make assumptions about their guilt. Following this simple rule will ensure that when you speak to the teen, their reactions will be less severe and extreme.

4. Being Put Down for Something They Did (poor grades, bad sports performance, ignored responsibilities, etc.)

Adults want adolescents to achieve their best. However, in pursuit of that goal, some grown-ups use comparisons or put-downs. They make remarks such as "Why can't you do as well as Bobby in algebra," "This stuff is easy. Anyone with half a brain could do it," "That was such an easy play; a five-year-old could have made it," or "You're just lazy!" It is understandable that these statements fuel this source of anger. Very often, a young person already realizes how badly they screwed up, and often they are harder on themselves than you could ever be. Harsh remarks just rub salt into their wounds.

Adolescents describe their reactions to these kinds of criticisms this way: "I know I [expletive]-up. Why does Coach have to make me feel even worse than I do," "Here's another time Mom treats me like [expletive]," "Why can't Mr. Harrison just stay off my case," or "So I'm not Miss Perfect? So what?!"

This manner of criticism should never be used; it produces only negative reactions. Instead, your focus should be on *exploring ways for improvement*. This can be achieved without put-downs or unfavorable comparisons.

Young people tend to blame others for their shortcomings. If this occurs, have them concentrate on what they could have done differently. Making a young person aware that they are in control of what they do and don't do introduces the concept of *personal responsibility*.

Listen impartially to what they think and how they feel. Hearing a teen's views of the situation helps satisfy their need for recognition; that is to say, it helps them see they are worthwhile enough for an adult to notice. Taking this approach sets the stage for both parties to work together to discover the road to improvement.

5. Being Told to Do Something Over and Over Again (chores, homework, etc.)

It is not unusual for a teen to need to be reminded to do something—usually the things they find difficult, bothersome, or less enjoyable than what they want to do. Their priorities include calling friends, using computers to scroll social media, texting, or watching TV. That's just the short list; there are, no doubt, many other distractions.

The most common response to a reminder is "I'll do it later," usually uttered more than once. Based on my previous experiences with young people, when the task is finally done, it is most often accomplished in a rushed and haphazard fashion, or it becomes one of those forgotten things a teen thinks the adults won't remember.

Even though these adult reminders are justified and logical, teens see them as another way to put them down or question their abilities. They think, *Does Dad think I'm stupid*, or *Does the teacher think that I'm deaf (I don't listen)?*

To successfully communicate with an adolescent, first acknowledge the possibility of this kind of thinking, and then share your thoughts in a way that avoids more stress between you and the young person.

6. Being Subjected to Another Person's Nasty Attitude (shown by sarcasm or tone of voice)

How an adult approaches a teen will determine the direction of their relationship. Coming at an adolescent in a loud tone of voice and making a sarcastic comment are two negative approaches that are going to evoke negative reactions.

This is not to say that you can't be upset with a young person. It is how things are expressed that causes an escalation of hostility from a teen. Constructive criticism—telling an adolescent about the troublesome behavior in a constructive manner, without worsening the situation—is an essential skill to learn if you wish to work with young people successfully.

One tool that is worth a try in this situation is the "I" statement, an anger manager to be discussed later in more depth. With this method, the adult speaks about how the upsetting behavior made them feel and the reasons why. "I felt angry when you cursed at me because it was a disrespectful thing to do" is an example of this approach. You are modeling this approach for a teen and, by doing so, making it part of the learning process. AMP participants felt this technique was useful.

The next step is to have the young person try using this method by responding to the adult's constructive criticism. "I felt happy when you didn't yell at me because you showed me respect" describes such a statement.

7. Being Betrayed by a Significant Other or an Adult

Let's look at the perception of adult betrayal first. In this case, two reasons for an adolescent's anger are possible. The first involves "being lied to" directly. The next arises when a youngster observes what they perceive as deceptive behavior. This can involve something as simple as overhearing an adult making excuses to avoid doing something with particular individuals or saying things that a teen knows are absolutely not true. This category of deceit also includes exaggerated details about a situation or about the individuals themselves.

The bottom line: An adolescent's trust in the adult suffers major damage when they catch them in this type of behavior. Without trust, the likelihood of a strong relationship diminishes drastically. The young person who sees this kind of behavior reacts to it in the same way they would were they deceived by their boyfriends or girlfriends.

In a close dating relationship, either party may say or do something different than what their partner was told. This may be about being somewhere other than where they said they would be or with someone other the teen feels they shouldn't be for whatever reason. Once this deception is discovered, the girl-friend or boyfriend loses trust in their partner. Their reaction may be to scream or hit the other person.

Without trust, the relationship is severely damaged or ruined, and often revenge becomes the reaction. This response takes the form of lying about what the other individual did or said, or turning peers against the offending person and treating them like an outsider, all of which can be played out in social media.

8. Having Private Conversations Divulged

Very often, an adolescent will tell an adult something in con-fidence. It may not appear important to the adult; however, it is significant to a teen. This information can be about a relationship or something they said about another person or incident. Once a teen's confidence is betrayed, anger quickly surfaces. The most obvious reason for this is that a trust has been broken.

In addition, revealing confidential information may cause embarrassment. An adolescent may react from the fear of looking foolish or appearing "soft" or weak to peers who find out the details of their secrets.

If the adult attempts to defuse this situation by saying, "I didn't think that it was that important," the idea of prejudg-ment enters the picture. The adolescent will almost certainly take this as the adult telling them what should be important to them and how they should feel.

A youngster's identity and self-confidence are constantly evolving. This type of adult response erodes the adolescent's progress and takes something away from their feeling of self-worth. "That person is trying to tell me what is important to me" expresses their reaction. No one likes to be told by another person what or how they are thinking or feeling or how much influence something should have in their life. This is especially true when working with young people.

<<*Sidebar—Confidentiality Exclusion: Some confidences may be about things that can potentially harm the teen or other people. Information about weapons, drugs, physical abuse, and threats fall into this category, and it must be reported to the appropriate authorities. In my role of guidance counselor, before I had any conversations with an adolescent, I let them know about the kinds of things that needed to be reported. This kind of honesty, when shown at the start of a conversations or relationship with a young person, ensures that you are a person who can be trusted and someone the teen can safely speak to.*>>

9. Being Ignored

When a teen is ignored, it sends the signal that what they have to say or want to do has little meaning. This conflicts with an adolescent's strong need for recognition, which involves valuing their achievements, thoughts, and opinions. When a youngster is ignored, they may become angry because they feel their adolescent self-worth is being questioned. "That person doesn't think what I have to say is important" conveys this idea.

Another more complex dynamic also comes into play. "If that person doesn't want to listen to what I have to say, why should I listen to what they tell me?" This kind of thinking reflects a need for mutual respect between an adult and an adolescent. It is a two-way street. The adult must be willing to understand a young person's ideas without making any judgments.

We are not talking about inappropriate behavior. Cursing, throwing tantrums, hurting others, and destroying property are not acceptable. This kind of conduct necessitates an adult choosing whether or not to directly confront a teen's behavior or ignore it. This message to an adolescent should be made clear: Act like this, and you'll get nowhere and nothing.

<<Sidebar—*You don't have to agree with what is said. Listening to and respecting what is said are the important things. The beneficial effect this approach has on your relationship with and influence on a teen outweighs the time and effort spent on using it.*>>

10. Being Made Fun in Front of Friends

For an adolescent, the value of peers is immeasurable. The need to belong is one of the strongest forces in their lives. With that comes the need to be respected by friends. When a youngster is put down in front of peers, reactions become nothing short of an emotional explosion or physical outburst. A teen will act in whatever way they think is necessary to save face and restore their status with peers. They may forcefully challenge an adult by using a loud voice, cursing, or hurling insults. At the other end of the spectrum, they may become severely depressed and withdrawn.

Some adults may feel that embarrassing an adolescent in front of their peers will force them to correct inappropriate behavior; some adults have even referred to this approach as "tough love." In reality, making fun of a young person in front of friends or *associates* (people in a peer group but not part of the teen's inner circle) is more likely to be a call to arms.

Public confrontations with an adolescent yield the most severe reactions. But for some teens, this kind of treatment works. What you have to decide is whether or not the course of action you have chosen is worth it in terms of the effect it will have on the adolescent and your relationship with them.

Reasons to Explore These Causes of Anger

Looking at these causes of anger has given us:

- Adolescents' perceptions
- Effects on teen behavior
- Ways to limit severe reactions by young people
- Ways to avoid these sources of anger in teens

This list can be expanded to include many other anger activators that adolescents feel apply to them. Use it as a means to open discussions and further them.

The Anger Scale: A Measure of Levels of Anger

To begin to understand more about the causes of anger in teens and how to defuse it, we must first use some sort of gauge to determine the intensity of an adolescent's anger when faced with different real-life situations. That is how the anger scale came into being.

Young people who participated in AMP were asked, "How can seeing how angry certain situations make you be helpful in managing your anger?" These teens quickly concluded that by being aware of situations that make them really angry, they can learn to avoid them. They were able to determine what situations caused them to reach the top of the anger scale. Armed with that knowledge, they could preemptively avoid the event or find a way to calm down before losing their temper completely.

To better understand this, we used the example of being in a car that is about to be involved in an accident. We asked, "What would you do if your car was skidding on ice and heading toward another car?" The teens quickly determined that an appropriate response would be to brace themselves to minimize the severity of injury.

The lesson learned: Foreknowledge results in a lessening of the impact. This is true whether you are referring to a car accident or using a tool to predict anger activators in an attempt to defuse emotional outbursts.

The Anger Scale

Visual aids present an idea in more concrete form. When a young person is able to visualize things, they become more real and are better understood; then your discussions become more productive. Let's look at this visual tool:

You are in control of anger   *Anger is in control of you*

1____2____3____4____5____6____7____8____9____10

Anger is under control   *Anger is out of control*

A teen may describe this scale differently than an adult would. For example, anything close to a 1 on the scale may be described by an adolescent as being "chill," "calm," or "cool." A person rated at 10 on this index may be described as being "crazed," "nuts," "psycho," or "losing it."

When you work with a young person, putting things in terms that they are familiar with makes ideas more relevant and acceptable. Having a teen describe each point on this scale in their own vernacular may provide them with the feeling of personal ownership and furnish a good reason to use this tool.

For our purposes, a score of 2 to 5 on this scale means the individual is still pretty calm and is able to express anger about a particular situation without causing harm to themselves or others. However, once a person passes a 5 on the scale, things can start to escalate as their reaction becomes more severe.

"At what point do you have to be to handle your anger without getting into hassles?" is a helpful question to ask a teen. Their response will help set goals and establish a foundation for using this tool again.

How to Use the Anger Scale with Individuals or Groups of Teens

Let's use being ignored, one of the top-ten causes of anger cited by young people, to illustrate how to use the anger scale. "Where on the scale would you be if you were ignored?" and "Why?" are two questions to ask to get things going. If you are dealing with an individual teen, have them indicate the number on the scale that best describes the level of anger this causes.

If you are working with a group of young people, you can use two possible approaches. The first involves having the group of participants choose the points on the scale that describe how angry they get when they are ignored.

The second approach, suggested by a teenage participant in the Anger Management Power Program, is to have people physically place themselves where they feel they would be if they were ignored. Have three people come up to the front of the room. Each one is given a number—1, 5, or 10—that represents three points on the anger scale. The other group members are then asked to stand at the point on the human anger scale that represents how angry being ignored makes them feel. The number of adolescents chosen to participate depends on the size of the group you are working with. Since this idea was first suggested, the method has become very popular, and it has proven to be successful with many program participants.

Whichever method you choose, the next step is to have each selected participant explain why they chose their particular position on the anger scale. Not only are you having them view this cause of anger from their own perspective, but you are also allowing them to see that, for others, being ignored may have a different meaning and overall effect.

A Teachable Moment with the Idea of Accepting Differences

At this point, you have a teachable moment and can explore the idea of accepting that not everyone reacts the same—another anger manager tool that can be used once the opinions of others are accepted without any negative comments being made.

Start with the question "How can this idea be useful?" If you get a shrug of the shoulders or an "I don't know" response—typical adolescent reactions—suggest that accepting differences can be a means of preventing anger from surfacing, or at least a way to keep another person from going too far up the anger scale.

Another approach is to ask, "Did anyone ever try to get you to change your mind about something that you really felt strongly about, such as the friends you have or music you like to listen to?" If a young person shows some sign of recognition, ask, "What happened?" The teen's response may be something similar to "The harder my mom tried to change my mind, the angrier I got." If this is the case, you've made your point.

You can take it one step further and ask, "How do you think your mom was feeling?" Then try to have the adolescent see the situation from the other person's viewpoint as a way to de-escalate anger in others. Describe the term *empathy* and what it means. This is another anger manager. If a youngster gives you the "I don't know" shoulder shrug, use a teen-relevant situation.

For young men, this could be something taken from sports. One example is to have them imagine a New York Yankee baseball fan trying to convince a New York Mets fan that the Yankees are a better team. This was used successfully with AMP participants, but remember that, depending on where a teen lives, the baseball-team rivalry may involve different teams. For young women, the example may involve using different styles of "cool" clothing or the types of boys they date.

What you want a teen to learn from this exercise is that certain beliefs—things that are important to people—are so strong that arguing about them leads only to frustration and anger. Along with this realization, point out that each of us is unique, and different ways of thinking about things is natural. Then move on from there.

Implications of Accepting Differences for Adults

It is a mistake to challenge certain beliefs an adolescent may have—for example, their thoughts and feelings about certain peer groups, their preferred styles of clothing, the way they wear their clothing (butts showing, etc.), their music (rap, hard rock, heavy metal), or the groups they think are cool or necessary to be a part of (teams or gangs). The point is not to argue about what you think is right or wrong about certain groups or preferences, but to find out why it is so special to the adolescent with whom you are working.

<<Sidebar—*This suggestion is not about judging the teen's preferences. The goal here is to understand the young person's thinking even though you may not agree with it. Keep in mind that both— accepting their ideas and trying to understand their reasoning—keep the doors to two-way communication open.*>>

The Role of Recognition and Belonging in a Teen's Life

Two very strong needs for teens come into play with this notion of accepting differences. The first involves the need for recognition—in this case, valuing an adolescent's opinions. It cannot be emphasized enough that only by listening to what a young person is saying and letting it be known that you understand their thinking—rather than jumping in with opinions and judgments—can the doors to an open dialogue, rather than an argument, remain open.

As a guidance counselor, this is what many teens told me they wanted and needed from adults. It is the kind of behavior that an adolescent will respond to most favorably. The more you listen to what a young person has to say, the greater the chances that they will be willing to hear your thoughts.

The Staring Incident and the Issue of Respect

Although being dissed (disrespected) was not listed specifically as one of the top-ten causes of anger in teens, some of the reasons for a teen's anger fall into this category. Being stared at is one major sign of disrespect described by many adolescents. A fight between two young people often occurs as a result of staring. These conflicts take place in the hallway at school or in any public area where teens congregate.

Individuals "looking hard" (staring) are often accused of looking down on the other person (dissing them) or wanting to start trouble. An adolescent recipient of a stare, the "offended," may notice the stare themselves or have it pointed out by peers. "That guy is staring at you. Don't take that from him" are remarks that signal a call for swift action by the "offended" youngster.

If this act isn't dealt with quickly, peers may regard the "offended" individual as weak or a person who takes [expletive] from others, both of which make the "offended" vulnerable to other such acts. The need to respond to being stared at becomes urgent.

Another reason for reacting to a person's "hard" look may stem from some previously unresolved difficulty that took place between these two teens. The staring becomes an excuse to refuel that fire.

An adult may view an intense look from different perspectives. They may think that the person is daydreaming, looking in the direction of some loud sound, or noticing some other person. In other words, they may view things more rationally. However, for a teen, when this situation occurs, it often doesn't call for calm thought. Instead, it becomes a signal to do something…and do it quickly.

After learning the reason for an adolescent's reaction to being stared at, the next step is to accept their evaluation of it. Keep in mind that in helping a young person manage anger appropriately, it is *their* perception of an incident and the feeling it arouses that matters, not yours.

<<Sidebar—*Accepting a teen's view doesn't mean you agree; it only means that you understand.*>>

Now that you have shown, without judgments or unwarranted advice, that you understand how an adolescent views the situation, the door is opened for a youngster to hear other reasons for staring. Steps can be taken to stop reacting based on emotion and to begin responding reasonably.

Your aim here is to help a young person reach a point at or below 5 on the anger scale, where positive anger management ideas may have a chance to flourish. It is time to test the waters to find changes in behavior.

Let's explore the effects of a teen's reactions to staring. This part of the process begins by asking a teen, "Was the fight worth it?" (Looking at the consequences of behavior is an anger manager that will be examined in more depth later.)

Even if you've paved the way for this discussion, an adolescent may respond to this question with an emphatic "Yes!" Don't be too dejected. With a young person, this is always a possibility.

<<Sidebar—Here's a place where many adults find themselves being frustrated. However, remember that teens often respond in a way that is purely about saving face; this is just a characteristic of this age group. Regardless of an adolescent's answer, proceed to discuss other possible reasons for an incident. They may be covering up an entirely opposite point of view.>>

Some adults may feel that a teen doesn't care what happens after an incident. This may be true. However, whether or not you agree with this view, the idea is to expose an adolescent to different ideas. The value of fighting over the "hard" look can be taken one step further by asking, "What are some of the consequences of fighting?" The responses of many AMP participants included being:

- Suspended
- Grounded
- Hassled by a parent, school or agency staff member, or police
- Deprived of certain privileges

The victim of payback (being hurt by the other person's family, friends, or other individuals coming back later to take care of "unfinished business") will see that the adolescent is punished for their actions.

After these consequences are explored, finding out if these results were what a teen really wanted brings them further down the road to reason. At this point, nothing is being suggested. Instead, an adolescent is given the opportunity to express what they see as the effects of fighting over the issue of "staring" and to evaluate whether the altercation was worth it.

This process may influence how a young person handles a similar situation in the future. Having a teen look at the consequences of their behavior can be a productive anger management tool. As a matter of fact, many AMP participants chose this method as a way they would prefer to handle situations in the future.

After having an adolescent look at some of the results of their reactions, finding ways they could have resolved the current situation without the escalation of anger becomes the next topic of discussion. One method, totally out of a youngster's control, involves the use of punishment, something certainly discussed as a consequence of fighting. Another form of dispute resolution involves some authority figure mandating that the two teens involved in the situation talk it out.

A third way of handling this incident involves both teens volunteering to discuss the incident by themselves without adult intervention. One form this kind of discussion can take is through peer mediation, a process facilitated in many schools and other youth organizations. The two disputants (people who fought) are involved in mandated mediation as an alternative to other more dire punishments and consequences of the fighting.

This approach often requires a forced truce and doesn't really involve any effort to discuss and resolve the issues that brought on the conflict. Right before sitting down to discuss the issue in mediation, young people often say, "It (the fight) is squashed (over)." The mediation merely puts a Band-Aid on the wound and doesn't deal with the cause of the problem. It often doesn't even take into account ways for a young person to prevent this kind of situation from happening in the future.

This is not to say that mediation and other forms of conflict resolution aren't productive. They all can be, and at the very least, they help to end particular conflicts. Keep in mind that a teen likes to feel in control of their lives. Having someone else decide how an incident is going to be handled demonstrates their inability to take care of their own business.

"Do you really want someone else to decide how to fix this situation, or do you want to have control of its outcome?" is something to ask when an adolescent is involved in conflict. This question alone may encourage a young person to find an alternative to handling an incident with violence or any other destructive means. Finding positive ways of fixing a problem can also prevent more problems from happening in the future; that possibility may influence a teen's willingness to try positive anger management methods.

Chapter Two

The Hidden Causes of Anger

The reasons for anger are many and varied. The more obvious ones were explored in the previous chapter. This chapter and the two that follow will examine the causes of anger young people find difficult to disclose because they are too painful, frightening, or embarrassing. They are things that require a teen's trust.

Without some type of intervention, an adolescent will remain angry and continue to react negatively. Before getting to the how-to of convincing a young person to disclose their particular hidden traumas, looking in general at the kinds of incidents that take place is helpful.

Physical Mistreatment

Physical abuse is the first category of hidden events. This type of injury may have resulted from a teen being the victim of sexual or physical abuse, or from being bullied by peers. As a consequence, an adolescent may show hostile behavior toward others or withdraw from any kind of relationship. You may notice that they flinch or move back from anyone who physically approaches them. They often resist all physical contact, whether only a handshake or an attempt to put an arm around their shoulder. A youngster will also clearly and often loudly tell others that touching is not acceptable to them.

More information on how to use these observations and get to the source of a teen's mistreatment will be presented in depth later in this chapter.

Emotional Mistreatment

Other less-talked-about causes of anger in an adolescent are emotional in origin. These are often more difficult for the adolescent to describe even though they underlie the irritation that is openly expressed. Emotional wounds take longer to heal than physical injuries. Emotional pain often leads to depression that, in its most severe form, can result in self-mutilation or even suicide.

The anger that is observed represents the tip of the emotional iceberg. Beneath the surface may lie many feelings that take a lot more effort to discover than the overt anger. Without getting to these feelings, a young person will only be able to see relationships and the world around them through angry eyes.

Sources of Emotional Pain

Finding the source of a teen's emotional pain is the starting point for helping them reveal, discuss, and find ways to lessen its impact on their lives.

Fear: This often lies beneath the surface of an adolescent's anger. It is an emotion that will not readily be expressed, and it may come from different sources. A young person may be afraid of being physically harmed; of losing a relationship with a family member, friend, girlfriend, or boyfriend; or of losing someone's love, respect, or attention. A teen often fears admitting this feeling to others because they believe it will make them look weak or "soft," which in their world means becoming the target for others to take advantage of or "be played."

Maintaining an outward appearance of strength is the reason for much of an adolescent's behavior. Keeping fear hidden enables a youngster to save face, remain strong in the eyes of his or her peers, and thereby secure a measure of safety and acceptance. It is the key to survival in their world.

These beliefs need to be addressed to help bring fear and other emotions to the surface. Once the fear is uncovered, a teen can be helped to find ways to cope more effectively with people or situations that create it; this affords them the opportunity to experience a more peaceful life.

Criticism: Repeatedly being criticized is another source of emotional pain in adolescents. Comments about an adolescent's physical appearance is a common source of pain. Being told over and over again they are fat or skinny, a slob, or look as if they just got out of bed typify this behavior.

How a young person looks to others is very important to them. Remarks about a teen's appearance attack their self-esteem. It affects their ability to have a girlfriend or boyfriend or be a person others want to hang out with. As a result, an adolescent might withdraw from any contact with peers, develop an eating disorder to make themselves more attractive, or act out against other young people or themselves by self-mutilation or even suicide.

Another source of emotional damage comes from constant references to a teen's behavior. They may be described as stupid, bad, or rotten. In this case, an adolescent may start to believe they fit this profile and act accordingly to maintain the mistaken image. The thinking behind this is *This is what my dad thinks of me, so why not be this way?*

A young person who doesn't achieve good grades in school may be described as thick, stupid, lazy, or irresponsible. These statements add to the list of emotional bullets aimed at the adolescent. With this kind of image, a teen who already sees school as a challenge may adopt a "Why try?" attitude.

Different preferences in dress, friends, music, or sexual orientation serve as other sources of criticism. Their friends may be described as weird, geeks, or losers. Young people react in a variety of ways to these judgments. One end of the spectrum is "I'll listen to whatever, or be with whomever I feel like. I'm old enough to make my own choices." The other extreme is "Screw them," especially when the criticism is coming from peers. These reactions are often followed by some form of physical or verbal confrontation. Disparagement may also be directed at an adolescent on social media, which can result in many others "piling on" and attacking them, further increasing the emotional damage.

These kinds of comments may come from a variety of critics—parents, siblings, peers, other family members, educators, or anyone else who is part of a young person's life. Some may say they make these remarks to motivate a teen to act in more positive ways. For others, these remarks are made out of frustration. Whatever the reason for such criticism, it can greatly contribute to a teen's anger.

Reactions to these onslaughts vary. The adolescent may just ignore them and refuse to speak. Or they may become defensive and lash out at the "attacking" individual.

Regardless of motivation or response, being the object of criticism lowers an adolescent's self-esteem. When this happens, a teen may think, *Why talk about something that's going to make me feel worse than I already do? My dad doesn't want to understand or help me.* As a result, the adolescent becomes even more alienated and harder to reach.

Discovering Hidden Causes

There are three steps that can be taken to help an adolescent reveal these anger activators and be willing to discuss them. This is a process analogous to peeling the layers of an onion. It requires time, a lot of effort, and much-needed patience.

There are two benefits to using this method. First, it can pave the way for a young person's emotional growth. By looking at the causes of their behavior, a teen is able to revisit painful or bothersome situations and learn how to confront rather than avoid them. Second, by taking these steps, an adolescent may finally exhibit a willingness to accept your involvement in their life.

A young person needs to be given reasons to feel comfortable talking with you. The first involves trust. This is demonstrated by your ability to keep what is told to you private and not use this information in any way that can damage them. What this means is that you will not use what was told to you in any way that would embarrass or make a teen feel more vulnerable to the comments or actions of other people. The next thing that he or she wants and needs is confirmation that their thoughts and feelings are heard, understood, and—more importantly—not judged.

With this foundation laid, the first step toward getting to the source of a teen's behavior can be taken. It involves letting them know that you are aware something is bothering them and that you are concerned. Care must be taken so that an adolescent feels comfortable enough to describe the source of unhappiness, rather than keep it to him- or herself. Your patience, ability to listen without saying anything, and refusal to judge create the type of atmosphere that may allow a youngster to reveal their innermost feelings.

Bringing up a recent incident that you have been made aware of is one way to discover the underlying causes of a teen's anger. Finding out what their reaction was to this event is the starting point for this process.

Typically, the teen will have responded in one of two ways. The first is the more obvious behavior—anger. It may include defiance and the yelling of curses and statements such as "What are you going to do about it?" or "I felt like [expletive]!" before the slamming of doors or getting into fights.

The second type of response to a situation isn't as clear or as easy to detect. It can be characterized by sad facial expressions, denials that anything is wrong, avoidance of eye contact, secrecy, or unwillingness to be around other people.

<<Sidebar—Pay attention to the general demeanor of an adolescent. If you have observed behavior over time that requires attention, be sure it is not an isolated reaction; however, remember that a single event can trigger hidden sources of anger. The behavior can also be the result of a situation the young person repeatedly finds him- or

herself involved in. It is significant if these behaviors go beyond the usual adolescent moodiness and need for secrecy and privacy.>>

The Three-Step Information-Gathering Process

The next step is to look at a method that can help you discover the underlying emotional causes of a teen's anger. You may become aware of an adolescent in different ways. Directly witnessing or being near enough to have heard the commotion represent two ways of finding out about an incident. Another means of getting this information comes from a young person's peers, a colleague, a neighbor, or a friend.

Regardless of the source, a teen's actions may become something you need to handle as a parent, guardian, family member, counselor, social worker, or youth worker. After finding out an incident has taken place, the next step is to discover the real source of an adolescent's anger.

Step One: Gathering Information About the Recent Incident

One of the hardest approaches for many adults after a youngster has publicly acted out is to stay silent and wait for a response. A teen may react to this tactic by giving an observer a long, hard look (the one with daggers), uttering a curt "So… what?" or saying nothing at all. Acknowledging that you are aware something is the message that needs to be conveyed.

Another way to approach this situation is to ask direct questions: "What's going on?" or "What happened?" And then be ready to follow these up immediately with some comments or more questions.

Typical teen responses to these questions include:

- "Nothing," to which you can reply, "People usually don't get upset over nothing."

- "You wouldn't understand," to which you ask, "Why don't you think I'd understand?"

- "Because I feel like it" or "None of your [expletive] business!" Leave the subject alone for the time being. A nerve has been touched, and the adolescent needs to have a chance to calm down before being expected to rationally talk.

- "I don't want to talk about it!" Sometimes the word *now* is added. If so, it is an invitation to discuss this subject later. The timing of a future conversation may come as a result of another "clue" the youngster may furnish.

Your knowledge of the incident may be considered a reason to be attacked. If this is the case, not immediately responding to a teen's reaction makes good sense. Waiting for an adolescent to tell you about the incident often is rewarded. In many cases, a young person is aware they did wrong or could have handled a situation differently, but they need to let their thoughts out without being interrupted.

The value of using this approach with a teen cannot be underestimated. Its benefits rest in making an adolescent more open to discussing what happened and more willing to hear what you have to say. "I only want the counselor to listen to what I have to say, not tell me what to do or that I was wrong" is a comment I heard often as a guidance counselor; it stresses the importance of following this advice.

<<Sidebar—This approach takes practice and much self-restraint. Using it does not mean you are agreeing with how a young person has handled a situation. It is a means of discovering what is bothering a teen and can result in helping to resolve this type of incident in more positive ways and prevent similar incidents from occurring in the future.>>

Looking at two different ways of explaining an adolescent's conduct can also be helpful. A comment such as "It's really not healthy for you to walk around so angry" is both a judgmental remark and one that makes an assumption about how a youngster feels. Instead, "When people slam doors, sometimes it is a way of telling others they are angry about something" is an objective, nonjudgmental way to describe a teen's actions. It prevents an adolescent from shutting down and gives them the chance to tell you what is going on. It is also a way to head off a "Don't tell me how I feel" response and avoid escalation of the anger with you as its target.

Keeping your opinions out of the discussion shows you are trying to understand their actions rather than criticize or judge them. The goal of this approach is to start to gather information about the incident that took place, not dead-end this possibility.

Once a teen accepts your interest as genuine and your approach as not accusatory, they are ready for you to discover the source of their behavior. This is not an easy thing to do. Here again, time must be taken, a lot of effort must be expended, and much patience is required. At this point, an adolescent may be ready to reveal the whys of their reactions to the situation. If this is the case, you can get right to it. If they aren't prepared yet to take that route, the next step is to ferret out the reasons for a youngster's resistance to talking about past incidents.

Step Two: Overcoming Resistance to Discussing Past Experiences

For many reasons, a teen may be reluctant to speak about troubling experiences. One cause for this silence may be they feel as if they are the only ones who have experienced these things. If this is so, they may also think others who hear their stories will think they are strange, different, weird, abnormal, crazy, weak, or any other negative judgment they fear.

Another explanation for not discussing these experiences is that they are too painful to talk about. Recounting these situations means reopening a deep wound or dealing with something the youngster doesn't want to acknowledge ever happened.

A third reason for a teen's unwillingness to talk about the past may be that it will make them feel more vulnerable. By revealing something they experienced, an adolescent may appear weak, which places their image or safety in jeopardy.

Whatever the reason for their hesitancy in telling their story, it needs to be overcome. To get through this resistance, speaking objectively rather than subjectively is useful. With this tactic, the focus is shifted away from the teen and their own experiences; generalizations are used instead. Broad statements illustrating this behavior include:

- "Lots of times, people go through experiences that they think no one else has gone through."

- "Other people have suffered abuse and recovered with help."

- "Other people have had feelings of shame and embarrassment over incidents that have taken place."

- "Don't worry that your behavior will be discussed with outsiders. It won't."

These types of remarks may permit a teen to identify experiences that have occurred in their lives. If they do, an adolescent will feel more comfortable about talking about these situations with you.

A young person may still not want to discuss these kinds of subjects when they are first brought up. But, later, they may refer to your first discussion. "You know when you told me that sometimes people get embarrassed by a situation" is one way a teen shows their readiness to talk. Other ways an adolescent may indicate their discussion readiness are by a nod of the head or a statement similar to "Stuff like that really does happen."

Whatever forms this willingness to talk takes, they have opened the door to more conversation. The question "Has something like this happened to you or someone you know?" can keep information flowing. When it does, ask, "What happened?" After you do, just let them give their response. Don't interrupt. For many teens, this conversational green light signals the time to open their emotional floodgates. It's a time when everything an adolescent has been holding in is allowed to come out, and the emotional injury can start to heal.

You may also get an "I don't want talk about it" or "I don't want to deal with it now" response. At this point, a youngster has been taken as far as they wish to go, and the subject has to be left alone. However, before it is, a teen must hear that whenever they are ready to discuss an experience, you will be prepared to listen.

When they put up a red flag on discussing an incident, it is often a test of your willingness to meet them on their own terms. In other words, an adolescent wants to see if you will give them the time and space to decide when they are ready to discuss a situation. In this way, they are exercising some control.

Building Trust

An adolescent has different ways of seeing if you can be trusted. Letting them know from the start that the conversation you are having with them is confidential is a small part of establishing whether or not you are trustworthy. Words alone don't determine whether someone is honest. How you describe your willingness to respect a teen's need for privacy carries a lot of weight. This trustworthiness test takes into account your body language and tone of voice, which communicate more about the sincerity of your message than words alone. An adolescent may also network with peers to check you out. This has great value to them because they have a strong peer culture. Much of what a youngster learns in just about any subject comes from other teens.

It is also wise, at the outset, to let an adolescent know that certain facts may require notifying the police or some other authority; this further helps to build trust. The rationale for giving them this warning is simple—if you are given information about something that can be harmful (weapons, drugs, threats, abusive behavior) and you haven't let them know about your obligation to report it, when an incident is reported and action is taken, the trust you are trying to build disappears.

A teen may respond to this disclosure with a doubtful or questioning look, or ask you for the reason you would report what was said. Whether or not they raise this point, it is beneficial to the relationship to describe the negative consequences of not reporting an incident. One point to make is that if someone is aware of something and doesn't report it, others may get hurt or even die. The question "How would you like knowing that, because you did not say anything, someone got hurt again or even died, and you could have prevented it?" drives home this idea.

Another reason to give is that reporting certain incidents is your legal responsibility. If you don't report an incident and something happens, you could risk losing your job or be charged with a crime.

How much influence these explanations may have is hard to predict. At the very least, you have given a young person honest reasons for reporting an incident. A teen is more likely to respect and trust you when you are up-front about what you say and do, than if you omit describing actions you might have to take. As a counselor, I found this openness and honesty typically had a positive effect.

Discovering the Emotional Effects of Situations

The emotional impact of past incidents on an adolescent must be discovered if you expect to be helpful. This information may take days, weeks, or even months to uncover. Imagining a *Patience Is Required* sign flashing in your head is helpful when trying to get to the whys of a youngster's hostile attitude.

Helping a teen peel off the layers of protection that surround these events requires not only hearing the words that are spoken, but also being aware of what is not said. There may be details left out, skimmed over, or told quickly. When an adolescent is anxious about describing an experience, they often tell their story rapidly.

Unfinished thoughts are also something else to pay attention to. They may start talking about something and then switch to another topic. Saying, "My dad was yelling at me and started to move toward me really fast," pausing, and then continuing with "The next day we went to the movies" illustrates this tactic.

Another clue to watch out for is a description of experiences that other teens encountered or saw in a movie, on television, or in a YouTube video. Attributing events to a third party allows a young person to tell you something without personalizing it—that is, give you information about a situation without saying it is about them. It's the objectivity method mentioned earlier. Looking at a situation as if it were happening to someone else has less of an emotional impact on an adolescent.

Listening Beyond the Words That Are Spoken

Interpreting all these signs necessitates recognizing that there is often more to a youngster's description of events than what you hear directly. Whether traumatic incidents are being described or they are experiences relating to school, peers, or everyday events, listening beyond the words that are spoken is important. You need to listen to the way a teen describes a past incident. The phrase "Listen not just to the words people say, but also to the music they play" makes this point.

Do the descriptions pour out, or are they related slowly with hesitancy? Are they uttered softly or in a loud tone of voice? Do you hear deep breaths or gulping? What facial expressions or physical gestures (eye-rubbing or foot-shaking) are noticeable? Is an adolescent looking at you or at other places in the room?

As you hear the information about their experiences, specific details about not only the events themselves, but also a young person's reactions to them, are important to observe. Questions should be posed in a matter-of-fact way, as though you were asking them to describe a party. This is a noninvasive approach to finding out about situations.

Details about the incident, the people involved, the frequency of an event, and the time and location of these incidents need to be explored. The following questions are helpful in obtaining this information:

- "What was going on (physical actions, put-downs, or threats)?"

- "Who was around when these things were happening, and what did they do?"

- "Did this kind of thing happen more than one time?"

- "When did this happen (a particular time of the day)?"

- "Where did it take place (at home, outside, in a hallway)?"

- "How did you feel when it happened or while it was going on?"

- "When it was over and things calmed down, how did you feel?"

- "Who did you talk with after this happened?"

Your goal is to make sure you fully understand what a teenager has gone through, both rationally and emotionally. Seeking to clarify what is being described communicates you are really trying to understand what they experienced. An observation made as an unfinished, fill-in-the-blanks statement is one way to do this. "When you were telling me about this incident, you looked down at the floor" illustrates this tactic.

After making this comment, silence is golden. If a young person doesn't respond to this communication gap within a minute or two, ask, "What was going through your mind?" or "What were you feeling?" If you get a typical shoulder shrug, hands raised in the "I don't know" position, or a "Nothing" reply, switch to an objective approach and say something such as, "People who have gone through similar situations talk about how upset they were." At this point, look for a gesture of agreement or denial. If you receive a negative response, ask, "What else do you think that they could be feeling?" If you still don't get a response, leave it alone. At some future point, they may decide to reopen this discussion. Once again, patience is required.

Using a phrase such as "it seems" or prefacing a remark by using "I thought" gives a teen the chance to admit or deny having a particular emotion because they do not feel as if you are dictating their emotions. This behavior prevents an adolescent from becoming angry, and that's usually enough to keep the conversation flowing.

Another way to help teens express their feelings is by interpreting their behavior. A statement such as "It seems a little frightening" or "When you did this, I thought you may have been feeling angry" is useful. They may respond then, sometime later, or not at all.

One last consideration should be taken into account. Sometimes, other people request to be present during a conversation between you and a teen. It is better to talk to an adolescent alone. The presence of another individual often inhibits a young person's discussion with you. A teen may fear the other person will not like what they have to say and/or do something to them for telling these things to a stranger. They may fear saying something hurtful. They may also be concerned about being embarrassed or made to feel dumb after describing a situation.

However, nonetheless, there are times another person will insist on being present during a conversation with a particular adolescent, and they will stay. This individual may be a parent, another family member, a staff member, or an agency supervisor. I have found there are only three reasons why a person wants to be in the room while a therapeutic conversation with a young person is taking place—fear for you or the adolescent, fear of manipulation, or fear of exposure. You may be told something similar to "I am worried his reactions may be too difficult to handle" or that the teen will try to con (manipulate) you to avoid punishment or other consequences for their behavior. In either case, acknowledge and express appreciation for these concerns. Let the individual know that you will take this information into account, thank them, but proceed to speak with the teen in private—just the two of you. This response both recognizes the other individual's misgivings and shows your confidence in working with the adolescent.

Fear of exposure may be another reason the other adult wishes to be in the room while you are speaking with the adolescent. If so, the individual will still insist on being present. This usually occurs when there is a fear that the adolescent will divulge something that may be potentially harmful or embarrassing to a family or agency—for example, substance or physical abuse in a family or failure of an agency to report or effectively deal with a situation affecting the young person. These types of incidents do occur and should be handled carefully.

In any event, for whatever reason, another individual may be present during your conversation with a teen. If they are, notice the nonverbal interaction that takes place between the other adult and the adolescent. In particular, be aware if either one shakes their head, vertically or horizontally, when particular subjects are being discussed. Glaring, gently pounding a fist against a hand, or holding up a finger by their mouth also fall into the "signals to notice" category. These gestures are often made subtly to escape detection; they furnish clues to the causes of behavior and often explain the reasons for an adolescent's hesitancy in describing all the details of past situations.

Getting to the root of a young person's anger is a time- and effort-consuming process. Once this task is accomplished, you are much closer to helping a teen effectively manage anger. Once an adolescent is able to reveal details of past experiences, they usually are ready to reach below the surface of their emotional icebergs. You both can now take the next step in this process.

Step Three: Using the Knowledge

The last part of this process is perhaps the hardest. You must decide what to do with the information you have gathered about a youngster and the causes of their behavior.

One possibility is that a teen doesn't want you to go any further. By discovering the source of their anger, they may have been able to open the door to the past and shake free from the pressure of having to keep these experiences a secret. This in itself is a big step and may be the only one they will be able to take at that moment.

Your attitude about what was described may also determine how much further this process can go. If you jump in with advice on what an adolescent should do or say something such as "That's nothing to be scared of (feel hurt about)," the conversation will be dead-ended.

However, if the young person's emotions have been accurately described, and you have shown a genuine understanding of the effect these experiences had on them, then the path to further discussion can be opened. Asking, "Now that you've been able to tell me what happened, what would you like to do about it?" or something similar can take you further down this road.

The response may be "I don't know" or the familiar shoulder shrug. If so, try "If I told you that you could learn to get over this fear"—if it's not fear that is the issue, use whatever word best describes the issue or feeling they are battling—"and not let it get you as upset as it did, would that be something you'd like to try?" This highlights the idea that it is up to them whether or not to continue working on their issues—they are in control, which is attractive to an adolescent.

Their tone of voice, smile, or "What ideas do you have?" responses indicate a readiness to proceed. If they say no, frown, or show some other negative sign, the process has been taken as far as it can go, at least for the time being. At the very least, you have opened another path for the teen.

Another avenue to pursue is to revisit the situations that were covered in your session(s). Using this approach and asking an adolescent how they think each incident could have been avoided or handled differently is helpful. If there is a pregnant pause, an "I don't know," or a shoulder-shrug response, ask them to try to remember how someone they knew handled a similar situation.

The energy a young person expends while responding to these questions, their expressions, or "Let me think about it" replies give you the green light to pursue this approach. If they frown or say, "Nothing," that is exactly what has to happen at this point—nothing.

Overview of the Information-Gathering Process

Keep in mind the goal of this process is to not only gather information about an incident, but also to focus on helping a teen deal more effectively with anger. In addition, revealing the source of anger often helps to reduce its intensity. Once this happens, an adolescent has the opportunity to discuss the effects of past situations and to find different ways of handling similar experiences in the future.

Chapter Three

Teen Frustrations

Adolescents today face many different types of frustration that affect their behavior. To effectively counsel young people, you must explore the sources of their frustration and then help them process their emotions more effectively.

Frustration

A large contributor to an adolescent's anger is frustration. Its sources vary. One trigger for this feeling is challenging a teen's beliefs. If you question their styles of dress, peer groups, or types of music they find enjoyable, the message they receive is "Your opinions don't count." The stronger the youngster's beliefs, the higher the level of frustration when they are not validated.

It is important to understand the role these beliefs have in a teen's life, but you must be careful not to judge them.

Accepting these things are important to an adolescent, without making any judgments, gives them value. By doing this, the adolescent's desperate need for recognition is satisfied. Asking a teen to elaborate on the pros and cons of their beliefs keeps the discussion flowing and eliminates or minimizes their frustration.

<<Sidebar—*When you take the time to hear and understand what an adolescent has to say, there's a good chance they will be willing to hear your thoughts in return.*>>

Following this pattern of interaction will add you to the list of adults to whom a young person will listen and from whom they may accept different viewpoints.

If you challenge their beliefs, you enter the "you're wrong—I'm right" zone. At this point, it is a lose-lose situation, the adolescent's frustration escalates, and negative reactions reign supreme. Again, any chance of influencing the young person plummets like stocks in a bad financial market.

Emotional Needs

The frustration caused by unmet emotional needs is a real sore spot for teens. When desires for *recognition, belonging, freedom, security,* and *safety* aren't met, they often react strongly. To understand more about this source of anger, you must:

- Define the requirements for meeting these needs

- Note what happens when they aren't met

- Discover how to handle a youngster's reactions

The Need for Recognition

Satisfying a teen's need for recognition involves giving value to their opinions, achievements, and decisions. It is important to an adolescent that someone notice they are achieving some level of mastery in a particular area, developing a skill, or completing tasks. This can involve accomplishments in school, in sports, or in dealing with situations that arise. It is important to focus on the efforts—not just the results or how they measure up to adult expectations. Any and all attempts by a teen to improve in any area of their lives must be recognized.

To illustrate this idea, let's look at academic achievement; however, remember that this principle applies to all areas of their life, not just school. For our example, we will assume an adolescent has improved their grade in math from a 70 in the first marking period to a 75 for the second marking period. For many parents, although there is an improvement, this better grade isn't high enough. They might remark, "You should be able to get an 80 or 85."

There is nothing wrong with a parent wanting their child to achieve high grades; however, in this situation, the child's actual improvement went unnoticed. This comment and oversight can negatively influence a young person and force them to give up altogether. Adolescents react negatively to being told what they *should* do. I once heard a person quip, "People get tired of being *should* on."

Another source of recognition for a young person is being heard. Adults listening carefully, not just to a teen's words, but really understanding the message, helps fulfill this need. Very often, we don't understand the *real* message—that is, what an adolescent communicates may not come from their words alone. If you hear a reaction similar to "You don't get what I am telling you!" or "You don't ever try to understand me!" you know you are misunderstanding what the teen is trying to communicate.

Communication Pie

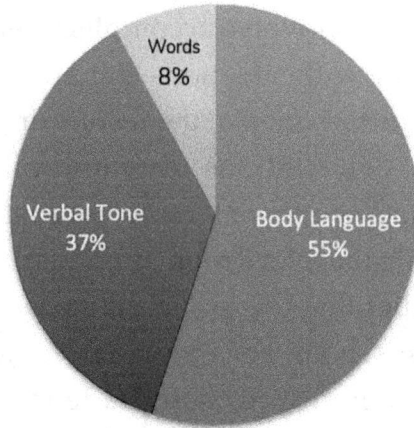

Words
8%

Verbal Tone
37%

Body Language
55%

■ Body Language   ■ Verbal Tone   ▨ Words

This communication pie will assist you in more fully understanding this concept. The pie above is divided into three unequal pieces. Each portion indicates a method of communication. As you can see, the most dominant is body language. It conveys 55 percent, or over half, of the speaker's mood. Folded arms, crossed legs, tightened facial muscles, or glaring eyes are messaging signals. The second dominant slice of the communication pie is verbal tone—that is, how loudly or softly the words are spoken. This accounts for 37 percent, or more than one-third, of the way we communicate our message. Finally, only 8 percent, or one-twelfth, of our message is delivered by our use of words.

What does this all mean? It tells us to look very carefully at our young person and to listen to more than their words alone.

Look, listen, then decide if their words are conveying the actual meaning of what they are describing. If all three components are consistent, the words being spoken actually are conveying the message.

If all three are not in harmony, however, we need to take note and describe what we are seeing or hearing. Statements such as "Your face is red" or "I noticed your arms are folded tightly around your body" may describe their body language. "I notice there seems to be something bothering you. Is it something you want to talk about?" will gently open the door for communication. If you hear an obvious inflection in their voice (raised or lowered), you may say, "Your voice got louder (softer) when you were describing the situation. What's going on?"

These *open-ended questions* (requiring more than a yes or no response) allow your teen to respond to your observation or perhaps say nothing. At this point, leave the subject alone if they choose not to engage. Whether they verbalize it or not, they know you are paying attention and really listening to them. They also know you are aware something happened and are interested in obtaining additional information.

Their response may come (or not) when such observations are made. The fact is you noticed the significance of what more than their words alone conveyed. It gives them a feeling of being understood and heightens their self-esteem. It also provides you the opportunity to understand more about their perceptions. "All I want is for someone to listen to me" is a comment made by many teens. It is something I heard frequently as a high school guidance counselor. It underscores the importance of communication in fulfilling the need for recognition.

Other sources of frustration with regard to fulfilling an adolescent's need for recognition come through social media and phone ghosting. This arises when a particular adolescent is abruptly cut off from all contact with someone. This comes in the form of unanswered texts, emails, being "blocked" or "unfriended," etc. In today's digital world, these acts are major sources of anxiety and anger in young people.

Obstacles to Fulfilling the Need for Recognition

A teen's desire for recognition often faces various roadblocks. The criticisms mentioned earlier describe one type of road-block. The how-to of getting through these roadblocks is learning how to verbalize suggestions and disapproving remarks in constructive ways. Listening is a key factor. Very often, a teen's anxieties over physical appearance, school, family, and relationships surface in everyday conversations about other things. These clues can come in the form of seemingly innocuous remarks such as "I can't stand how dumb I am in math" and "I hate to look at myself in the mirror."

They may also be masked in comments such as "Sally's mom doesn't put her down about her weight. Instead, she waits until Sally asks her for ways to lose weight before she says anything." Or "Brian's parents don't yell when he gets a bad mark."

By making these types of direct or indirect remarks, an adolescent furnishes a conversational lead and opens the door for a discussion. Sometimes, you can ferret out the teen's concerns in a nonthreatening, matter-of-fact way by asking general questions such as:

- "What's happening?"
- "How are things going for you?"
- "What's new with school?"
- "How are things going with your friends (girlfriend or boyfriend)?"

Often, these questions are answered with a shrug or short, evasive responses like "Nothing" or "Okay." Knowing youngsters frequently want privacy makes these remarks predictable. The key is to keep asking questions. At some point, perhaps in some indirect way at another time, you'll get additional details about their life.

Continued interest also shows concern. Keep in mind an adolescent will pick the time and place to speak with you. Be ready for it.

Another strategy for eliciting more information is asking *open-ended questions*. The information you are trying to obtain is based on previous knowledge about specific things an adolescent revealed, either directly or indirectly. Using *how*, *when*, and *where* questions may help you tap into these parts of a teen's life.

The Need to Belong

Closely related to the need for recognition is the need to belong. Being part of a group is as essential to a young person as having food, clothing, and shelter. Being familiar with peer groups is of tremendous value in understanding teen behavior. Though in no way complete, previous studies have identified the following groups considered important by teens:

- Jocks
- In-group (the "cool" group)
- Druggies/stoners
- Racial or ethnic groups
- Loners (identified as those most likely to be involved in school shootings)
- Gangbangers (members of a gang)

Newer, less familiar groups include:

- Good-ats (are well-rounded; exceed in academics, sports, and extracurricular activities; and associate with college-bound students)
- Floaters (go from group to group)
- Anime/manga (wear clothing representing characters in video games and resemble geeks, dorks, etc. of yesteryear)
- Emo/goth (exhibit countercultural behavior, are focused on today's music and aesthetics, wear all black, dye hair dark, sport black nail polish, and see beauty in darkness)

Knowing the individuals who are viewed as weird or are on your adolescent's "shouldn't know" or "don't want to know" list offers tremendous value in understanding your teen's behavior. Showing you understand and are validating their choice of group(s), even though you do not necessarily agree with it, may set an example for how your adolescent can manage negative reactions and differing opinions from peers in more positive ways.

Being part of a peer group fulfills the need for recognition. "I feel important because people (peers, particular groups, family) want me to hang out (go places, do things) with them" illustrates the connection between the need for recognition and belonging.

Fulfilling this need also extends to family and other intimate relationships. When peers or adults ostracize a teen for their differences in dress, music, or lifestyle, the teen feels as if they are an outsider and being rejected.

The need to be a part of a community, school, or peer group can lead to frustration if not met. Anger and resentment may set in, which can start the emotional chain reaction that may escalate to the point of senseless violent behavior against others. Shootings exemplify this kind of reaction to alienation by groups or other individuals. A youngster may also react to this source of frustration and/or exclusion by turning their anger onto themselves with a self-inflicted injury or, in the most severe cases, even suicide.

Another source of this form of frustration occurred during the pandemic. With school closures and distant learning, adolescents were kept from their peers and teachers. In addition, they were asked to stay at home to protect themselves from possible exposure to people who had contracted COVID-19. This meant they couldn't congregate with friends in their neighborhoods, on athletic teams, or in places they usually met. Frustrating this need to belong occurred in families too, where close relatives also were forced to isolate themselves.

In my estimation, this isolation probably caused the highest degree of frustration in the lives of teens. Belonging and being recognized are two of the strongest desires for young people. Understanding how intensely a teen experiences these feelings that color their reactions is helpful in learning how to communicate with them effectively.

At this point, ask them to identify where on the anger scale (noted in chapter one) they think they find themselves. Alternatively, have them list situations in which this desire is frustrated. Once the degree of anger is noted, analyzing the incident becomes the focus of the discussion. How to prevent their reactions from rising higher on the anger scale then becomes the emphasis of the conversation. Using this visual tool, as mentioned previously, offers a concrete, more understandable way to effectively work with adolescents.

The Need to Be in Control and Independent

Another source of frustration arises from the pressure of having a teen do something they don't want to do. This stress can come from peer pressure to go certain places or be with a particular group of friends. It may also come from parents who want to impose a curfew or assign certain chores. In these situations, the adolescent perceives that their need for freedom and independence is being threatened.

Limiting their freedom is a major source of frustration for adolescents. Put another way, adolescents desire to have control over their own lives. They want to be viewed as being capable of handling different responsibilities—school, sports, chores, and relationships—on their own. A teen also wants to be viewed as being capable of making the right choices. Doing certain things, being with particular people, and going where and when they want are the kinds of decisions they feel they should be able to make independently. If they are regarded as responsible, their need for both freedom and recognition is met.

Typical adult objections to allowing an adolescent the freedom to act independently are:

- "Tony makes the wrong choices."

- "Carla doesn't have any sense of responsibility."

- "Joey needs me to be on top of him."

There is no doubt teens may have a history of not doing things, not achieving, or not caring. This behavior certainly needs to be addressed. Handling it in a way that results in the fewest conflicts offers the greatest opportunity to gain influence with adolescents.

What happens when a youngster's need for freedom is not satisfied? You can expect their reactions to be delivered loud and clear. Their responses can take on many forms. Some typical teen remarks are:

- "You treat me like a little kid!"

- "You don't trust me!"

- "I can do what I want when I feel like it!"

- "I am fifteen years old. I can do what I want without you being on my back."

Some adolescents in AMP described the following reactionary behaviors when their freedom was challenged:

- Yelling

- Storming out of the room

- Slamming doors

- Cursing

These participants also expressed that when their freedom was restricted or taken away, they did exactly what they were being told not to do. This type of rebelliousness included:

- Staying out late on purpose
- Getting involved with the wrong people
- Participating in illegal activities
- Hurting others
- Doing something harmful to family members (stealing, hurting a sibling, or being physical with a parent or other caregiver)

These actions carry the message "I'll show them! I don't have to take their [expletive]!" A teen usually knows the things they are doing are wrong, but anger takes over their behavior when a major nerve is struck, and especially when a teen's control over their own life has been taken away.

Remember what you are trying to accomplish—teach an adolescent how to deal more effectively with their anger. This cannot occur if, in the process, you add to their frustrations.

<<Sidebar—*This is not to say that an adolescent shouldn't have structure. In fact, having guidelines to follow, whether they admit it or not, is something they want and need. This period in a teen's life is when it is crucial they feel both free and secure in the knowledge they can go to a parent or other adult for help. But be aware that, many times, these mixed needs result in an internal conflict that becomes another source of confusion for them.*>>

The need for freedom was thwarted by the pandemic as well, which was beyond anyone's control. Our youth were unable to go to school, participate in sports and social activities, or go anywhere they would encounter others. The mandated quarantine prevented adolescents from being exposed to COVID, but over an extended period of time, it also greatly increased their frustration. The inability to leave their homes was far more aggravating than most other forms of confinement imposed by adults during their lives.

Educational Frustrations

School can be another source of frustration for adolescents. These include, but are not limited to:

- Articles of clothing that cannot be worn (hats, "butt-showing jeans," do-rags, etc.)
- Items that cannot be used (cell phones, iPads)
- Exams
- Grades
- Subjects described by teens as "useless in real life"

The comments of parents, caretakers, and educators often heighten this frustration. Remarks illustrating this kind of criticism include:

- "How come your little brother can do this stuff, and you can't?"
- "You really don't want to learn."
- "You're wasting my time and yours in this class."
- "Why don't you go for your GED (equivalency diploma)?"

Add to this feeling of incompetency the frustration of not being able to satisfy their needs for recognition, safety, security, and freedom, both at school and in the world in general, and you begin to see a more complete picture of the impact the educational environment can have on a teen.

Some remarks adolescents make about school include:

- "I just don't get this (subject)!"
- "There's no way I am ever going to graduate, so why should I try?"
- "I'm quitting!"
- "Screw school, the teachers, and you!"

These types of reactions often come after an exam, a report card, or in anticipation of some other indicator of academic progress. Avoiding doing assignments, cutting classes, or dropping out of school entirely are common reactions to educational frustration.

These feelings were exacerbated during the pandemic. Many schools were closed for an extended period of time, so school systems instituted "distance" or virtual learning. Access to a computer became a problem. Students had to deal with teachers who themselves had to learn how to use this new and often-challenging educational technique. Many youngsters found they didn't pay attention or tune in to many of their classes.

Keeping the attention of teens is often difficult enough with in-school learning. Imagine having to learn while watching the teacher on a small computer screen. Background noise, siblings, parents, weather, windows to a forbidden outside world—all could easily distract a teen's attention or serve as convenient excuses. During this time, there was a dramatic decrease in the motivation to learn because there was no real one-on-one contact between students and teachers, or even students with their peers.

The COVID effect is certainly something for adults to consider when dealing with a young person's performance in school. Once this epidemic ended and youngsters were able to return to school, great deficits in learning became apparent. For some teens, it meant they had lost a year or two of their education. I believe this is one way in which adolescents suffered the most from COVID. These learning insufficiencies heightened their lack of confidence, which led to a higher level of frustration and a related decrease in motivation for learning. "What's the use in trying? I'll never catch up or be able to graduate" became the attitude many teens exhibited toward achieving educational goals.

<<Sidebar—At the end of chapter six, you will find replies from teens to pandemic-related surveys. Their viewpoints may assist you in better understanding how this event may have influenced their educational lives.>>

To help an adolescent overcome educational challenges, different strategies are required. The first approach involves gathering information on how strong the frustration with school is and what about education or school upsets them. The questions "How frustrated does school make you?" and "What about it makes you feel this way?" focus on these details.

The anger scale from chapter one is a good barometer for determining how strong a teen's reaction is to this source of dissatisfaction. If they say it's a 3 to a 6, you know their displeasure with school is annoying and bothersome, but not overwhelming. If their assessment is 7 or above, then there is a chance their reaction will become more severe. If they can't come up with a place on the anger scale, then have them compare the frustration school creates with other sources of irritation.

Another indicator of how intense a young person's reaction to school is can be gleaned from their description. A teen's tone of voice (matter-of-fact, forceful, soft) and facial expressions (glaring eyes, puzzled look) provide clues to how angry they are. Observing and listening are often more effective ways than words to deal with an adolescent's frustration with school. Once you understand how angry they are and why, you can make the assessment of whether or not they are just venting (letting off steam) or about to act out more severely.

If it's just a matter of venting, create an atmosphere in which the adolescent is able to freely discuss their feelings. Doing nothing but listening gives a youngster the opportunity to sound off about annoying things or people at school. Their grievances may come out all at once or in bits and pieces.

After they are finished describing their source of frustration, they may sigh or take a deep breath. If this occurs, it is a sign their "siege of frustration" is over. It is the peace that follows a storm. At this point, an adolescent may be ready to describe calmly why school is so frustrating and discuss what can be done to help them feel less upset. Or it is possible the teen just wants to leave the subject alone for the moment. Whichever path the teen chooses, follow their lead and respect their choice.

If an adolescent appears extremely agitated and is describing themselves as being at an 8 to 10 on the anger scale, or exhibiting behavior consistent with that level, they are heading toward a crisis point. If this is the case, steps need to be immediately taken to diminish the intensity of their feelings. The first step involves acknowledging the frustration without judging it. The remark "Yeah, when something like this happens, a lot of people just want to forget about it or not deal with it at all" illustrates this tactic.

Watch and wait for a reaction from the teen. If they smile, nod, or show any other sign that you are on target, try to determine what caused their feelings toward school to spiral out of control. "What's stopping you from doing better in school?" represents a good starting point for this discussion. A young person may remark, "I'm just dumb," or blame teachers, the educational system, or any number of other people or things for their problems with school.

If they describe themselves as someone who lacks intelligence or ability, accept this feeling without agreeing. Instead, offer insight. "Some people feel that way when they have a difficult time doing or understanding things" is one way to accomplish this.

Remind the teen that even though they may not be doing something well, they can still try to do better. The question "What kinds of things can people do to improve themselves?" addresses this idea. If a teen can't think of a response, describing other things they *can* relate to may stimulate their thinking. This can be accomplished by asking what athletes do to improve their game or get out of slumps, or what musicians and singers do to win a spot in a band or become recording stars.

If a youngster plays the "blame card," asking, "Besides that (whatever is being blamed), what else is getting in your way?" helps them focus on what they may not be doing to succeed in school. If there are some areas in which they can take responsibility and improve, the path to a lower level of frustration can be opened.

Another approach is introducing the idea of control. Asking if they like the idea of being in control starts you in this direction. They may respond to this seemingly "dumb question" by commenting:

- "Who doesn't?"
- "You've got to be kidding!"
- "Are you serious?"
- "Yes!"

After this obvious conclusion is reached, stating, "What you can't control is how others (teachers, counselors, principals, other school staff, or parents—the objects of the teen's blame) behave toward you or the requirements for a diploma," can nudge the teen down the road of leaving blame behind and looking for ways to achieve more in school.

Let this thought sink in for a moment. Then add, "You have the power to deal with school, if you choose, and do something about all the things keeping you from passing. It's your decision." You have now empowered the youngster to take charge of this part of their life. Whether they do or not is another story. Their reaction to this train of thought will determine whether this approach will be effective.

Another tactic is having a teen think of a time when someone had a seemingly unsolvable problem at first, but then successfully handled it. If they recall a situation, have them describe how it was resolved. If not, look at what might have been done. Previous experiences can be helpful. There is more about this in a later chapter.

Looking at the big picture is another road to take. In this case, try to put their difficulty with school in perspective by pointing out problems others face. Describing individuals who have to deal with a physical difficulty (disabilities) or some life-threatening disease serves this purpose. Make the point that many individuals with severe limitations don't just quit or stop doing what they need to do to get on with their lives. This may help the teen see the light at the end of their educational tunnel.

If the teen opens their eyes wider, nods, or makes a "Maybe my problem with school isn't all that bad" remark, their frustration level with education has been diminished. If, however, you receive an expression of doubt, a "Yeah, but I'm not smart," or a "So what!" respond with something similar to "When someone goes through a tough time, they often don't want to look at anyone else's problems" shows empathy toward the youngster. This attempt to understand a teen's viewpoint may soften their reaction and spark their thinking. Often, having their thoughts and feelings heard and understood is all an adolescent really wants or needs to get past a situation.

<<Sidebar—Trying different approaches—that is, using "trial balloons"—often pays off. When dealing with a young person, your gut reactions to situations are often right on target. Go with them. It is something I have found useful in working with teens. You never know what idea is going to make sense or when they will use it.>>

Frustration with Peers

The last, and perhaps the strongest, source of frustration for a young person comes from their relationships with peers. Much of a teen's life centers on friends. Identity and recognition are parts of this picture. "If I have friends and belong to a group, I am a worthwhile person" expresses this idea. Having a network of friends can fulfill these desires, as well as the need for security and safety.

There are many ways an adolescent can experience frustration with peers. Not wanting to do what friends want or go where peers want them to go is one type of frustration. Not being a part of a particular group—jocks, good-ats, emo/goths, anime/manga, geeks, or gangbangers—illustrates another frustration with peer groups. What makes peer groups even more upsetting, however, is the inherent conflict between needing to be independent (free) and needing to belong, to fit in, to be accepted by peers. This can lead to immense internal tension and anxiety.

If a young person chooses independence over fitting in, not only can they face criticism, but they also leave themselves open to ridicule, ostracism, and sometimes verbal or even physical hostility. Some of the remarks they face when demonstrating their need for freedom from their peer group's influence are:

- "What's the matter? You think you are better than us?"
- "You're a snob."
- "Forget you!"

Ghosting or being excluded in chats or posts on the Internet are other common reactions to an adolescent's display of independence.

<<Sidebar—*The effects of social media will be explored in chapter five.*>>

When suffering this kind of behavior, an adolescent often reacts strongly. In their most extreme, these reactions may be violent and directed toward others or themselves. The young people responsible for the Uvalde Elementary School and Apalachee High School tragedies illustrate this response in its most extreme form.

"[Expletive] them!" and "I'll show them," coupled with hand-pounding, fist-clenching, banging objects, bullying, and frequent fighting represent other reactions to being criticized, ostracized, or subjected to other forms of alienation.

These responses may result in self-destructive behavior—that is, hitting something hard, punching a window or other objects. Another way a youngster may hurt themself is engaging in risky behavior—frequent fighting, dangerous activities (walking across railroad/subway tracks or busy streets), or unhealthy habits (smoking, taking illicit drugs, or participating in unprotected sex). Self-mutilation and attempted suicide are the most extreme examples of self-destructive behavior.

We often don't know what triggers such reactions; however, frustration from a variety of sources certainly contributes to these extreme behaviors. It is difficult not to note the frequency of violence in our society in general, and in school settings specifically. The more we understand what actually fuels adolescents' emotional fires, the more effective we can be in guiding them in other directions. As the saying goes, Knowledge Is Power!

Less obvious isolating behavior may also occur. It can develop at any time and is often hidden from parents, other family members, teachers, boyfriends, girlfriends, and close friends. A young person may physically distance themself from others. A teen may *frequently* tell others they want to be alone or need their own space. They may push others away by yelling, sulking, or behaving in ways that prevent others from wanting to be around them. Some go on eating binges or starve themselves, which can be symptomatic of bulimia or anorexia, respectively—both serious conditions that are often hidden. (For additional information regarding these illnesses, consult a mental health agency or search the Internet.)

Sleeplessness is another red flag that may indicate frustration with peers. Problems with friends may increase anxiety and keep young people awake. During these sleepless times, an adolescent thinks a lot about ways to handle the problems with their friends. They may feel, if they are unable to resolve the difficulty, they have nothing to live for. This idea may seem overly dramatic to an adult. However, this kind of thinking is common, and it expresses how seriously teens take their problems.

Sleeping too much offers a way to escape dealing with an issue. When an adolescent sleeps a lot and refuses to go places or do things they used to eagerly do, these may be signs there is a problem. It is true that red or droopy eyes may be caused by allergies, something in their eyes, or waking up late. However, when persistent, these symptoms and behaviors may also be attributable to drug abuse, frequent crying, or depression.

All these reactions require serious attention. These indicators do not necessarily mean your worst fears are coming true; however, they are warnings that you should become more attentive to what is going on with your adolescent. When such behaviors last over two weeks, it may be time for an intervention. Without professional help, the consequences to young people, their families, and others may be catastrophic.

The behaviors attributed to an adolescent's frustration with peers may also be reactions to other sources of anger or an inability to express feelings. They should be noted, discussed, and handled directly.

Acknowledging behavior is a good first step. What you see or hear needs to be objectively described. "I noticed you have been hanging around by yourself lately," "I saw you punch the wall after you walked away from your friends," or "You look like you haven't gotten enough sleep" illustrate this type of recognition. If you've observed this behavior over a period of time, acknowledge that as well. "It seems to me you've been unhappy for a while" describes this observation. Then watch and wait for a response.

An adolescent may say, "So what!" or "Yeah," stare, nod, or not react at all. When this happens, they may be waiting for you to keep the ball rolling.

Respond with "You looked like you wanted to react to what I said." Once again, pause, be patient, and give the young person the chance to respond.

If there is still no response, remark, "What I said seemed to be something you want to talk about." Then wait again. If the silence continues or you receive a curt response, ask, "What's going on?" and see what happens.

Keep gently probing, no matter how many attempts you make. This should be done periodically over a period of time—not all at once—so you don't get the "Get off my case" response and ruin your chances of discussing this issue. You are trying to establish a cause-and-effect between the teen's behavior and the reasons for it. When the adolescent responds, the path to easing their frustration and limiting its effects is opened.

If a teen gives you a hands-up gesture, a look of doubt or disgust, or just walks away, the conversation has gone as far as it can go, at least for the time being. DON'T BE TOO FRUSTRATED! The adolescent will often revisit the subject at some later time. It may occur spontaneously or perhaps when a similar situation arises. Discussion readiness may also be signaled by descriptions of situations other teens are experiencing or from television or movie characters.

After discovering and discussing the reasons for your adolescent's frustration with peers, devise ways of limiting the effects of this feeling. Rather than repeating strategies already described, return to the section entitled "Educational Frustrations" for additional ideas.

The Need for Security and Safety

Other sources of anger in young people are connected to unmet needs for recognition, belonging, and freedom. Unfulfilled desires for security and safety represent two additional reasons for teen frustration. The root causes of problems associated with security and safety are not easily discerned because these issues usually cause the most embarrassment, shame, or fear.

Meeting the Need for Security

The need for security can be met in different ways. One means takes place when youngsters feel part of a stable environment—a strong adult relationship, a steady family income, and healthy caregivers. Food, clothing, and shelter all factor into the adolescent's need to feel secure.

The pandemic brought with it many losses and changes, all of which exacerbated feelings of anxiety and insecurity all over the world, and especially in our youth. If their parents or caregivers no longer felt secure, how could they?

The knowledge that a teen's home and neighborhood are safe contributes to a feeling of well-being. This need can be threatened in many ways, as it was during the pandemic. A parent losing a job threatens the ability to pay for essentials—food and utilities—and may even result in families losing their homes. The pandemic also resulted in many hospitalizations, long-term and terminal illnesses, and deaths of loved ones. A fire or natural disaster could also destroy a family's home and economic security.

When these events occur, adolescents may find themselves separated from parents and siblings, living with unfamiliar relatives, or being housed in a foster-care or group-home setting. The peace and comfort they once felt is replaced by anxiety. They may have face the possibility of not knowing when or if they will live with their family again. When these types of changes occur, a teen may also be forced to move to a new neighborhood, attend a different school, and, worst of all, be unable to see their friends as often or ever again.

When these drastic life changes occur, it is no surprise teens become angry. This can manifest in many ways. They may appear defensive when asked about their family. A quick and loud "Why do you want to know?" expressed in a distrustful manner may be the response to "What's going on in your life?"

An adolescent who has experienced difficulties is sometimes resistant to forming close ties with others. Their thinking can be "Something else may happen and make me move again, so why bother with other people?" A youngster experiencing this insecurity may walk around with constant scowls and get into frequent confrontations. They may also cut classes or be hesitant to return to wherever they are living, whether it's in their own home or somewhere temporary. This kind of behavior represents a desire to avoid having to face uncertainty.

No matter if this feeling is based on reality or created by fear, its lasting effect is great. It is safer for a teen to show anger to camouflage this insecurity, rather than admit to being afraid. The thought process is "If I show I am worried, people will think I'm soft (weak) and think they can play (take advantage of) me." Being tough in appearance and action is the key to survival for many adolescents.

As with other causes of anger, objectively describing their actions represents a good starting point for most young people. The remark "Seeing you staring into space when someone asks you about your family makes it seem like something is really bothering you" illustrates this idea. The more specific the details of their actions, the clearer the path to telling you what they are experiencing.

Using a pregnant pause after making an observation gives a teen the opportunity to decide whether or not to speak. The absence of sound can really be uncomfortable, so they'll probably want to break the "quiet barrier" quickly. Looking at it another way, for an adolescent, it can be their opportunity to take control of the moment.

If there is no response, asking directly, "What happened?" may result in the sharing of some information. However, if there is still no reaction, you have reached the end of this path for the time being.

A youngster may provide information at some time later through conversational leads. This information can come veiled by descriptions involving a peer, a character in a movie or television show, or something they read on the Internet.

After a youngster has dropped this hint, remarking "You spoke about what happened to your friend. Some people your age think that is going to happen to them," or something similar, may reopen the road to getting to the root of their fear. If after a minute or so they haven't responded, ask, "Do you see this kind of thing happening to you?"

Once you have discovered the reasons for their insecurity, the next step involves helping them find a way to experience some degree of comfort and well-being. Uncovering the source of their fears and frustrations can help reduce the intensity of the teen's insecurity.

Discussing previous experiences is another way to help an adolescent contend with their sources of unhappiness. Asking, "Have you seen anyone else deal with (divorce, illness, or whatever situation they are facing)?" is a way to obtain this information. Continue this information-gathering process by asking probing questions, such as "What happened," "How did they deal with it," "What helped them," "What was not helpful," and "Do you see any of these ideas being helpful in your situation?"

If no response is forthcoming, encourage the teen to think of how a character on a television show or in a movie handled a similar situation. Have them describe how the person managed their problem. This method keeps the spotlight off the youngster, while encouraging them to deal with the situation. It is called the *"objectivity method."*

Confronting change is another area to explore. Moving from one neighborhood to another, advancing from elementary to middle school to high school, and processing the loss of a close relative or friend represent these types of adjustments. Asking them to recall the changes and how they previously handled them may provide some degree of confidence in dealing with their present situations. "You were able to handle that situation, so I really think you will find a way to take care of this now" reflects this belief.

Reminding a young person of the sources of stability still remaining in their life is another approach. If, for example, the situation involves a divorce, discussing what will remain consistent is worth trying. Focusing on ways to routinely see the person who may no longer be living in the same house is something to discuss. Reaffirming the individual works or lives close enough to be seen easily and frequently can be helpful.

Discovering if decisions affecting an adolescent's education, health care, and behavior will still involve both parents describes another consistency in their life. Thinking about the family members who remain in their household and the roles they play is also worth mentioning. By discussing these possibilities, they become aware that even though there are major changes taking place within their family, some consistencies remain.

Consistent relationships in a teen's life, outside their home, represent other sources of stability. These may include friends, classmates, teachers, guidance counselors, other school personnel, priests, rabbis, social workers, agency interns, or store owners. These are people they feel comfortable speaking to and spending time with—point out they can continue to do so. Revealing these stable relationships may help diminish the intensity of feelings of insecurity, isolation, abandonment, or rejection often accompanying the changes taking place in their life.

Another source of solidity entails any activity still a part of their lives. Attending school, participating or attending sporting events, parties, rock concerts, and dances remain the same in spite of a changing family environment. A young person's reaction to this may be a resounding "So what!" The unwillingness to accept the changes in their life, or the idea there won't be anything positive once the family is split up, is common. Often, a teen simply cannot accept these differences emotionally.

The key to regaining stability rests with their ability to get through their emotional upheaval and calm down enough to cope with these changes in a rational way. After any loss, there are emotional stages that map the road to healing. These steps can involve a variety of feelings, including anger, denial, fear, disappointment, and pain.

Acceptance—the final stage in this process—allows them to reach a rational point. When they realize what has happened in their life is a reality and cannot change, they are ready to deal with the situation differently. Helping an adolescent reach this stage may mean giving them time to express these feelings. By hearing, understanding, and not giving advice, their thoughts and feelings are validated.

Once this venting has occurred, you can expect a calmness. It is at this point some of the sources of stability suggested to them can be reconsidered. The goal in revisiting these approaches is helping a young person understand that as disruptive as things may be in their life, there are people and parts of it that remain constant.

Once this idea is accepted, they may also see their world is not totally falling apart. By accepting this reality, they may see their need for security can be met, at least to some degree, and may not feel as frustrated.

<<Sidebar—Gut-Reaction Advisory: There are ideas that just pop into your head. Call them gut reactions, instincts, or mental thunderstorms. They are thoughts that have been stored in your memory bank. For whatever reason, they are knocking on your mind's door, ready to be called into action. When dealing with an adolescent, don't be afraid to let them out and follow their lead.>>

Meeting the Need for Safety

Safety is another powerful need for a young person. Meeting this need requires them to feel protected from both physical and emotional injury, and even death. We all know too well the rampant epidemic of gun violence occurring in our society. School shootings have become an all-too-common occurrence. Students and staff members have been taught to shelter in place in their schools, doors are locked, and in some cases, armed officers are present.

Being shielded from physical pain and possible death can be handled in many ways, depending on the circumstances. A teen experiencing physical abuse at home often avoids this treatment by coming home late, spending time in other people's houses (friends, other family members), or getting involved in extracurricular activities, good or bad.

Another threat to physical safety can come from violent peers. To avoid this source of hurt, a teen may cut classes or school entirely, do things outside of their neighborhood, or join a group, often a gang, for protection because "they (other gang members) have my back." Self-preservation is a powerful motivator.

The ways a young person finds safety are often those they see and hear from their peers. Gang membership or payback (retaliation) are methods learned from close friends or other peers, often referred to as "associates." Using these kinds of methods involves a strong belief you should fight violence with violence—an "eye for an eye" philosophy. Challenging this attitude only alienates a teen and shuts down any further conversation on this subject.

<<Sidebar—*It is important to note that in no way am I saying gang involvement and violence are positive ways for an adolescent to gain protection from physical harm. However, hearing and understanding their reasons for thinking gangs and violence are necessary is important. The more you know about what adolescents think on these subjects, the better the chances of finding safer alternatives.*>>

Finding a Positive Path to Physical Safety

Physical and sexual abuse against teens must be reported to the police or some other governmental agency as mandated by law. All the methods described below do not replace or substitute for this means of protecting them.

Violent acts can occur within families, in dating situations, or in other intimate relationships. They can also occur between members of the same or different peer groups. Wherever and with whomever these incidents of mistreatment occur, agencies and groups are available to help the victims. On the Internet, there is a wealth of information about referral sources from state, city, and other mental health agencies and organizations. Without some form of intervention, the risk of repeated abuse and perhaps even death is extremely high.

Physical abuse is, no doubt, a very sensitive and emotionally painful subject for a young person to report and describe. Discovering the how, where, when, and why of physically harmful situations is the first step. Use open-ended questions that require more than a yes or no response. They are useful in gathering the most details and keeping the conversations going.

Getting this information from an adolescent requires time, patience, and trust. A teen is often reluctant to admit what happened or resistant to discussing it.

There is much that must be discovered. Ask how the injury occurred. Was the adolescent struck with open hands, fists, or objects like irons or brooms? How often has this type of incident happened? Does this behavior occur once in a while, every day, or weekly? Find out whether or not the person hurting the youngster does so when they experience stress (financial, job, school) or when they are drunk or high. Look at what events led up to the incident and the steps the youngster or others took to stop, prevent, or avoid the abuse; this could be an important piece of the abuse puzzle. Does the abuse take place at home or somewhere else, out of sight or in public?

Once you have answers to these questions, strategies can be developed for helping the teen protect themself from future injury.

There are several different steps that can be taken to get information from a victim of abuse. The use of objective descriptions for an adolescent's behavior is helpful. "Often, people your age who have been abused need lots of space and don't like to be touched" is an example of this kind of remark. It is a statement that can be made and then left alone.

Whether in response to this statement or while describing an incident, careful attention must be paid to the youngster's tone of voice, pauses, and nonverbal cues. Does a teen's body look rigid or relaxed? Are their hands and arms folded or resting on their legs? Do you see tears welling up? Do they look sad, angry, or scared while describing abusive situations? Only by asking these questions and sharpening your observation skills can you fully understand the effect of this type of treatment.

Once the fact-finding is complete, there are several ways to help prevent the recurrence of this mistreatment. Some of these have already been described in the safety section above. Another direction to take is to look at past successful attempts to prevent the abuser from hurting them. You can also have them describe what peers or characters in movies, television programs, or other forms of media did to successfully prevent themselves from being mistreated.

<<Sidebar—Cultural and family patterns often play a role in knowing why abusive behavior takes place. These are things that are sometimes inadvertently mentioned by a young person. "This is how people in my family do it" and "In my culture, hitting a kid is the way we get punished" describe how this information is revealed. This is the kind of knowledge counselors, social workers, and youth workers should take into account when dealing with teens.>>

For some adolescents, using weapons or physically striking back at an abuser can be a way of handling the abusive behavior that is hurting them. To an adolescent who describes this pattern of behavior, the consequences (another anger manager to be explored) can be pointed out. The reply to "What happens to your mom, brothers, sisters, or other family members if you are sent to jail, or if the abuser isn't hurt and comes after you and does more damage to you or others in your family?" expands on this idea.

Sometimes young people who are reluctant to see any other way of dealing with an abuser will say, "I don't really care." If this is their response, "To stop this from happening again, what action can you take that won't get you in trouble with the law or hurt?" should be the next question. You are not agreeing with the teen's vengeful thoughts; you're only listening and giving them the opportunity to find other ways to manage this situation.

Prior to reporting an incident, victims and their family members may not want these situations disclosed because they fear retaliation by the abuser. There are several ways to handle this objection. One thing that can be done is to let an abused person and their family know there are places they can go where the abuser won't be able to find them. These may be the homes of relatives, friends, or temporary shelters.

Inform the victim that people under investigation may not attempt additional acts of violence out for fear of facing jail time or financial penalties if they are found guilty. Even if abusers aren't punished as a result of a particular investigation, if accused again, they may have less of a chance of escaping punishment. This may cause them to think twice before physically harming anyone else. It is important to stress to the victim that not reporting this behavior may allow the abuser to hurt other people or possibly cause someone's death.

Even after using this approach, young victims may not want you to file a report. Fear sometimes outweighs all the reasons for turning in an abuser. This is an important consideration for the professional working with a teen victim of physical abuse. The professional has a legal responsibility to file a report, but may fail to fulfill this obligation for many reasons. Feeling sorry for the victim, not wanting to be the cause of any more of their pain, and thinking they can help prevent further abuse are three such thoughts.

However, if you have knowledge of mistreatment and fail to report it, there is the chance the adolescent could be physically injured again or even die at the hands of the abuser. It's an outcome no one wants to have on his or her conscience. Not to mention the legal liability, severe penalties, and professional repercussions that may result from the lack of reporting. It's a professional dilemma many people face. The expression "It is always better to err on the side of caution," I believe, can help resolve this confusion.

Your role as an advocate for a young person involves taking the action that will best serve them and have the least negative effect on their life. This isn't always the easiest road to travel. Your support takes on many faces.

Emotional Safety

Emotional safety has its partner in the need for recognition. Rather than feel the pain resulting from criticisms described earlier in this chapter, a teen will seek those who provide protection from this source of pain. The individuals who will listen without making harsh judgments about them and their interests, opinions, or friends. These "emotional safe havens" include school counselors, teachers, coaches, custodial personnel, school safety agents, ministers, social workers, relatives, friends and their parents, or any individual whom they trust.

Helping youngsters handle this source of frustration can involve a three-step analytical approach. The format used in this method is the same as that found in an anger journal, another anger manager explained in subsequent chapters. Using this approach requires a teen's readiness. This occurs when their emotional reactions have run their course, their anger—the power fueling heightened reactions—has been released, and an adolescent can express their anger without hurting themselves or others.

Many anger managers have been revealed—others will be introduced later—to help young people reach this goal. Once their anger has dissipated, the following approach can be used.

First, analyze the situation that led to their frustration. Look at *what was said* to cause this emotional injury. Find out why it was upsetting—that is, discover what hot button was pushed.

Next, focus on *ways to diminish or eliminate the effects* of the situation. View the incident from different perspectives in order to think of better ways to manage it. This stage enables the adolescent to answer the questions "What else could the other person be trying to tell me?" and "How could I have handled this situation without getting so upset?"

Finally, look for *ways the teen can protect themself from experiencing future emotional pain and trauma.* If they care about their relationship with the offender, they may decide to tell you how and why that individual's remarks were so damaging.

The "I" statement, another anger manager to be discussed later, helps accomplish this task.

In this stage, a youngster may also consider the reasons people criticize others. The critics may be individuals who themselves received much criticism in the past or those with low self-worth. Putting down others may make them feel bigger or better than those they criticize. When presented with these two possibilities, teens may decide to ignore hurtful remarks.

Chapter Four

The Effect of Gun Violence on Teens

Mass shootings in schools have greatly increased since the Columbine High School incident in Colorado in 1999. At that time, this type of incident was rare. According to a report issued by *The Washington Post*,[1] since Columbine, there have been 392 school shootings, and a total of 396,000 youngsters have experienced severe trauma after hiding during these incidents. This number will no doubt increase. These are not facts that comfort anyone, especially students, parents, family members, communities, and educators.

Let's not forget some examples of these horrific incidents, as described and highlighted in the media, and their impact on the communities in which they occurred. These tragedies have affected us all.

- Sandy Hook Elementary School (December 14, 2012), Newtown, Connecticut
- 20 students and 6 adults killed

- Marjory Stoneman Douglas High School (February 14, 2018), Parkland, Florida
- 17 students and staff killed, 17 students and staff injured
- Robb Elementary School (May 24, 2022), Uvalde, Texas
- 19 students and 2 teachers killed, 17 people injured
- Apalachee High School (September 4, 2024), Winder, Georgia
- 2 students and 2 teachers killed, 7 people injured

An *ABC World News Tonight*[2] commentary revealed 6,000 young people, aged one to seventeen, were injured or murdered by gun violence in various settings in 2022. These statistics are mind-boggling! In this author's opinion, gun violence in schools (elementary, middle, high school, and college), as well as throughout our society, has reached epidemic proportions.

In order to provide a better understanding of the severity of this problem, statistics were furnished by the research group Gun Violence Archive[3] and by Everytown for Gun Safety,[4] an organization advocating more stringent gun control. Some sources describe mass shootings as those involving four or more people killed or injured, while others go with a definition in which three or more victims are involved. No matter which definition you use, the number of incidents and their effects recorded thus far in 2025 are provided below:

- Mass Shootings—347
- Mass Murders--14

- Teens (12–17) Killed—827

- Teens Injured—2,290

Although we are focusing our attention on the incidents taking place in educational settings, it is important to mention how frequently these occurrences influence people's lives— where they live, work, pray, socialize, and enjoy life. People of all ages feel the impact in different ways, often lasting many years, if not indefinitely. As these horrendous events continue to occur in so many places in our society, measures have been put in place to protect all members of the public, and new ones are being instituted every day.

Since we are mainly focusing on teenagers, their safety in various settings will be described. However, our discussion is not meant to exclude preventive measures for younger children and adults who find themselves in these locations. For example, methods used in school settings also apply to adults, teachers, support staff, etc.

Gun violence occurs as a result of extreme reactive behavior stemming from the intense anger of the perpetrators of these crimes. With teens, our job is to help them learn how to handle and express these powerful feelings without causing harm to themselves or others. The numbers of those injured or killed are hard to fathom—these shootings irreparably damage families, friends, survivors, and even bystanders.

The effects of gun violence on teens, the measures designed to protect them, as well as the ways to provide help will be explored. Where teens live and spend their time is a huge factor in understanding how they respond to gun violence. A spontaneous conversation with a few students regarding gun violence in their schools and surrounding neighborhoods can furnish some thoughts and feelings many adolescents experience.

School Safety—A student in a suburban Connecticut high school revealed feeling secure only after both a metal detector and a school resource officer were placed in her school. She described how, one year prior to these instituted measures, her school had been in lockdown several times due to threats of gun violence.

Fear of Gun Violence—Now a freshman in college, a young woman disclosed how classmates in her Long Island, New York, high school feared violence could happen, even though no such events had actually occurred there. However, in areas surrounding her school, many violent incidents had been reported. This knowledge created much anxiety in many of the students in her school.

Lockdowns and sheltering in place are two methods of protecting our youth and staff members in schools throughout the nation. Sadly, in some locations, these drills are performed on a regular basis. Unfortunately, they are reminders that additional school shootings may occur, and more people could be injured or killed. This has become an all-too-common reality. It has instilled fear in so many of our youth who feel anxious over the necessity and reason for these drills. This heightened awareness oftentimes leads them to overreact to sounds and people who may appear threatening. Discussing different types of situations and their effects may prevent adolescents from reacting to others in negative ways. An active consciousness of their surroundings may be helpful in reducing a teen's level of anxiety and anger. In other words, paying attention to where they spend time outside the classroom is an important factor in understanding the manner in which teens may respond to gun violence.

In the James Garbarino et al. article "Mitigating the Effects of Gun Violence on Children and Youth,"[5] the authors describe some effects of gun violence on young people. This exposure to gun violence can occur in a variety of environments—their communities, schools, homes—or through various forms of media. Sharing actual incidents of violent behavior—schoolyard confrontations, street fights between peers—on social media takes on a life of its own. Instead of two individuals ending their conflict, it is forced to continue.

However, whatever/wherever youngsters observe violence, they may suffer a variety of psychological effects, both long and short term, that manifest in anger, withdrawal, post-traumatic stress, and/or desensitization. The end result often leads to a continuation of the cycle of violence.

Some adolescents are at a higher risk of having problems with violent behavior. Individuals directly exposed to gun violence—for example, those injured by a gun or those who have grown up in a violent home or community environment—are the most susceptible.

However, getting help can be difficult; the long waiting lists for mental health professionals often mean assistance is not provided when needed. Adding the young individual's name to the waiting lists of as many mental health facilities as possible is one key strategy. This may increase the chances of psychological help being more timely.

According to Garbarino,[6] parental monitoring—he believes this includes television, movies, or the types of video games played—is a strategy that should be used to limit exposure to violent behavior. School administrators and mental health professionals should target the youths at risk of committing violent activity and develop therapeutic interventions to both forestall the violence and help traumatized youngsters. Influential members of communities should contribute to efforts aimed at preventing additional gun violence and helping the healing process of those who have suffered from the effects of violent behavior.

There have been numerous articles written about teens and gun violence. The following commentary in a *Harvard Health* blog, written by Claire McCarthy, entitled "Gun Violence: A Long-Lasting Toll on Children and Teens," adds additional information to what was previously noted. It takes into account a medical perspective on gun violence and youth. In it, Dr. McCarthy describes the atmosphere in which many young people live with not only the emotional effect of violence but its physical result as well.

> *There is increasing research that growing up amidst violence, poverty, abuse, chronic stress, or even chronic disease can cause both kinds of results. These adverse experiences put the body on high alert, engaging the fight-or-flight responses of the body in an ongoing way. These increase the risk of depression, anxiety, and substance abuse, but it does so much more. The stress on the body increases the risk of cancer, heart disease, chronic disease, chronic pain, and even shortens the lifespan. The stress on the brain can literally change how it's formed and wired.[7]*

Dr. McCarthy sees the need for people to work together to develop more united communities with resources to contend with this condition. By using this approach, the feelings contributing to the frustration and reactions of young people, along with the degree of violence, can be somewhat diminished. In Dr. McCarthy's words:

> *The communities our children are growing up in, and the world they are growing up in, are increasingly becoming scary places. If we care about our children, if we care about our future, we need to stop fighting among ourselves and come together to create solutions that support the health and well-being of children, families, and communities. We need to nurture our children, not terrify them.*

Let's keep in mind, within communities, there are resources already in place. If you are a part of a supportive agency, reach out and get involved. Exert your influence in helping to stem the tide of gun violence. There are national groups and local organizations you can join—for example, Moms Demand Action, Everytown, Sandy Hook Promise, and United Against Violence. Members of these organizations are typically those who have suffered personal tragedies in schools, public places, and houses of worship due to gun violence. Their efforts and these groups need to be publicized, supported, and expanded. They are brought into local communities as another path to decreasing gun violence and its effects on the lives of youth and their families. These organizations focus more attention on the urgent need for stronger and more effective gun control legislation.

Do What You Can! Get Involved!

In Dr. James Garbarino's article cited above, he describes other factors that in how gun violence affects our youth.

These include whether young people are directly exposed to gun violence or indirectly involved through, as he calls it, "contamination of the consciousness" of youngsters. Here, the author references an apathy toward the frequency of gun violence that has developed in some adolescents. This certainly affects their reactions to it. In a majority of cases, as Dr. Garbarino indicates, the result of a single incident and its effect on youngsters is most often resolved within a year. Dr. Garbarino states, "It's a terribly bad day in a generally safe and supportive life." Interestingly, he goes on to report that most of the trauma experienced directly by youth in our country today is a result of the coverage of murders on social media, which he terms "fed consciousness."

However, there is an exception to Dr. Garbarino's observations. It occurs in single, isolated incidents of gun violence. Nevertheless, as we found with the Sandy Hook, Parkland, Robb, and Apalachee school shootings, the emotional and psychological effects on the survivors, families, and communities aren't short-lived at all! The trauma resulting from these horrific incidents lives on for an indeterminable amount of time in the witnesses and those suffering the loss of loved ones. Many youngsters and the families of victims of these awful events utilized support groups, psychotherapy, and medical assistance. However, as stressed in Claire McCarthy's blog, these traumas may lead to physical ailments as well as emotional difficulties.

As a direct result of these tragedies, multiple organizations have been formed for the purpose of preventing further occurrences of these senseless acts of violence. Through massive efforts aimed at promoting changes in gun control legislation, they have turned their grief and anger into action.

Awareness of these organizations needs to be continuously shared with others whenever and wherever possible. With an expansion of this knowledge and these efforts, and an increase in the number of people involved, these endeavors may have more of an impact on legislators and gun manufacturers—the fundamental mission and driving force of these groups.

Let's turn our attention to gun violence and its impact in schools. Safety drills are regularly scheduled, and staff and students are taught how to prevent themselves and others from becoming additional victims. Resource officers are assigned to many schools, doors are secured, and metal detectors are installed. Fortunately, the implementation of these methods has already saved many from death and injury caused by perpetrators of this form of violence. However, this heightened awareness has created much anxiety in our schools and communities, as previously noted in this chapter.

Dr. Garbarino goes on to describe the greater influence gun violence has in communities. It is an everyday part of a youngster's life, or what he notes as "multiple-incident chronic trauma." He describes these neighborhoods as "war zones." He communicates the idea that adolescents in these communities most often are unable to receive the therapy needed after they experience these traumas. The idea of things "getting back to normal" is incomprehensible to them. Constant exposure to these incidents develops what he describes as "a range of problems, both experiencing and normalizing gun violence related trauma." Dr. Garbarino cites a 1999 study of trauma outcomes by Solomon and Heide. They reported, "Beyond (normal) PTSD, chronic trauma produces poor self-esteem/self-concept, interpersonal distrust, feelings of shame, and dependency."

In addition, Garbarino describes:

> *When other chronic trauma (including child maltreat-*
> *ment in the home) occurs in the context of community*
> *violence, it also yields a more dangerous symptom:*
> *development of a war-zone mentality. Viewing all this*
> *violence as "normal" might develop a "hypersensitivity*
> *to threat and a validation for preemptive assault."*

Some insulate themselves from these feelings. These adolescents are primarily males living in environments where poverty, racism, and beating of others is commonplace. Positive male role models are rare. They may join gangs for a variety of reasons.

Dr. Garbarino had conversations with one actual and two would-be school shooters who were "psychologically and socially vulnerable." Through media descriptions (particularly Columbine), he saw what troubled, angry, and sad teenagers could do when lethal weapons were easily available. He goes on to describe how, in these cases, the adolescents' plans to harm others were revealed on social media. As Dr. Garbarino reports, "In these adolescents' troubled minds, if anger or sadness is the question, gun violence is the answer."

Teens are extremely susceptible, and many have access to guns. In communities in which we are involved, awareness of what Dr. Garbarino describes as the "war-zone mentality" is helpful in understanding what some teens face both inside and outside of their homes. There are ways of discovering what might be troubling a teen:

- Consult school staff who are often aware of harmful occurrences within the community and/or families

- Contact people living/working within a community regarding troubled youngsters

- Seek out peers who often are aware and eager to help a friend going through hard times

Gathering any information takes time and patience. Part of what we as parents, educators, counselors, etc. can do with regard to gun violence and its impact on youth is to become keen observers. See and hear what adolescents have to say and how they feel—*not by words alone,* but by listening to their tone of voice and carefully noticing their behavior. Anger is often quite visible through the sound of a teen's voice and by body language, curtness, rudeness, and facial expressions. If we understand what to look for, we might be able to help a young person diminish the intensity of their feelings and rationally deal with its cause—either by ourselves or with the help of a colleague or other resource.

Knowledge Is Power!!

Asking a teen questions can give you additional insight about their thinking. In addition to the resources previously mentioned, the following information is the result of surveys administered to teens during the 2024–2025 school year. It reflects their opinions on this subject. These analyses provide insight into the reactions of young people. They also serve as a guideline for assisting them in navigating this reality in their lives.

After each question we asked is a list of its *most frequent responses*. Interestingly, these answers aligned with the results of the surveys we conducted about social media and the pandemic. Keep in mind many responses other than those listed were made.

Composition of Survey Respondents (All Three Surveys)

Males: 64

Females: 48

Ages: 12 (1), 14 (1), 15 (5), 16 (10), 17 (8), 18 (72), 19 (14), No Response (1)

Grades: 7 (1), 9 (1), 10 (5), 11 (13), 12 (4), College Freshmen (87), No Response (1)

Gun-Violence Survey Results

1. **When you think of gun violence, what word comes to mind?**
   - Murder
   - Death
   - School Shootings

2. **When you say or hear the words *gun violence*, what thought comes to mind?**
   - School shootings
   - Murder or death
   - People dying for no reason
   - Kids ruined for life

3. **What goes through your mind when there is a lockdown or shelter-in-place drill?**
   - Something is happening in school.
   - It is for safety, or we are unsafe.
   - A shooting
   - What if it is real?
   - We're practicing for something that might happen.

4. **Do you worry about gun violence?**
   - Yes—69 (61%)
   - No—40 (36%)
   - Both—1

5. **Where do you worry about it happening?**
   - My school
   - Public places
   - My home

6. **Do you feel safe in school?**
   - Yes—78 (84%)
   - No—14 (15%)

7. **Why do you worry about it happening?**
   - Because of the many school shootings that have happened
   - Thoughts of losing my life or a loved one
   - I don't

8. **What can people do about gun violence?**
   - Crack down on gun laws

- Have a gun to use when you are in a life-or-death situation

- More background checks

- More school security

- Stop selling guns to anyone

9. **How can people protect themselves from gun violence?**
   - By knowing what you need to do

   - No real way

   - Buy a legal gun

10. **How can adults in your life help you deal with gun violence?**

    - Not keeping guns in the house and around teens

    - Have a gun home for defense

    - Adults educating adolescents about safety and defense

    - Making you feel safe

    - Teach me how to use a gun.

    - Teach us how to deal with situation when gun violence is happening.

11. **Have you personally witnessed someone threatening another person with a gun or seen an incident with gun violence?**

    - Yes—23 (21.1%)

    - No—86 (78.9%)

12. What did you do?

- Nothing, just watched, or mind your own business (many responses)
- Ran away
- Stood there; it wasn't my problem.
- I stayed calm and didn't intervene.
- After it was over, I called the cops.

Conclusions

1) The fear created by gun violence often manifests itself in anger or other intense emotional responses. These reactions may be evident after:

- Reporting of shootings on media
- Incidents occurring in different neighborhoods
- Shelter drills held in school on a particular day
- Reluctance to go to school or other places

This feeling is often not expressed. If an adult is aware of situations or thinks their teen's behavior may be due to any of these factors, using a hypothetical statement such as "Sometimes when (use any of the possibilities suggested above), people don't feel safe or are worried. Is this how you feel?"

2) In some neighborhoods there are more frequent—even daily—incidents of gun violence, so owning a gun or using one to defend themselves is the more likely response for youngsters living, working, or going to school in these environments. Overreacting to this fact is not helpful. If you are

dealing with teens in unsafe environments, remind them that safety goes beyond owning or using a gun or other weapon; there are other methods for remaining safe and reducing fear. And then begin that discussion.

Chapter Five

The Effects of Social Media on Teens

The first edition of this book was written at a time when social media was in its infancy. Since then, it has become a significant part of almost everyone's life. Both its positive and negative uses are for all to be aware of, particularly young people, who often lack judgment when using social media and leave themselves vulnerable to serious negative consequences.

In Buck Black's article "Anger and Social Media,"[8] he describes the ease and rapidity with which social media is used for communicating with others. It is important to remember, however, all thoughts remain on the Internet well beyond the time they were originally sent. In fact, they remain indefinitely. When considering this fact, the question Black poses is "Would the two people who are writing these things have such an argument in front of a huge crowd of people who can hear every word?"

People who view something posted on social media may take sides and gang up on the party with whom they disagree, which could lead to harassment and ridiculing. This sequence of events is worth describing to young people who may or may not be aware of the negative cycle of behavior caused by sending angry messages to others over the Internet.

Another factor to consider is teens do not think logically when they are angry, so what they say may be hurtful. Once something is said in anger, generally it can't be taken back. The best time to speak to another person, whether online or face-to-face, is not in the heat of the moment. Instead, you should wait until all parties have calmed down. Some de-escalation techniques are described later.

Noted in an article by staff members of the Mayo Clinic, a 2018 survey facilitated by the Pew Research Center asked 750 teenagers about their use of social media. In those ranging in age from thirteen to seventeen, 45 percent were online almost constantly, and 97 percent used a social media platform such as YouTube, Meta (Facebook), Instagram, Snapchat, or X.[9]

<<Sidebar—Some of the names of these platforms may have changed by the time this book is published.>>

These statistics reveal social media is a prevalent part of adolescent life. That's why it is vital that we take a serious look at its effects.

Social Media Benefits

Black also credits social media with having the following positive effects on the lives of young people:

- Communicating with others
- Building social networks that provide valuable support

- Allowing those with disabilities or chronic illnesses to connect with others

- Preventing or alleviating some forms of depression

These positive effects come from socializing with others—that is, staying connected and often receiving help and support from peers. Social media can be beneficial for youngsters who are despondent or uncommunicative. Some teens may feel more comfortable getting help from peers through the computer rather than in person. Contrary to what some adults believe, young people can often provide worthwhile advice to their friends. Peer networking can lead to positive results by relieving teen pressure and the burden of concerned, powerless adults. This peer-to-peer interaction can be quite helpful.

<<Sidebar—*Keep in mind an adult's perception of what is a difficult problem may differ from that of a teen.*>>

However, if not resolved, these issues can lead to serious emotional reactions, including acting-out behavior, anxiety, or depression. Many schools have peer counseling and conflict-resolution programs to help students deal with issues that often arise. After proper training by staff members, these groups can often prevent extreme reactive behaviors such as fights, other violent behaviors, and even gun violence.

<<Sidebar—*For staff-training opportunities, check with state, district, or national education associations.*>>

Social Media Disadvantages

Black also discusses the negative effects of social media on teens. These include:

- Distractions
- Disruption of sleep
- Exposure to bullying
- Rumor spreading
- Unrealistic views of other people's lives
- Peer pressure

Researchers have pointed out additional harmful effects. Teens ranging in ages from twelve to fifteen who spend more than three hours a day using social media may be at high risk for developing mental health issues. Another study found, with greater nighttime social media use and what they called "emotional investment," young people unable to access social media sites risked poorer sleep quality and higher levels of anxiety and depression.

Lack of feedback or communication (ghosting), whether on social media or cell phones, was also linked to depression. Older adolescents who viewed photos of peers living the "good life"—pictures of parties or beautiful girls and handsome guys in provocative poses—were more prone to view their own lives as unsatisfying. Those who experienced interactions via social media and posted information about themselves did not feel this type of negativity.

In addition, with this same age group, another study showed the longer these young people used social media, the more they believed others were happier than they. This was not true for those who socialized in the physical company of friends.

Needless to say, regardless of age, adolescents not connected with others remain onlookers and use social media as a source for gauging how positive or negative their lives are.

Being aware of how teens react can help us better understand their moods. With this knowledge, we can forge a path
to discussing these issues and helping teens overcome the
negativity, adolescent stress, and obstacles that, for some, are
caused by social media.

The nature of teens is to be impulsive, so they often post
without considering the consequences. This may make them
the object of negative sources of recognition—bullying,
harassment, or even sextortion. This is particularly true with
some of the social media behaviors dealing specifically with
relationships. In the end, the teen may suffer great emotional
pain and embarrassment, which sometimes lead to depression, anxiety, and even thoughts of suicide.

Ghosting, sexting, and sextortion are three types of online
behavior responsible for causing a variety of negative reactions in teens. *Ghosting* is the practice of ending a personal
relationship suddenly, without explanation. In other words,
withdrawing from all forms of communication with another
individual. This behavior leaves the object of this treatment
totally confused and upset. It may cause depression or even
result in thoughts of suicide. This is a negative example of
subtlety—excluding or blocking another person from communication, which frustrates that person's need to belong.

Sexting is the act of sending sexual text messages. It may
include sending nude or seminude photos and/or videos.
This type of behavior is often done to attract or please a
partner. The teen sometimes doesn't realize these photos will
be made public, regardless of what form of social media is
used. Parents, future employers, and sexual predators may
be viewing these pictures. In some cases, peers may seek
to humiliate or embarrass the individual by using these

photographs as objects of ridicule. They may also be used as a means of revenge after a breakup.

Sextortion is the use of intimate photos to embarrass, threaten, or force an individual to do something against their will. These are consequences teens must be aware of *prior to* considering sexting. Whatever the reason, the ramifications of such actions need to be discussed.

Many teens often forget their actions always have consequences, and many are not pleasant or satisfying. This is a common phenomenon we can label "judgment insufficiency."

In the documentary *Childhood 2.0* by Winans et al.,[10] we are shown that sexting, for some teens, is used as a means of sex education. In addition to this form of "education," online pornography is prevalent and available to young viewers without parental control. Some teens feel whatever is seen or heard online must be perfectly acceptable. Others learn abusive behavior when exposed to pornography at an early age.

Adolescents are typically hesitant to discuss the subjects of sex and relationships with adults. This lack of communication often comes from fear of being judged or lectured. These perceptions need to be discussed. One approach in opening communication is to do so in the context of general conversations about their daily lives. Often a teen will describe a situation in which a friend dealt with one of these topics. This is an opportunity to explore the thinking and ideas of a young person and to begin a discussion about responsible use of social media.

The negative effects of social media on the lives of adolescents were pointed out in the Mayo Clinic article cited above. They recommend the following:

- **Set Reasonable Limits**—Talk to your teen about how to avoid letting social media interfere with their activities—sleep, meals, homework, etc. Encourage a bedtime routine that avoids electronic-media use. Keep cell phones and tablets out of teens' bedrooms.

- Set an example by following these rules yourself. You may mention how in your own life, watching an action-packed television show or reading something suspenseful might affect you in the same way as being on the Internet prior to going to sleep.

- Limiting the use of technology before bedtime may be difficult to enforce since it is not uncommon for homework to be completed on the computer. *But it is worth a try.* Use whatever logic makes sense to your teen.

- **Monitor Your Teen's Accounts**—Let your teen know that you'll be regularly checking their social media accounts. You might aim to do so once a week or more. It is imperative that you follow through with what you tell your teen. You must be consistent if you expect your vigilance to have a positive effect.

- Your teen may complain and tell you your monitoring is an invasion of their privacy, but weather the storm. Both you and your teen will benefit from such watchfulness.

- **Explain What's Not Okay**—There are many ways to help limit the toxic effects of online behavior. Here are a few:

  - Discourage your teen from gossiping, spreading rumors, bullying, or damaging someone's reputation online or in any other way.

  - Talk to your teen about what is appropriate and safe to share on social media.

  - Make them understand how posting photos and comments could hurt others they care about, or even themselves.

- **Encourage Face-To-Face Contact with Friends**—This is particularly important for teens vulnerable to social anxiety disorder. It is best to communicate with others in person so that both parties' meaning, tone, and attitude are clear, and feedback is immediate. This keeps your conversations private, avoids the misunderstandings inherent in posting messages into the void of the Internet, and prevents the "piling on" that results online as social media "surfers" react to your posts.

- **Talk About Social Media**—Talk about your own social media habits. Ask your teen how they are using social media and how it makes them feel. Remind them social media is full of unrealistic images.

- Information gathered directly from teens is a tremendous source of knowledge. It enables us to find out about their lives, beliefs, activities, and effects of social media.

A social media advisory issued by US Surgeon General Vivek Murthy[11] on the potential dangers of social media for children highlights its negative impact on their mental health and overall well-being. This advisory was the result of a request from the American Psychological Association in 2022 for Murthy to raise awareness about the potential risks of social media because nearly 95 percent of all young people, ages thirteen to seventeen, at that time were using a social media platform.

Murthy's report focuses on children and teenagers, ages ten to nineteen, whose developing brains are "particularly vulnerable." The advisory states, while social media can be beneficial as a creative outlet, studies show excessive social media use is linked to problems such as cyberbullying, exposure to harmful content, disrupted sleep patterns, negative body image, and reduced physical activity.

Spending more than three hours per day on social media was found to double the risk of symptoms related to depression and anxiety—at the writing of this book, teenagers were averaging around 3.5 hours of social media surfing per day. The report also outlines recommendations for technology corporations and policymakers to strengthening safety standards, enhance data privacy measures, and consider age restrictions.

Once again, a worthwhile resource for understanding youth and social media is found in the documentary *Childhood 2.0* mentioned previously in this chapter. Many of the ideas discussed above are highlighted in this film. Teens are interviewed, and their responses are helpful in understanding the whys of social media. Young people in this film also emphasize the necessity for the adults living and/or working with teens to be open to *really understanding them, really hearing* their needs and how, *without making judgments*, they are fulfilled.

Adults need to "get it." Young people want to share their ideas if they feel understood and are sure the adult listener is "with them" unconditionally. Being successful at this will encourage adolescents to seek adult assistance when encountering difficulties in their lives.

It cannot be stressed enough—*the effects of social media on teens and their peers is a must-have discussion.* Adults may have the opportunity to discuss this topic when an adolescent brings it up on their own—completely unsolicited. This should not be forced or conducted with a sense of urgency. Important issues need to be aired naturally, as do any other issues about a teen's daily life.

Social Media Survey Results *(Because of their anonymity, teens were able to respond honestly.)*

1. At what age did you begin using social media?

Teens in middle school seem to be the most prevalent age group in the responses to this question. So it is at this age that adults should become more aware and vigilant, looking into sites and the reasons their adolescents are using social media. The adult's best approach to this phenomenon should be from curiosity and awareness, just as they would act if asking about the teen's friends or places they are going.

2. **How much time do you spend each day on social media?**
   - 1–3 hours
   - 4–6 hours

3. **Which social media sites do you visit most often?**
   - TikTok
   - Instagram
   - Snapchat

4. **How long can you go without using social media?**

   Responses varied widely from between an hour to days or longer. This is a question to ask youngsters and, after their response, the reasons why.

5. **What are the biggest benefits from using social media?**
   - Connecting with others
   - Information
   - Education

6. **What are the most harmful effects from using social media?**
   - Cyberbullying
   - Rumors and false information
   - Fears and threats

7. **Have you had any negative experiences from using social media?**
   - Yes—42%
   - No—57%

8. **How can people prevent these bad experiences from taking place to them and their friends?**

   • Being aware of these comments

   • Making accounts private

   • Blocking sources

   • Not using account

9. **What do you think adults in your life should know about social media?**

   • It's not all bad.

   • What kids are doing on social media

   • It has a big impact on teen lives, both bad and good.

10. **How can adults in your life help you deal with harmful things happening to you on social media?**

    • Talk without being judgmental

    • Report cyberbullying and harassment to police

    • They can't.

11. **Do you connect with random people?**

    • Yes—34%

    • No—65.3%

12. **Why or why not?**

    • Easy to do

    • Connect with random people

    • Connect to share information

    • **Conclusion:** Youngsters believe what a random person tells them. This is *blind trust.* This factor is worth exploring with your teen by asking, "How do you know someone is really providing accurate information?"

13. **What are questions you would ask other teens about social media?**

   - Do you learn anything from it?

   - Why do you use it?

   - How do you keep yourself safe?

   - How often do you use it?

   - How do you benefit from using it?

These are areas many adolescents felt were most important for their peers to explore with adults.

Chapter Six

The Effects of the Pandemic on Teens

Although the pandemic is in our rearview mirror, many of its effects are still lingering. Long-term physical consequences, as well as those evident by their impact on families, education, and emotional states of adolescents, are still apparent. Looking at its aftereffects, we see this epidemic may have contributed to the following causes of adolescent anger, which aren't easily discovered.

- Environmental stress, as entire families remained at home together

- Disruption in families resulting from financial hardship and trauma due to the hospitalization or death of one of its members

- Societal stress, as violence and racial tension occurred during this period of time

- Frustrations brought about by virtual education

- Worries about sickness and loss because there was a real possibility of the virus spreading from one person to another, of hospitalization, or even of death

- Threats to the need for security due to the loss of a parent's job and the resultant financial devastation of the family, which could leave the family without heat or electricity, or even homeless

- Threats to the need for belonging due to the isolation of lockdowns and quarantines

<<Sidebar—*When working with adolescents, it requires much patience and trust to uncover the full extent of the pandemic's emotional residue.*>>

There have been many studies about the effects of the pandemic on teens. The overall decline in the mental health of adolescents is noted in the three studies utilized in this section of the book, as are the contributing factors cited by their authors.

In Maria Abenes's article,[12] a new diagnosis of post-traumatic stress disorder (PTSD) has been added as many teens deal with "multiple issues including trauma, the effects of isolation, and a shattered sense of security and safety." The author notes the increase in the number of teens with this condition is due to the "fear of what *might* happen, instead of what *has* happened." This fear stems not only from the pandemic; it is also the result of exposure to other events occurring in our society. To name just a few:

- Violence and racial tension fueled by the deaths of George Floyd, Breonna Taylor, and Ahmaud Arbery

- Storming of the Capitol

- Mass shootings and killings
- Seemingly out-of-control havoc provided by Mother Nature

Another pandemic element that greatly affected families was remote learning. Adults needed to create the space and budget time for work and school, a problematic adjustment for many. Students found it difficult to concentrate without the assistance of teachers, and educators found it challenging to hold the attention of young people through a small screen. In some communities, access to the Internet was another barrier as some students had no access to this alternative form of education. Needless to say, many teens and young students were severely hindered in their learning process. When schools reopened, educators found huge gaps in students' academic abilities.

Additional stress was placed on many minority families. Parents/guardians in Black, Hispanic and multiracial communities encountered additional concerns centering around the loss of jobs and employment stability. This added to the stress of their children, which manifested itself in additional anxiety, problems sleeping, and increased insecurity. Asian Americans experienced an increase of racism and even violence since many people held them responsible for the spread of COVID-19.

The Role of Social Media

Although social media is discussed in the previous chapter, it is worthwhile repeating its impact on teens during the pandemic. It did serve, as previously noted, as a connection to friends and family. Some described it as a means of "feeling better" when depressed, stressed, or anxious. When the killings of George Floyd, Breonna Taylor, and Ahmaud Arbery caused racial unrest, teens turned on their phones to keep up with the news. After George Floyd's death, the George Floyd Challenge encouraged some teens to re-create and post online scenes of the crime.

Black and Hispanic youth used social media to expose racist content, and this approach expanded into describing homophobic incidents reported by LGBTQ youth. It was a reminder to many young people of how harmful social media can be.

Social media affects teen body image. According to Abenes,[12] "Body dissatisfaction and body shaming weighed heavily on them, so much so admission to hospitals for eating disorders rose particularly for those in the twelve-to-eighteen…age group." This is not surprising since so much attention on television, in magazines, and in online ads is devoted to "selling" the idea that being slim or muscular will make you happy and desirable.

<<Sidebar—More recently, ads have shown women of all sizes and shapes, something this author feels helpful in addressing the concerns of young people worrying about body image.>>

For perceptions to change, this issue needs particular attention. The focus should be on what is *really valuable* about an individual, things such as:

- Academic achievement
- Talents/special abilities
- General health
- Simple growth and natural capabilities

This is certainly a difficult task. Instilling this value system in youngsters requires patience and a willingness to listen, *without judging or lecturing*, to what body image means to them. As an adult, speaking about others whom the teen might respect, and who possess positive qualities beyond that of physical appearance, can be helpful. Those you refer to may include family members, friends, entertainment/sports personalities, teachers, coaches, or clergy.

The Role of Reopening Schools

When it was deemed safe for students to return to school, loss in learning was reported by many educators. Pupils described feeling unprepared to return to socializing in schools, and they doubted they'd be able to succeed in their education. Many still felt anxious about contracting COVID-19 while in school.

In an article by John Allegrante,[13] the author described the nature of parental supervision during the pandemic. He notes, since families were homebound and more adult supervision was available, the instance of alcohol abuse in teens declined. This was not the case when a family member needed to work outside the home in order to maintain their livelihood.

However, once the pandemic ended, this tightened structure no longer existed, so negative teen behavior increased. Some adolescents actually slipped back into abusing alcohol and other more readily accessible substances.

Questions such as these can be helpful in assessing this aspect of the pandemic's effects on the adolescents with whom you are working:

- "What was it like staying home and being unable to hang out with your friends?"

- "What were you able to do?"

- "What couldn't you do during this time?"

- "How are things different for you and your family now that the pandemic is over?"

The above questions are deliberately open-ended. They cannot be answered with a yes or no response. By avoiding questions that can be answered with one or two words or the raise of a shoulder (a common way teens communicate an "I don't have any idea" or "I don't care" response), you will be able to gather more information.

In addition to addressing the role of adult supervision during and after the pandemic, Allegrante's study focuses on the subject of rest. This could be more readily monitored by adults during the pandemic. According to his research, getting enough rest is "linked to decreased substance use among teens because it helps with emotion regulation and mental clarity. They have a much clearer sense of discretion."

As you know, good judgment in young people isn't a particularly fine-tuned skill. Lack of pre-sleep stimulation (violent or scary television shows, emotional conversations on their phones, or stimuli from social media), however, enhances the chance of a good night's sleep.

<<Sidebar—*Lack of stimulation prior to sleep is also a theme presented in the chapter on social media.*>>

Another idea explored in this article is the role of adult *support* rather than *supervision*. Allegrante describes this form of adult influence as having the greatest impact in helping young people resolve their stress. Taking an interest in teens' opinions provides a path toward the idea "someone cares about what I think or feel" and helps fulfill the need for recognition. What young people seem to react most favorably to is being taken seriously, not ignored.

<<Sidebar—Recognition (acknowledgment) is an important emotional need for teens. This subject and other sources of emotional satisfaction are discussed in chapter three.>>

One last thought regarding the post-pandemic effects on teens' mental health relates to issues currently affecting our society—political polarization, climate change, and gun violence. These are excellent subjects to discuss with an adolescent anytime they arise. Let's call these teachable moments.

Andrea Hussong's research article "The Impact of COVID-19 on Adolescents' Mental Health"[14] is described in an interview conducted by Kim Spurr, a student in the College of Arts and Sciences, University of North Carolina. Many of the findings reported by Dr. Hussong are consistent with those of other investigators. In this study, written in the midst of the pandemic, she notes steady increases in adolescent levels of anxiety, depression, and stress, particularly in African American, Latino, and LGBTQ youth. Hussong concludes this is the result of a lack of resources for dealing with the emotional and psychological conditions in these populations. The following represents parts of this interview:

Q: What are teens saying about how this has impacted their mental health?

A: One adolescent described, "I know multiple friends who were diagnosed with different things like depression, and I know that was very hard on them."

Linked to these issues are problems with focus and motivation in school, reconnecting socially, and loneliness. Many youths are recovering from traumas experienced during the pandemic, including the loss of family members, the burden of growing up quickly to care for younger siblings or ill relatives, financial hardships involving food and housing insecurities, and more.

One high school senior shared, "I think low-income households are being affected the most because, in the very beginning, the jobs weren't open, and so that probably took a toll and had a lot of stress on parents."

<<Sidebar—*These effects were mentioned in various ways in all the articles cited above. All are worth repeating. However, it must be noted some teens experience events more dramatically than others.*>>

Teens often help friends discuss some of their issues and reactions. They may also direct their peers to adults who have more knowledge and resources available. Often, this intervention can help troubled youngsters release the emotional pressure heightened stress may create and prevent reactive behavior. Youngsters helping their peers can have tremendous value in alleviating unwanted responses to many situations. Observations of contemporaries are helpful in uncovering problems many youngsters won't outwardly admit.

Q: How does COVID-19 and mental health fit in with your overall research?

A: The experiences youngsters had during the pandemic were both a shared and a personal experience. The pandemic came at a time when issues of racism, poverty, and addiction contributed to a rising mental tsunami. Youth development was being reshaped. Rather than asking high school seniors to go back to normal—which returns them to their sophomore years—we need to ask them and the systems that serve them to recognize their new developmental path. It is a changing path young people need help navigating. Our role as an adult, is to provide support and assistance; this needs to be emphasized once again.

In addition to filling the gap in helping adolescents deal with challenges to their mental and physical health, Hussong calls for policymakers and educational systems to provide financial and regulatory resources for "educational and family policies that support recovery as well in mental health services." She further justifies satisfying this gap by stating, "Funds were already insufficient before the pandemic. They are now depleted and exhausted. Incentives for recruiting and retaining teachers and counselors are imperative."

An important point Dr. Hussong emphasizes is the recognition of support staff. She states:

> *Critical positions such as bus drivers, cafeteria workers, and custodians must have more attention paid to their needs because, without them, schools cannot function. We need to recognize that a return to normal is not good enough, nor is it even possible. We are learning much from the pandemic, about what went wrong and what was already wrong before. We can do better; we must do better than a return to where we left off.*

Dr. Hussong describes a broad societal approach to helping adolescents survive the challenges of teenage and young-adult years. It is imperative to pressure policymakers and school systems to do better than what has been provided in the past if we are to afford this generation the opportunity for greater emotional and psychological health.

Keep in mind, by the time this edition of *Peace: The Other Side of Anger* is published, the pandemic will have become part of recent history. However, factors associated with it are worth remembering and addressing. This two-year plague has left residual effects on many teenagers, their families, and society.

Survey on the Effect of the Pandemic on Teens

1. What bothered you most during the pandemic?

- Being away from family and friends

- Online school

- Wearing a mask

- Not allowed outside

2. **How do you think the pandemic affected your family?**
   - It didn't.
   - Not seeing each other
   - Drifting apart
   - Financial stress
   - Sickness and death

3. **How do you think the pandemic affected your education?**
   - Loss of motivation
   - Negatively
   - More difficult to learn
   - Not at all

4. **Did you have use of a computer during the pandemic?**
   - Yes—99%
   - No—1%

5. **Did you pay attention during your school's Zoom?**
   - Yes—46%
   - No—54%

6. **Was it hard going back to school?**
   - Yes—54%
   - No—46%

7. **How did the pandemic affect you socially?**
   - It didn't.

- Social media helped me to connect with friends.

- Youngsters promoted contact with each other.

- Harder to make friends

- Unable to react with friends in person

- Kept me away from my friends

- Terribly

8. How did you connect with your friends?
- Social media

- Phone/texts

- Video games

<<Sidebar—*Technology assisted teens by helping to satisfy their need to belong and connect with others during this time of isolation.*>>

9. During the pandemic, what were you able to do that made you feel good?

- Sleep

- Sports/physical activities

- Play video games

10. How did you make up for things you couldn't do during the pandemic?

- Spent more time outside

- Nothing was different.

11. What was the most helpful thing to do during the pandemic?

- Help with chores and errands

- Play video games

- Learn how to cook

- Read

- Wear a mask

- Sleep

- Time with family and friends

12. **How did your family handle the pandemic with you?**

- Spending time and doing things together

- Kept each other safe

- Became closer

- Not well

<<*Sidebar—Delving more into the answers by asking how, for example, may be helpful in assessing the possibility of long-term effects for a teen in these areas.*>>

13. **How are things different for you with your family now that the pandemic has ended?**

- They are the same.

- We became closer.

- We can go out when we want.

- Unrestricted socialization

- More distant relations

14. **Did anyone you know die during the pandemic?**

- Yes—34%

- No—66%

15. If someone you know passed away, who was it?

- Parents
- Grandparents
- Aunts/uncles
- Family friends

16. If someone you know died, how are you handling it?

A variety of responses were given. Death is a difficult subject for everyone—youngsters as well as adults—to discuss. Possible conversation starters may include:

- Mentioning death was something to which they were exposed daily in the media during the pandemic
- Relating your own experiences with death

However, as previously discussed, adolescent responses may come at some time later than the initial conversation. Patience and time are necessary. This conversation may come as a result of an incident, either personally experienced, witnessed, or described to them.

17. Who helped you cope with the pandemic?

- Parents
- Other family members
- Friends
- Therapist

- No one (*something to explore with the teen*)

18. How did they help you cope?

- Being present
- Talking

19. What questions would you ask other peers?

- Did you pay attention during school Zoom classes?
- How did you connect with friends?

Chapter Seven

Other Sources of Anger

I n this chapter, we'll focus on different sources of anger, such as:

- Unmet expectations

- Injustices

- Traumatic experiences

- Domestic violence

- Drug abuse by a family member

While there are methods to help handle these situations, it is essential to make sure an adolescent is safe after an abusive situation is reported.

Unmet Expectations

Unmet expectations are major contributors to anger in young people. When the hope that something will happen or someone will do something is smacked against a wall, the disappointment that follows can lead to varying degrees of anger. Whether or not this is a frequent occurrence can determine the intensity of an adolescent's reaction. Specific events also carry their own weight. Cancelled plans to go to a movie or a ball game, to celebrate a special event like a birthday or graduation, to work on a special project, or to visit with a parent are some of these sources of unhappiness.

Managing Unmet Expectations

Once you've discovered what expectations were not met, several approaches are possible. A good starting point is having the young person rate each source of disappointment on the anger scale. Once the intensity of all setbacks is defined, strategies for handling those reactions can be developed, beginning with the unmet expectation that evoked the strongest reaction.

Another way to deal with unmet expectations is attempting to depersonalize the offending behavior. In other words, have the youngster think about whether or not this behavior occurs with others. If so, "What does this tell you about the person who disappointed you?" is a good question to ask. Seeing the incident from the perspective of the disappointer may help diminish its effect on the youngster.

Having a teen look at the disappointing behavior as a "promise deficiency" describes another way of helping them handle the offense. This can be accomplished by comparing this deficiency with other limitations (for example, being unable to walk) or educational challenges (for example, being unable to read well or succeed in math).

Self-talk and self-affirmations are two anger managers that can also be used to empower the teen to deal with this source of anger. "This is something I cannot control" and "I am not going to get upset" illustrate two examples of self-talk. "I am a patient person" and "I am an understanding person" are self-affirmations used in handling changes in plans. These techniques will be discussed later in more depth.

Another approach is having the teen remember when they managed disappointment well. Past experiences are useful tools. Once a youngster makes this connection, the thought *I know being let down can be handled, so I have an idea of what to do now* may come to mind and supply the confidence needed in this situation.

No doubt, these ideas may be difficult for a teen to understand and accept. As with many other suggestions, you never know what might appeal to your particular adolescent at any given time. It is important to develop a repertoire of ideas. The motto Try, Try Again bears repeating and keeping in mind.

Injustices

A young person often describes injustice as something being "unfair." Some reasons for this may be directly expressed and observable, while others may be harder to detect. Others can be both.

The frustration from unmet emotional needs leads to other areas of grievance. This may occur when a teen views a request for compliance as a deliberate attempt to take away their freedom—for example, regulations dealing with dress codes, use and possession of cell phones, smoking or drinking, curfews, and academic requirements (homework, papers, examinations, courses needed for graduation).

Criticisms over appearance, lack of achievement, and choice of friends are some of the top-ten causes of anger in teens. Discriminatory statements made about teens as a group or the use of derogatory stereotypes are triggers as well. And, all too often, individuals who are from a specific culture, have different sexual orientations, profess a particular religion, or live in a certain neighborhood are frequently referred to as "you people," "those people," or any number of prejudicial slurs.

Sometimes these statements aren't expressed directly, but are overheard. Where these remarks are made—whether in public (school, workplace, mall, movie theater, or street) or in private—and who makes them (people in the same or different groups, parents, siblings, teachers, police, supervisors, coworkers) determines a teen's reaction. It may be immediate, but often a teen does not respond at the time of the incident.

When responses are not immediate, the anger gets buried and rears its head at a later time. You may see an adolescent walking around with a scowl or cursing and yelling for no apparent reason. When asked about their mood, you may be met with silence or hear "I don't know," "I don't want to talk about it," or "Get off my case!"

Asking, "Does something happening seem unfair to you?" is one way to begin delving into a teen's dissatisfaction. If you receive a positive response, the question "What's making you feel that way?" can keep the information flowing. In the absence of a direct response, listen closely for a conversational clue that will assist you in discovering more about the cause for the teen's anger. Questioning a teen's behavior by remarking, "You seem to really be upset about something the coach said a while ago," or mentioning a past situation can be helpful in getting information.

A great resource to tap into is the teen's peer networks at school, in neighborhoods or any other place they hang out, or on the Internet. These are rich sources of information about potentially harmful or upsetting events—fights, weapons, grudges, rumors, or anything potentially damaging. Peers will often tell you about things they feel just aren't right, are unfair, or need to be addressed. As a guidance counselor, I found students often apprised an administrator or dean of an act of violence—past, present, or future.

Once these sources of unfairness are uncovered, you must help the adolescent find ways of handling them. Discussing the reasons comments were made is a good starting point. The answer to the whys of the actions of others furnishes clues on how a teen deals with different types of injustices. Their responses may be:

- "It makes the person feel big." (effectively means "bigger than I am.")

- "They think they are 'all that' (cool, knowledgeable, fashionable) when they put me down over what I (wear, listen to)."

- "They just don't know anything about us (teens, ethnicities, religions)."

- "He (she) is just stupid."

No matter what they say, just listen—*don't judge!*

Discovering how an adolescent reacts to these unfair judgments is necessary. They may say, "I yell at them and tell them how stupid they are," or "I walk away really mad, and don't want to talk to them."

After hearing the description of their behavior, ask, "What's another thing you can do to keep their remarks from getting you so upset?"

A teen's response to this question indicates whether or not they are capable of resolving this source of anger. If not, try another approach. For example, the question "If the person says things to get you angry and you become upset, who is in control?" This indicates the instigator was the one in power, something every teen desires. Once this sinks in, the teen with whom you are working may be ready to listen—you've just opened a path for them to regain control of their emotions.

Another element to discuss with an adolescent is the "ignorance factor." The remark "Some people don't know anything about the groups they put down" may start you in this direction. Follow this up by asking how the teen discovers information about teachers, programs, organizations, neighborhoods, or subjects such as sex. Knowing their information network is important in understanding a teen's thinking.

More than likely, they will tell you they hear "things" from friends, siblings, or other family members. This is a good time to remind the teen some of the information gathered from these sources may not be accurate, may be based on hearsay, and may be skewed by personal bias. A young person more than likely can understand these concepts.

Remember our motto—"You don't know what's going to appeal to a teen unless you try it." There is no magic bullet, no single method that works all the time with every person. Different approaches are *trial balloons*. They are attempts to find a method of communicating that is effective with your adolescent, one that fosters better understanding of a situation and paves the way for less reactive responses in the future.

Traumatic Experiences

Traumatic experiences may include divorce, death, financial instability, or loss of a home by fire or some other means, all of which are major life changers for a young person. These types of occurrences took place during the pandemic. Many families' lives were disrupted by the pandemic-related deaths of loved ones. When businesses were closed, moms, dads, and other caregivers lost their jobs, which added financial pressure. With the loss of income, came the inability to pay bills and eventual homelessness for many families. These effects are ongoing and, with them, a corresponding increase in teen frustration, difficulty concentrating in school, and more easily triggered emotional outbursts than prior to COVID.

Our job is to find out as much as possible about the issues influencing behavior, whether from teens themselves or from those who live or work in their communities. To those who think the pandemic is behind us, I say, "Yes, but so many of its effects are still evident in the lives of our young people, as can be noted by their behavior."

Chronic Illness

This can be a disease or condition in the young person or a member(s) of their family. In both situations, there are constant pressures to control the illness without letting it severely limit the lives of the affected person or other family members.

During my career as a guidance counselor, I had occasion to work with a young man who had muscular dystrophy. He was referred to me because of his frequent angry outbursts in class. My understanding of the anger and frustration he faced on a daily basis began when he asked, "Why can't I be normal?" He later admitted over 90 percent of his anger was caused by the disease and frustrated need to be "normal." The other 10 percent was due to a combination of the pain he faced on a daily basis and comments made about his appearance by insensitive peers.

So the road to diminishing most of his anger relied on his accepting his disease and disability. This was a difficult task. For him and others who have similar limiting conditions, whether themselves or a family member, one path that can bring solace and acceptance is using the five stages of grief. Though originally developed for those grieving the death of a loved one, every one of those stages must be experienced, without lingering on any one step, when coming to terms with a permanent disability. A mental health professional can help navigate the entire process until the final stage—acceptance—is reached. After that, a youngster can move on with their life.

This approach takes time, specialized effort, and often the assistance of a professional. The American Cancer Society, the American Heart Association, and those who deal with specific illnesses provide these types of services. You can help open the door for a teen going through this experience by mentioning the stages of grief and then guiding them to someone who has the specialized knowledge and experience to assist them to move on with their life.

As with any kind of disruptive influence, the idea of connecting with others who have gone through the same thing and still developed a positive outlook on life can also be helpful. In the case of a physical illness, as with this young man, perhaps his doctor or an association specializing in the particular disease can offer some sort of support group for helping him move past his anger and successfully navigate life.

Abnormal Behavior

This category includes depression, eating disorders, brain injury, or substance abuse, which may or may not be related to the pandemic. These conditions usually go unnoticed initially because they develop over time. Even if a disorder has been diagnosed and is being treated, certain behavioral signs can provide clues to conditions still hidden. Among these indicators are:

- *Increased Nervousness and Anxiety:* A teen may seem fidgety, constantly look around, cough (not from a cold or an allergy), blink their eyes often, or pace a lot. This behavior may be new or one that has increased over time and is now noticeable.

- *Withdrawal from Previously Enjoyed Activities:* An adolescent may have enjoyed going to the movies, hanging out with friends, or participating in sports or other activities, but now they no longer have a desire to participate. "I just want to be alone" is a statement often accompanying this behavior.

- *Changes in Eating and Sleeping Patterns:* Eating or sleeping too little or too much, especially when it is not the young person's usual pattern, should be addressed. Both of these behaviors can be accompanied by a lack of energy or enthusiasm. If you notice these behaviors lasting more than a week or two, they cannot be attributed to a mere cold. Something is really bothering the young person, and it should be addressed.

- *Increased Irritability*: This is beyond the usual moodiness, accompanied by unusual displays of temper, and need for independence often very much a part of the teen years. This behavior appears more quickly, intensely, and frequently over incidents that previously hadn't bothered the adolescent.

- *Drop in School Performance:* This is not only reflected in a drop in grades, but also in a youngster's lack of effort and energy when it comes to anything related to their education. The way assignments are done, the desire to stay in bed instead, or being oblivious about when tests are given and assignments are due illustrate this behavior.

- This isn't about their usual complaints and attitudes toward school. These reactions may have resulted from a particular incident involving a teacher or peer, threats or bullying by other students, or some sort of trouble taking place near or around the school. It may also have resulted from the limited or complete lack of learning that occurred during the pandemic. The comment "What's the use? I'll never catch up" describes this attitude.

- *Increased Acting Out and Reckless Behavior:* These actions can include frequent fighting, cutting school, shoplifting, taking drugs, or engaging in careless acts such as walking across train tracks and hanging on to moving buses or trucks. They may be reactions to divorce, a parent's illness, or bad treatment a teen has observed or been subjected to. Regardless, this behavior is a red flag that shouts, "I need some help. Something is really wrong, and I can't handle it myself."

When any of these behaviors are noticed, they must be addressed immediately. "What's going on?" and "I've noticed you shut yourself in your room more than you used to" move the conversation in this direction. Whether or not a teen says anything, the fact these signs were noticed is a good jumping-off point for getting at their causes. School personnel, close friends, or family members are excellent sources of information about a particular adolescent who is exhibiting these signs.

Environmental Stress

During the pandemic, we were forced to stay at home to avoid exposure to the COVID-19 virus. Many pressures accompanied the lockdown; the loss of income, the real possibility of utilities being turned off, and the threat of homelessness are but a few. Illness and sometimes the death of loved ones from this disease heightened the emotions of all family members. Some of the effects of this outbreak are described by youngsters in the surveys on the pandemic appearing in chapter six. Some causes of environmental stress include:

- *Noise:* Anxiety can be created by the noise in different living conditions—for example, a teen's home or their neighborhood. Different sounds ranging from parents arguing and younger children crying, to screeching sirens and blaring horns, are contributing factors.

- *Living in Crowded Conditions:* Whether an adolescent lives in a house with many people or in an overpopulated neighborhood, they face unwanted circumstances outside their control. In a household with many people, the need for privacy and quiet is often frustrated. Whether they want to listen to music, work on a computer, read, or do things requiring concentration, too many distractions prevent them from doing so.

- These were all-too-common circumstances during the pandemic. When a teen lives in a crowded neighborhood, they often cannot participate in activities as quickly as they desire, or even at all. An example may be waiting for a basketball court or finding a place to play ball. Space just may not be available. The need for freedom to do what they want, when they want, is greatly challenged. Often, the frustration experienced is extreme enough to translate into violence.

Once environmental stresses are uncovered as the source of a teen's anxiety, our focus is in helping them handle their circumstances and be less stressed. In other words, we must find ways to fulfill the need for privacy and space without changing neighborhoods or their family.

One way to accomplish this goal is by discovering some other bothersome situation they couldn't change but learned to deal with. Perhaps, it was a teacher they didn't like and wanted to transfer to another class, but couldn't. In this example, as a means of avoiding additional issues, they might have kept out of the teacher's way and not answered questions in class.

The teen's ability to develop a successful plan in that instance may provide the confidence they can find a way of managing their present uncomfortable environmental situation. Now is a good time to ask, "What do you think you must do to get the privacy and space you need?"

They may respond:

- "Talk to my parents."

- "Move out."

- "Make time to do what I need when I know people in my family are doing other things (watching TV, doing their own homework, or going to their room to play games)."

- "Wait until my brother (sister) is asleep."

- "Keep yelling at whoever is bothering me until they stop."

Have the teen attempt to implement these ideas. If any of the methods work, they have found a way to reduce their own level of anger. If these techniques aren't successful, make other helpful suggestions.

If a youngster hasn't dealt with this unchangeable condition or devised a solution, suggesting the possibilities of moving to a different neighborhood or having their brother/sister leave may result in doubtful expressions. You may get a funny "Are you crazy?" look or a "Yeah, right" response. However, you've made your point loud and clear—current conditions most likely won't change, so a solution must be found.

With these possibilities eliminated, discovering things a teen can do to accomplish what they want becomes the focus of attention. One of the most *powerful motivators* is knowing ways to *control a situation*. Asking additional questions and offering suggestions will help accomplish this goal. It's surprising—it often startles even them—how ingenious and creative teens can be when they are given the opportunity.

<<Sidebar—*Bear in mind a strong reaction brought on by extreme stress or rage usually comes from a loss of control. Once a young person begins to feel they have some power over a situation, their anger will decrease.*>>

"Where do you think you can go outside of your home when you want a place to hang out and no one will bother you?" is an approach to take. A relative or friend's house; a youth center in a church, synagogue, or other organization like the Y; or a bookstore, coffee shop, or restaurant are all possibilities.

If an adolescent is unable to formulate a plan, guide their thinking. "Some people go to (any of the places mentioned) for peace and privacy. Which of these places might be somewhere you can go to get the privacy and the space you need?" prompts them to think outside the box of their usual frame of reference. If there is still no response, at the very least you have given the adolescent some new ideas to consider.

Visualizations are a form of "mental escape" and another tool for helping to diminish anger. It is an anger de-escalator explored in a later chapter. Asking, "Do you ever think about a place where you have privacy and can just relax, or a person who makes you smile or feel good?" You may get another "Are you crazy?" look, a frown, or, if you are lucky, a response.

If there is still no reaction, try, "Some people see themselves on a beach or in the country, or remember something funny someone did or said." This gives the adolescent an idea of what you are suggesting. You can also recommend they mentally picture a special place or person when things get hectic.

Using visualization, whether it's imagining something or actually looking at an actual picture, is a useful tool for calming down. I had a photograph of my oldest grandson, Julian, on my office desk when I was a guidance counselor. When stressed, I looked at it and smiled. This is an example I used with AMP participants, who responded with nods of acknowledgment.

For many adolescents, physical activities are important. Whether it's football, basketball, handball, baseball, soccer, dancing, or singing, these activities are an essential part of a young person's life. In crowded neighborhoods, courts or playing fields are often not available. To a young person who really enjoys any of these sports, waiting or not getting to participate in the sport on a particular day is a source of great frustration. Difficulties also arise when a teen feels others are taking too much time on a court or field or when competition for a particular area, whether by groups or individuals, is intense. Sometimes these delays last over a period of time, and the anger heightens. In any event, as the level of dissatisfaction rises, fights often break out.

These problems are inherent when living in a crowded neighborhood. Methods for handling these challenges need to be explored. At this point, you can apply a method similar to that used for handling other issues of space and privacy. Asking a teen how they deal with limited time to participate in a particular activity is a good starting point. They may come up with the idea of getting involved in organized team sports taking place in evening centers, Ys, churches, temples, and other organizations.

If this idea is not applicable, suggest courts or playing times that can usually be reserved without being a member of a team. The adolescent may respond that making a reservation doesn't guarantee people would be available to play when they chose, or the facilities may not be close to their home. If so, say, "Isn't it better to be able to know you can definitely play (whatever sport), and the time is yours, than not being sure when you can participate or play at all?" This thought may make sense to a teen.

You never know what will work!

Disruptive Family Situations

As with other environmental stressors, a disruptive home life is out of a teen's control. It can severely affect their moods and ability to cope. While many of the approaches already discussed can be used, situations in which adolescents are in danger require contacting outside services promptly. *A youngster's safety cannot be compromised or overestimated.*

Living with a Family Member Who Is Unemployed

In homes where this reality exists, entire families are under stress. Here again is a circumstance all too common during the pandemic. Those who have lost their job become frustrated with themselves and often feel like failures for not being able to provide for their families. They often have short tempers and may physically or verbally take out their frustrations on their spouse or other family members. In turn, those living in this environment may take their frustrations out on each other.

Without a doubt, much tension exists in these households. Their reactions often reach beyond the nuclear family. It can affect relationships with peers, boyfriends, girlfriends, teachers, or anyone with whom teens come in contact.

In families with an unemployed member, addiction or violence often accompanies this problem and may become very much a part of the teen's life. These associated problems necessitate additional tactics. For an adolescent, dealing with a parent's or other caretaker's loss of income requires an understanding of what this means, not only to the young person and other family members, but also to the individual who no longer can provide for the family. This type of awareness requires a willingness to observe the situation from another viewpoint and empathy (an anger manager to be explored in subsequent chapters).

Granted, adolescence is usually a time when young people primarily focus on themselves. Use this phenomenon to help the adolescent understand the frustration these circumstances bring to the unemployed adult. Remarking, "Without an income, how has your father (mother, grandfather, grandmother, or other adult) reacted to losing their job?" becomes a way of having an adolescent view a situation through others' eyes.

Be prepared for "My (dad/mom) yells a lot" or any number of other reactions, including being told there is physical violence in the home.

"How does this make you feel?" is a follow-up to their reaction

Possible answers may include "Scared," "Angry," "Worried," or "Like I want to (hurt/punch) my (dad/mom)."

Asking, "Do you see a way of keeping the other person from making you feel uncomfortable?" may encourage a youngster to suggest methods for managing their own situation.

They may shrug, give you a glazed-over or "I have no idea" look, shake their head, or even come up with an answer. An adolescent may say, "Stay away from my (dad/mom) until they calm down," "Leave the house," or "Not say anything when they are yelling." Avoidance is one way these types of reactions can be managed.

For a youngster who has no idea, respond, "Some people walk out, don't answer back, or let the other person finish yelling." Then adding "Which one of these do you think may work for you?" can be helpful.

"What kinds of other things should you do to prevent your (mom/dad) from getting upset?" is another approach to take with a teen. If there is no response, ask, "How would they feel if you asked to go to a movie/arcade or purchase clothing they couldn't afford?"

Adolescents may respond, "They'd feel bad," or "Get angry." By following this train of thought, they may understand how another person feels and reacts and begin to develop empathy for their unemployed family member's state of mind. By using this approach, teens can learn what needs to be done to keep situations from escalating and avoid having more problems with the person who lost their job.

Living with a Family Member's Addiction

Many of the behaviors evidenced by a family member who has suffered a loss of income may be evident when addictions occur. And much of the avoidance advice is similar. Violent or aggressive behavior when an abuser cannot obtain drugs is one source of anxiety for adolescents. The addicted individual may also take money or other possessions from family members to turn into cash or substances to feed their habits. Either of these behaviors threatens a youngster's safety and security.

Hiding the addiction is another stressor for families with addicted members. They fear the embarrassment and shame if this problem is made public. There is also the concern the abuser may try to hurt others or commit a robbery in order to get the money they need to buy drugs. These behaviors may land an addict in jail or result in their injury or death.

Once a teen has revealed having an addicted family member living at home, different elements of the situation need to be clarified. The behavior of the substance abuser and how it impacts an adolescent and other family members need to be addressed. The question "What does your (father/mother) do when they come into the house?" starts this information-gathering process.

A young person may describe a situation in which the abuser is high or strung out because they are without drugs. Yelling, throwing objects, taking their anger out on the nearest person, or at the other extreme, going into a room, shutting the door, and crying describes this state of affairs.

"When your (father/mother) acts like this, how do you feel, and what do you do?" gets to the impact of an abuser's behavior on a teen. Once this information is gained, the focus of the remaining part of this discussion becomes what can be done to help the young person and the rest of the family handle this situation. Finding out what attempts have already been made to prevent an addict's behavior from escalating is a good starting point. These efforts can include:

- Leaving the house when a teen knows the person will be coming home
- Being quiet when the addict is yelling
- Leaving the room when negative behavior arises
- Going to a friend's or family member's house
- Participating in extracurricular activities

In other words, some form of avoidance is the usual response. With some individuals, this method works; with others, it causes an addict to escalate their behavior.

If an adolescent hasn't mentioned talking to other people about the problem, find out why. Most often, it is either because they are too embarrassed or afraid the abuser will find out. Verbalizing their feelings is a way for teens to limit the effects of these emotions.

"What was it that allowed you to feel it was okay to speak with me?" is something that can work. Trust is the main reason an adolescent feels comfortable enough to reveal private information. Achieving that trust is one of the most important goals for anyone working with young people.

<<Sidebar—Keep in mind, if a teen reveals an abusive situation in their family, it is information that must be reported to the proper authorities. The adolescent should be apprised of this for the reasons mentioned earlier in the "Building Trust" section.>>

A problem arises if you are in an educational or social service agency setting. As a teacher, counselor, social worker, or youth worker, you often don't have the time to slowly gain a young person's trust and then ferret out important personal information. There is only so much time in your schedule, and obviously their case needs more attention.

If this arises, you must discuss it in detail with the teen. You don't want to have them feel you are abandoning them, their trust is going to be violated, or you are not concerned with how they are coping with having an addictive family member. Explain the concept of a support system and how it is helpful to have others whom they trust and know will be there for them when you cannot be. Isolating themselves and feeling they have to handle their circumstances alone often lead to depression or anger.

"Find others with whom you can trust to talk about your (relative's) addiction" is a good first step. If not, suggesting a close friend, family member, girlfriend, or boyfriend may open a teen's thinking in this direction. It should be noted that talking about this uncomfortable situation and no longer keeping it a secret are signs of strength, not weakness.

There are support organizations: Families Anonymous, Al-A-Teen, Al-Anon, Phoenix House, and Narcotics Anonymous. Let the teen know these organizations value anonymity— hence, the use of the word *anonymous* in their titles—and *never* provide the names of their members to outsiders. This factor can overcome any resistance to joining such a group. In addition, these organizations may assist in building their trust and overcoming their resistance to seeking outside help. Information regarding these organizations can be found online. The more material the teen gathers about them, the greater the confidence they will have to attend meetings.

Part of empowering a teen is providing resources for dealing with a variety of problems underlying their anger. If and when they take advantage of your suggestions is their decision to make. At the very least, you have given them choices.

Living in a Violent, Unpredictable Family

This atmosphere is a more obvious threat to an adolescent's need for safety and security. Questions that express this type of stress are:

- "What's going to happen next?"
- "What's (the household member) going to be upset about today?"
- "Where can I go until they are in bed (or passes out)?"

The approaches to helping youngsters and their families deal with violence follow many of the same paths described for addictive families. Often, staying away from home and avoiding the people or situations that are unpredictable in a family work well for a teen. Using different types of avoidance and obeying the mandate to report physical or emotional abuse are the first steps to take. Speaking with friends, family members, girlfriends, and boyfriends is another way to relieve some of the pressures caused by the secrecy surrounding the abuse.

A great starting point for help in the area of family violence is contacting the Domestic Violence Hotline (1-800-799-SAFE (7233)) or local, city, and state mental health agencies found online. The experience and resources these organizations provide are essential to an adolescent's physical and emotional safety.

Sometimes, prior to seeking assistance, situations must reach a crisis point before people feel they have endured enough and need outside help. Providing young people and their families with resources is often the greatest assistance they can receive.

Some of the ways to meet their need for security were pointed out earlier in this chapter; these can help them deal with the instability occurring in their household. Getting a handle on coping with this source of stress will help a young person feel they have some control. Once this occurs, their reactions and level of anxiety become more moderate.

Knowledge of the Causes of Anger

Several chapters in this book have been devoted to describing various reasons for anger in youth. One of the purposes of giving you information on the causes of anger is helping you and the adolescent become aware of what creates this emotion.

The many causes described in the chapters themselves should be considered a menu of ideas from which to choose. When working with teens, their behaviors and conversations offer clues to the most relevant causes and situations in which they find themselves. This should provide hints as to which techniques to use.

Chapter Eight

Challenges in Working with Teens

Effectiveness Blockers

Before taking this process further, your readiness to handle an angry adolescent's needs must be addressed. Being prepared for this task requires an *"attitudinal checkup,"* which can reveal conditions that need to be addressed. The judgments you make and the different feelings you have about a young person's behavior may turn up during this self-reflection.

You may think how a teen acted was just plain dumb, made absolutely no sense, or was a deliberate attempt to hurt other people. "What was that kid thinking to get themselves (suspended, into a fight) over this stuff?" sums up these types of evaluations. You may find their reactions disappointing, annoying, unacceptable, or chronic. No matter what you have tried to do to influence them, nothing has worked. You may feel you should write this adolescent off as incorrigible, not worth the effort.

It is easy to become irritated or tired of being involved with a difficult teen. You have your own life, and this type of individual tends to take up too much time. These sources of dissatisfaction are important to know as a parent, teacher, counselor, social worker, or youth worker. Your goal is to help the youngster manage anger in ways that won't be harmful to themselves or to others. Letting your emotions override your ability to help them work through anger management issues is *not* helpful.

Maintaining objectivity when working with a young person is crucial. Stepping back takes a real effort. The how-to of developing this skill will be discussed shortly.

Your readiness to handle a teen's anger also involves knowing some of the roadblocks hampering your efforts. One possible obstacle is becoming a victim of "*contact anger*"— when you experience the same anger toward whoever or whatever caused the anger in an adolescent. This occurs when individuals get caught up in an individual's or a group's emotional reaction over an issue. This reaction is a form of "*mob mentality*" that occurs in groups of people in reaction to news events, pop culture, religion, or politics. The intensity of these shared emotions is often greater than a single individual's. You lose the ability to use reason and, instead, emotionally unite with the angry young person or mob.

If you experience contact anger, both you and the teen have allowed anger to take control. Being aware of contact anger is the first step in preventing it from happening. Once you find this reaction starting to surface, using self-talk (an anger manager to be explained in more depth later) can be helpful. "I am not getting caught up in this teen's anger," "I am in control," or "I am here to help this individual deal with their anger, not be controlled by it," said silently by you illustrates this tool.

Sometimes an adolescent will make a negative remark about you. It may be about your appearance, your role in their lives, or your ability to be helpful. "You look crazy (sick, sloppy, fat)," "You are a lousy (parent, teacher, counselor, etc.)," or a statement such as "You don't really know how to get me to stop fighting (or any other negative reaction)" are remarks exemplifying this tactic. The youngster's goal is to upset you. Somehow, they know just the right button to push if you allow them to use it. If it is a successful distraction, any efforts you make to assist them in changing their behavior become sidetracked. Once again, keep your mind focused on helping the teen manage their anger.

There are various strategies for avoiding these roadblocks. Using "focus protectors," which involves letting adolescents know you are aware of their game and don't want to play it. is one such technique. A statement such as "You are trying to keep us from dealing with your anger. Let's stay on track" illustrates this approach. You can also take deep breaths or use a self-talk phrase—such as "I will remain focused" or "I am going to stay on track"—to prevent yourself from colliding with these obstacles.

With this knowledge of the roadblocks that can occur when dealing with a young person, take whatever steps are necessary to remain calm and keep them—and yourself—focused on the behavior to be corrected. Some suggestions on how to accomplish this goal have already been made, and more will follow.

Additional Techniques for Staying on Target

- Counting forward or backward

- Saying, "I am a calm person," or "I am the parent/professional." These are self-affirmations and describe your qualities rather than your behavioral goals.

- Thinking of a humorous or pleasant experience with the adolescent

- Silently chanting a phrase repeatedly—for example, "Needles and pins, pins and needles" (recommended by an adult participant of AMP)

- Speaking to someone regarding the teen and their behavior.

Additional ideas on reducing the intensity of anger will be presented later. Although these methods are explained for an adolescent, they also apply to you for overcoming contact anger.

Is a Third Party's Intervention Needed?

Once a young person has described past incidents and their effects, an important decision must be made. Two factors are significant. The first deals with your ability to serve the best interests of the teen. The next focuses on whether or not the trust you have gained with the adolescent can be taken to another level. The question "Does what the youngster described to me require assistance going beyond my expertise and experience?" sums up these concerns.

Several factors need to be taken into account to address these uncertainties. The first involves knowing whether or not you can be objective enough to help a teen fully understand and handle the situations being described. Can you prevent your feelings for a teen from getting in the way of being helpful? If you feel their pain too strongly, relate too closely to the situation, or develop a strong negative attitude toward those who have harmed the teen, then you cannot be as helpful as you may want to be.

Another area to examine is your ability to help an adolescent understand the meaning of their present situation and connect past incidents with their recent behavior. The issue is whether or not you know what to look for when events are described. Besides the obvious reactions young people reveal through their use of words, asking the following questions is helpful:

- "Can I recognize other feelings being expressed by the teen's body language or tone of voice?"

- "Do I know what to look for in what is *not* being expressed?"

- "Do I know how to get beyond any roadblocks a teen may put in my way to prevent me from understanding the impact incidents had on them?"

- "Do I have the knowledge, experience, and expertise required to help manage their anger and help them heal?"

This *mental soul-searching* calls for complete honesty.

Another area to consider is your ability to help a teen to move past the effects of earlier incidents in their lives. This part of the helping process necessitates having a repertoire of ideas and the skill to use past experiences with these tools. It makes use of an individual's instincts in taking specific actions and their faith and confidence in doing so.

Additional factors may also come into the picture when a third party is involved. Some of the hidden causes of anger involve different forms of abuse and trauma. Some carry the burden of mandated reporting. For those, it is important to know the answer to the question "Is some type of therapy or follow-up provided by the agency when a report is filed?" If not, there may be other referral sources an organization can recommend to help a mistreated youngster.

In addition, siblings or other family members may have been mistreated or may have witnessed the abuse. This dynamic can call for knowledge of group or family treatment methods and may also require more expertise than you possess.

Finally, your comfort in dealing with depression, violent behavior, or any other subject a teen may describe as important must be considered. If a particular topic makes you feel uneasy—for example, rape, extremely violent episodes, or LGBTQIA+ issues—or makes you think you are ill-equipped to be effective, then it is time to refer the teen to another mental health professional or source of assistance.

The decision becomes "Does this adolescent need someone who can give them more help than I can provide?" If your response to this question is yes, then reading the next section will be helpful. It describes ways of assisting the adolescent realize the benefit of speaking to another person.

If you feel comfortable continuing to help a young person, then skip to the "Setting Behavioral Boundaries" section of this chapter.

Helping a Teen to Accept the Idea of a Third Party's Help

Once you have made the decision to step back and refer the adolescent to a third party, the challenge becomes convincing them to accept this idea. There are several ways to approach it. The first involves applying the trust developed toward you one step further. It requires a teen to believe you—the person with whom they shared their upsetting experiences—would only suggest something in their best interest. This is an idea that may be difficult for an adolescent to understand.

Providing the reasons for referring them to someone else continues this process. One approach involves using yourself as a role model. This becomes another teachable moment. This is the time when you acknowledge having limited experience and knowledge in dealing with the situations the teen has described. The message being conveyed is "When I need help with something beyond my experience, I ask someone with more understanding of the situation." This admission shows you are not afraid to say you don't know something or are weak in an area. It's not just your words and tone of voice, but your behavior carrying the strength of this message. It can be an ego-shaking admission to ask for help, but one paying great dividends in accomplishing this transition.

Without allowing too much time to elapse, the reason why another person can be more helpful to them needs to be addressed. "This individual (social worker, therapist, psychologist, counselor, priest, rabbi, etc.) has worked with many other people your age who have gone through similar experiences. They can give you the best chance of understanding your situation and finding ways to get past it" addresses this concern.

A teen may strongly resist this idea. They may walk away, start cursing, slam doors, or show some other strong sign of disapproval. These are common responses. At this point, leave this suggestion alone. They need time to calm down and think through this idea.

Reasons for a Youngster's Resistance to Working with a Third Party

There are many reasons a teen resists working with a third party. The first is difficulty in repeating painful or embarrassing highly personal details. Young people do not open up easily. It was probably extremely difficult for them to open up to you. Now, they are being asked to reveal their fragility to yet another person who is most likely a complete stranger.

This discomfort needs to be acknowledged. "I think it was hard enough for you to tell me about what happened. Now, you are being asked to tell this experience to someone you don't even know. I can understand your being uncomfortable" addresses this resistance. Follow this up by explaining the benefits of retelling their story. Tell them the first time people speak about something difficult is usually the hardest. This may soften their opposition to describing events again.

A second reason is the adolescent may be reticent to revisit their pain. If so, reassure them; by taking another look at a situation, they may remember details that were left out the first time. It is also an opportunity to look at what happened in a different light. By getting varied viewpoints, they may hear more ideas on how to better handle a similar situation in the future.

Regardless of their reaction, continue to follow this train of thought. It is at this point you can explain the best source of help often comes from people who work with a specific organization (child protective services, victim assistance agencies) or specialize in the types of situations they experienced. If you know of other adolescents who have spoken to a particular individual and felt better afterwards, let the youngster know.

Another objection a teen may have to talking to someone else may be their fear of *"image busting."* They may feel, by speaking to another person, their peers will view them as someone who is incapable of handling their own problems—in other words, someone who is unable to be in control of their own life.

"Sometimes people think, if they ask for more help, they look weak or stupid. Is that what you think?" addresses this idea. A positive response lets you know you are on the right track. If this is the case, you can again point out *you*—not they—are the one seeking another person's help and ask, "Do you think I look stupid or out of control?" It gives the message you are walking the walk, not just talking the talk. You are doing what you are telling them to do. They may still be opposed to speaking with someone else; however, you have given them another idea to consider.

"I don't want to go to a shrink. I'm not crazy!" is another reason for a teen to object to this kind of outside intervention. Question the reasons they think only crazy people speak to "shrinks"—using their words shows a willingness to try to understand their perception. After hearing their response—which may even include an admission similar to "Not only crazy people go for counseling"—find out if they know people who weren't "nuts" and went for help. If so, discover the reason the individual needed to speak to a third party.

If a youngster doesn't know anyone who has been in therapy, gives you a "you've got to be kidding" look, or offers no response at all, steer the discussion to why, in general, people seek help. "Who do people go to when they get sick?" and "If someone doesn't understand something in school (or an incident occurs), whom do they turn to for help?" illustrate this approach. You are focusing the spotlight on other people, rather than on the teen. This results in a greater likelihood the teen will respond.

"Have you ever gone to a doctor when you were sick or received help with an incident occurring in school?" is a more direct approach. If positive responses are given, the idea of seeing a third party is reinforced. A youngster may or may not admit they have obtained these sources of help. Regardless, the thought can't be unspoken, so the adolescent is bound to consider what you've said. Possible teen reactions are "So!" or "What's your point?" or "Going to these people isn't like seeing a shrink."

No matter what response you receive, and even if you receive none, you must stress this point: Whatever help people need, going to someone who specializes in their problem offers the best chance of fixing what's wrong.

An adolescent may still remark, "I don't need anyone else's help," "I'm the only one who can make this right," or "I've told you about my problem. No one else can do anything about it or me." If they do, leave this idea alone. You have taken them as far as they can go at this point.

Another reason a young person may be reluctant to speak with a third party is they may feel rejected…again. They may have already experienced a painful rejection, and it may be the underlying trigger for their anger. If this is true, you must make it clear you are not rejecting them, and you must do so immediately after suggesting they speak to a third party.

An adolescent may verbally lash out by saying, "You're like my dad. When things get tough, he has someone else take care of it." At this point, you must do two things: not react to this tirade, and let it run its course. Once the teen has calmed down, have them explain the similarities and differences between their relationship with you and the one they have with a parent or other caretaker.

Using this approach demonstrates you have taken the teen's comments seriously, without judgment, and you are not rejecting them, as other important people in their life may have. Point out you are referring them to a third party because you have limited knowledge, not because you just didn't want to be bothered with them. This alone may help put your referral in a positive light and contrast it to their experiences with a parent or others who have rejected them.

When an adolescent believes no one but you can solve their problems, defining the role of the professional to whom you would like to refer them may change a teen's thinking. Explain the professional is a person who:

- Is not there to tell them what to do

- Will look at the situation and suggest different ways of viewing it

- Is there to help them come up with ideas they may never have considered

Stress to the teen it is *their decision* what solution, if any, they want to use.

An adolescent may fear the third party will find something "really wrong" with them or cause them more pain. This fear may or may not be verbalized. If not, ask, "What uncomfortable things do you think this person will find out about you?" Responses can vary. They include:

- Embarrassing or harmful things they may have done to themselves or others
- Behavior that reveals weakness
- Involvement with drugs
- Acts of vandalism, violence, or self-harm

Adolescents fear exposing what they perceive as their character flaws. They are rarely rational enough about their own actions to realize they were only reacting to painful, fearful, and harmful acts by others.

Assisting the youngster to view their actions as *responses to circumstances, rather than innate character flaws*—in other words, changing their perceptions of themselves—is another way to break down their resistance to speaking to a third party.

When a teen has been hurt by another person, they often bury the pain and don't want to experience it again because when the pain is revisited, it may be more intense. Reassure the teen that the more they discuss their situation, the easier it becomes to describe and resolve. This may offer a path to working through their fear(s) and objections.

These *guesses* are *trial balloons* you can launch to discover the reasons behind young peoples' reluctance to speaking with others. They can also be productive tools to stimulate additional thinking and gain more insight into the teen. The time and effort you expend addressing the idea of working with a third party is an indicator of the value you place on it. By trying many different tactics, you may find one that will influence the teen. You never know what and when something you've mentioned is going to work. Again, the maxim Try, Try Again should be your mantra when working with adolescents.

Infrequently, a young person may readily agree to talk to a third party. Their reasons, however, may not appear sound. "I'll go to this person if you want me to" or "I'll go just to prove the shrink can't help me" illustrate this example. Others will set specific conditions for their compliance. "I'll go two or three times" illustrates this idea.

Whatever reason they give or condition they make, don't be concerned. These assertions represent a means of showing some control over what they are being asked to do; they are face-saving remarks. Acknowledge their decision, and then see what happens. It's up to both the helping individual and the adolescent to determine how far their relationship will go. You've led the horse to water.

The idea of seeing a third party may take some time for a young person to accept. If they decide to take this step, whenever possible, offer to go with them the first time. By accompanying them, you are physically and psychologically supporting their decision, not to mention showing them once again that you are not rejecting or abandoning them. By helping teens decide to take this step, you bring them closer to ridding themselves of a part of their painful past and provide them with a way to move toward a more peaceful future.

Setting Behavioral Boundaries as a Way to Overcome Obstacles with Teens

Developing behavioral guidelines for young people is one of the hardest tasks for an adult to undertake. The example in this chapter serves only as a behavior modification model that can be used with teens. Feel free to apply it, modify it, or completely change it to fit your specific needs. The dialogues are fictional and for clarification only. They are illustrations of how to communicate in a way that encourages an adolescent to change their behavior.

One of the sources of anger in young people was explored in chapter three. It dealt with unmet emotional needs. One of these was the freedom to go with whomever, wherever they chose and whenever they wanted. Challenges to this need are often met by yelling, cursing, slamming doors, or even running away. This gives rise to the question "How can you set limits an adolescent will obey?" The following description will provide an answer.

The Initial Approach to Working with Adolescents and Meeting Their Needs

Using the anger scale is one approach to determining the intensity of teen anger when they perceive their freedom and control is being limited or taken away. Have the adolescent rate their reaction to each of their restrictions.

Another way to view the intensity of their reactions is to have them list three to five of the most bothersome restrictions and rank them from the most upsetting to those with the least impact. Once accomplished, you and the teen should look first at the limits causing the least amount of frustration. These particular boundaries are the easiest to work with since they cause the least emotional reaction. That means they provide the greatest opportunity to develop an emotional-reaction structure an adolescent will be willing to follow. This will become their model for dealing with more difficult limits to their freedom.

The next step is to develop an "adolescent-friendly" plan to deal with this restriction. Inform the teen a component of this plan should include ways to *avoid, remove, or diminish the length of time* their freedom is restricted. This alone may ensure their compliance.

Guidelines can be discussed before or after an incident has occurred. The views of both the teen and the adult about the merits of these limits being imposed should also be considered. This information-sharing process allows each party's perception to be expressed and acknowledged. At this point, you can fruitfully exchange ideas and jointly develop a plan for going forward.

Conditions for Setting Guidelines

Let's get to the how-to of setting behavioral boundaries. There are two conditions that are necessary:

- *Condition Number One—Timing of the Discussion:* Readiness, in this case, means when all parties are calm. Nothing can be accomplished when the atmosphere is charged with hostility. Allow all parties, particularly the young person, the time to calm down after a situation has occurred.

- *Condition Number Two—Adolescent Involvement in Creating Guidelines*: Adolescent involvement is crucial to the success of setting guidelines. Both parties must state clearly what they need, and a mutually agreed upon framework must be established. If the adolescent is not on board, no matter how many guidelines you set, they will not be successful in behavior modification.

Keep in mind miscommunications and conflicts often occur because the specifics of what was wanted, needed, or expected were not clear. Active listening skills—paraphrasing and clarifying—were not used. The statement "What you are saying is you feel confined" or a question clarifying expectations was missing. Assumptions were made. Once that occurs, relationships almost certainly head in the wrong direction.

Let's add another reason for being specific. Many young people have a knack for manipulating what is said. To illustrate this point, let's use the case of the nonspecific rule.

The Situation

Parent: "I want you home at a reasonable hour."

Adolescent: "Okay," but they have their own idea of what is "reasonable."

This is a school night. The young person strolls in at midnight. The parent thought the "reasonable hour" was around ten thirty. The parent waited up even though they had to get up for work at six in the morning.

The Result

The parent was enraged at the child and yelled as soon as the child entered the house. The idea of a "reasonable hour" became the subject of a much-heated and lengthy battle. The parent "grounded" the youngster until they "acted more responsibly."

The teenager storms out of the room mumbling, "I'll show you!" The next night, they stay out until two in the morning.

Summary

This example illustrates what often becomes a source of conflict and anger between parents and adolescents. It shows how the lack of specifics in rule setting—in this case, telling the teen a specific time when they should be home—leads to the frustration of the needs for both freedom and structure.

You must be very specific when setting parameters for the rules you want to establish with a youngster. We'll continue with a curfew-setting situation to illustrate how to develop effective behavioral guidelines with a teen. Before starting this process, keep in mind:

- This approach can serve as a model for developing other guidelines.

- Whatever behavior needs to be improved, you must come up with rules that are easy to both implement and measure. That is, for both adult and child, this plan should involve simple steps to follow and monitor. Success is a great motivator. This is an opportunity for an adolescent to experience a sense of accomplishment for both setting up the structure and adhering to its guidelines.

- A young person is empowered to "own" the results if they have been a part of the planning process. By helping develop this idea, the adolescent feels an obligation to see it through.

An Illustration of Establishing Guidelines

It is essential teens know and accept the reasons for establishing guidelines. This is the starting point for this process. Using the above example, before the adolescent walked out the door, there should have been a discussion about the curfew so both the reason and the time established were clear.

Among the most common reactions adolescents may have for resisting a curfew is they view themselves as responsible, trustworthy, or old enough to know when to come home. The question "Why do I need a curfew?" expresses a youngster's attitude.

There are two possible responses to this. You can list all the things a teen has done wrong up to that point: getting poor grades, skipping school and you receiving calls from school regarding the lack of attendance, not doing homework, and hanging out with peers who get into their fair share of trouble, etc.

This approach, however, may escalate the discussion into a full-blown conflict because the adolescent feels attacked. They then get more upset and react accordingly. For the teen, having their freedom restricted while being labeled irresponsible is similar to being stabbed twice.

This is often the way many issues have been handled in the past, and it describes one reason why youngsters resist having limits set. Who wants to get repeatedly hammered about what they do wrong? The answer is no one, particularly teens. Many times, they are well aware of their own failures and feel bad enough, even if they don't overtly show it.

<<Sidebar—*This is not about whether or not a young person has been doing the wrong things.*>>

An alternative approach deals with a teen's difficulties in a different way. This method involves adults listening to what an adolescent has to say and accepting their views—even if they don't agree.

The next step is deciding what to do with the information the teen shared. One way to deal with a youngster's lack of achievement in school is by expressing your concern. This can be done in various ways. To show your worry without making any judgments, you may say:

- "I am concerned about school."
- "I noticed the low grades on your math tests."
- "You passed four out of seven subjects on your report card (accentuating the positive while letting them know you are aware of the three failures)."
- "Mrs. Jones called to suggest you get some help in algebra."

Once this has been done, you have laid the groundwork for explaining the reasons you think a curfew may be helpful. "I know you are capable of doing better. I think time is a factor. This is why I think we need to look more carefully at the time for you to be home" describes this rationale.

Safety is possibly another discussion point for setting a curfew. "I worry about bad things happening to you out there. I know you are a good kid, but there are some others who hang out looking for trouble. A lot of things happen later at night when there aren't many people around" expresses this cause of anxiety.

With both of these sources of concern, it's not *what* is said, but *how* that determines whether the adolescent will heed your instructions or ignore you. This approach emphasizes *reason over hostility*. Without the emotional interference caused by feeling verbally assaulted, a teen is more capable of understanding and addressing your fears. When this state of reasonableness exists, a productive discussion is more likely to occur.

Benefits of Curfews for Teens

Once an adolescent hears the reasons for setting a curfew, the "What's in it for me?" factor has to be considered. The most convincing answers to this question come from the adolescent. If they have a response, it's time for the next step in this process. If they can't see any benefit to having this limit placed on them—the most common situation—making some suggestions is helpful.

Try to think as a teen does. They don't like to be hassled. "Wouldn't you like it if I didn't have to argue with you, and we both were cool with each other?" takes you in this direction. The answer to this no-brainer will undoubtedly be a resounding yes. However, raised eyebrows, quizzical looks, and frowns can also occur. Or the question "What does this have to do with a curfew?" may follow your remark.

One response to an adolescent who has doubts about the setting of a curfew may be to tell them they would then have time to complete their work without being hassled. Expect to hear these typical responses to this rationale:

- "I can get those things done when I come home from school."

- "I'll do it when I come back." (Then comes the "I'm too tired" excuse.)

- "I'll do it before school tomorrow." (Then it's often done in a rush.)

At this point, saying, "So far this year, you haven't been able to do what needs to be done at any of those times," gives a youngster something to think about.

Assuming they haven't taken a *mental leave of absence* by this time, have them attempt to see a curfew as something that hasn't already been attempted and just might work. Mention it just may be a way for them to get what they want; this will almost certainly sweeten the curfew "pot."

No doubt, the question "How?" may be raised. Patience—and a lot of it—is required. Take a deep breath, and then continue this tennis-match-like exchange. Using the example of improved grades, tell them, besides avoiding the "hassle factor," by obeying the curfew and getting better marks (be specific—whether it's achieving a specific grade in one subject or passing all their classes), they:

- Are showing they are both trustworthy and responsible

- Have given themselves the opportunity to do more of the things they want

- Will have more time to hang out with friends, play video games, go shopping, play basketball (or any other sport they like), or go to the movies

These results answer the typical teen question "What's in it for me?"

Once these benefits are described, the success of this rationale will be determined by an adolescent's response to "Wouldn't these things make a curfew worthwhile?"

If the answer is yes, it is time to move on to setting the time for the curfew. By accepting the idea of this time limit, a young person has become part of this process and "owns" it. It becomes a joint venture in which both of you have an opportunity to reach your goals.

However, before setting the time for the curfew, it is important to pause and point out what the adolescent has already accomplished during this process. They have:

- Accepted the idea of a curfew

- Agreed to it as a means of getting things done

- Given themselves the chance to be seen as responsible

- Seen a curfew as the means for gaining more freedom

The idea behind this pause for reflection is to show an adolescent they have been successful in using this method so far. It also instills a sense of pride of ownership. The maxim Success Breeds Success summarizes this idea and is something young people, as well as most other individuals, need to experience.

Setting the Curfew

This process requires trusting a youngster's ability to make responsible decisions. The why and how of this involves two ideas:

- Allow the power of positive expectations to be your jumping-off point. "I am counting on you to come up with a time that allows you to do what you agreed to" describes this leap of faith. Here, the adolescent has a chance to prove they can act responsibly.

- Do not take this step in isolation. In your mind, you already have a specific time for this curfew, and it will act as a reasonable guide for this process. Your power of positive thinking is being tested by handing over the reins to the adolescent for this part of the process.

Keep in mind the goal in this case is to see an improvement in grades—something that has not been accomplished in any other way up to this point. As with some of the other things discussed earlier in this book, you don't know if an idea will work unless you try it. These ideas can be useful in resolving issues with teens, whether or not, in this instance, the adolescent agrees to a curfew.

Let's say the curfew you set in your mind is somewhere between eight thirty and nine thirty. If the adolescent's idea of a time to be home coincides with yours, no further discussion is needed. If the teen's curfew is within fifteen minutes of yours, it can work. Accepting the teen's curfew may send a positive message and satisfy their need for trust, control, and independence.

If, however, a youngster's curfew is a half hour or more later than yours, ask them if they think their deadline will allow enough time for them to not just complete, but thoroughly accomplish what must be done. Their reply will determine whether or not further discussion is needed.

<<Sidebar—By appealing to a youngster's reason, you'll be surprised how much more willing they are to reconsider the idea of a curfew or a particular time for it. This idea requires you to make another leap of faith.>>

However, if there is a big difference between the time you feel will work and theirs—let's say nine thirty is yours, but the teen thinks eleven will be okay—other strategies need to be employed. Ask the teen to justify their choice of curfew. Explain the reasons for your time, but indicate you are willing to listen to their reasons for proposing a much later curfew.

If after this the teen insists their time is fine, but you are still not convinced, propose another alternative, perhaps a compromise. Suggest a short-term "test" of the teen's curfew —perhaps a week or two.

A teen may bargain with you. They may tell you they will be able to accomplish a task without a curfew, and then plead with you to give them a chance to prove it. "If I don't get better marks by the spring term, I'll come home earlier" illustrates a familiar adolescent strategy. Making this deal may avoid further resistance to a curfew. It gives a youngster the opportunity to either prove or disprove the necessity of having a curfew. This approach makes the teen an active participant in the solution and satisfies their need for trust and control.

Whether it is setting a curfew or avoiding one by using other means, *specific details are necessary* as part of the plan to obtain better grades.

Components of the Curfew-Setting Process

In this example, completing chores and homework, and ultimately an improvement in grades, are the reasons for having a curfew. Setting this limit involves:

- **Listing** all elements involved—all assignments and work to be completed, times to carry out these actions, which should not be immediately before going to bed or leaving for school. The methods for monitoring these behaviors should be written down and agreed to by all parties.

- **Setting** guidelines—the specific place the teen should leave the completed work (a kitchen table or a person's desk), the time it will be checked daily, and the specific person (parent, guardian, staff member) who will be responsible for consistently checking the work. If the teen is aware these steps are being *consistently taken*, they will be less tempted to avoid fulfilling their responsibilities. All of the information in this step should be identical to what both parties agreed to when they first discussed this jointly developed plan.

- **Including** ways of evaluating the curfew's effectiveness—for example, an improvement in grades must be accomplished over a defined time period. In this case, it might be after an exam, an oral report from a teacher after a given week or two, a month, a marking period, a report card, or a term.

- **Emphasizing** specific behaviors throughout this entire process. The involved parent, counselor, social worker, youth worker, and youngster must clearly understand the rules and expectations of the curfew.

Results of the Curfew-Setting Process

Opportunities for expanded privileges when the adolescent meets their commitment, or negative consequences if they don't, must also be specified. If the system is working consistently, then a young person is establishing a positive habit. By doing so, they are exhibiting a sense of responsibility and earning the opportunity to do more things and go more places. Their need for freedom is being met while your desire to see positive results are being satisfied. It is a win-win situation.

Fine-Tuning the Behavioral Guideline Process

This process doesn't happen in just one sitting. Allow for multiple meetings to establish the guidelines between you and the teen. Ideas should be written down so those involved can view them, have a chance to think things over, and understand what has been discussed. This document can take the form of a single page as long as it is easily readable and understandable; short sentences and bullet points are useful in this regard. Periodic intervals for evaluating the effectiveness of the curfew should be stipulated in this agreement. In that way, adjustments to its terms can be made as needed.

Once the process is completed, both the adult and adolescent sign this declaration, indicating they agree to its terms. An "official" document has been created by both parties. By spelling out all conditions and consequences, there is less of a chance for misunderstanding, and accusations and denials are prevented. It is also easy to refer to this document when there is a disagreement later about how and when things are to be done.

This guideline takes time and effort. It is a chance for both an adult and a teen to work collaboratively. This method can prove to an adolescent their opinions are valued and they are capable of working with an adult in a responsible way. Those are two of its most significant benefits. Others include:

- A teen is part of this process, which makes the agreement more likely to be followed.

- Reason, rather than emotion, dominates this approach.

- Decisions are not forced or arrived at hastily.

- The needs for structure and freedom are both being met.

- The adolescent has a chance to show they have a sense of responsibility.

- Both parties agree to specific behavioral guidelines and consequences. Everything is clear to both the teen and the adult.

This method serves as a model for establishing other guidelines. Its benefits and influence on a young person and your relationship with them can be tremendous!

Many may be wondering if this amount of time and effort is worthwhile. It is if you:

- Have tried other methods that haven't worked
- Feel it can help remedy a situation
- Are willing to do what is necessary to implement its use

As with other ideas expressed in this book, these are *only* suggestions.

Chapter Nine

The Effects of Anger

Knowing the effects of anger on teens is the first step in empowering them to handle this emotion differently. In a conversation with an adolescent who had "lost it," I introduced the idea of being in control of his behavior by asking, "When someone says or does something to get you angry, and you hit them, who is in control, you or the other person?" He thought for a short time, nodded, then replied, "I never thought of it like that." This is one way to have a young person understand they are relinquishing control—something they absolutely do not want to do—whey they react with anger or violence to a person who is trying to push their buttons.

In this chapter, the different effects of anger on a teen will be examined. Three categories will be explored. First, the body's physical reactions to this feeling, and then we'll look at other emotions connected to anger and teen thoughts about it.

Physical Effects

Why identify physical effects?

The first step in answering this question involves explaining what happens to a person's body when they experience anger. Some of the responses from AMP participants indicate, when anger is aroused, a force inside them starts to build, and it needs an outlet. Their heart starts beating faster, muscles begin to tighten, and they feel their face begin to flush. As these effects keep building, the more intense the anger becomes, and the quicker they reach a level of 8 to 10 on the anger scale. At that point, they "explode," "go ballistic," "go nuts," or any other term adolescents use to describe anger. The remark "It is similar to a person being underwater so long their lungs feel as if they will burst unless they can release their breath" explains this idea.

For a youngster who isn't able to visualize this situation, use the analogy of a balloon—"When you start blowing up a balloon, what happens when it gets too much air?" Describing the effects of too much pressure building in a water pipe or when steam builds up under a manhole cover are two additional examples that illustrate your meaning.

Once this idea of pressure building is understood, and the "what happens" question is answered, ask the teen how they respond to anger. Do they yell, curse, hit someone or something? In this way, an adolescent is able to connect the increasing intensity of the anger with negative ways of releasing it. Then, helping the young person build a bridge between knowing these effects and learning how to control them is essential.

In other words, if a teen can find a way to chill out before their body gets to the blowing-up stage, they can prevent

themselves from doing something with negative consequences. This is reason enough for teaching them how to
prevent themselves from reaching this level of anger, and it
effectively answers the questions "Why should I know what
my body does when I get angry?" and "What's in it for me to
know this stuff?"

The question "What happens when you lose it?" takes this
process further. You can expect a variety of answers, some of
which include:

- "I feel better."
- "Whoever bothered me knows to stay away."
- "People think I am crazy."
- "I get grounded."
- "No one wants to deal with me."
- "I hurt someone; then the cops or other people
  get involved, and I get hassled."

Some of these responses may seem totally wrong to you.
Nevertheless, these are typical adolescent replies.

<<Sidebar — Being nonjudgmental and accepting what a young
person thinks and feels keeps communication open so they will hear
what you have to say.>>

Once a teen expresses these outcomes, ask "Which of these
things would you like to prevent?" One response may be
"I don't care (about the consequences)!" If this is the case, it is
important to find out why they feel this way. If they just hold
up their hands or say, "I just don't," accept that response.
Your conversation with them has gone as far as it can for the
time being.

The remark "If you decide there might be things you don't want to happen when you explode, we can discuss them at another time" leaves the door open. It also provides the opportunity for an adolescent to make a choice—that is, be in control of when or if they want to continue this conversation.

Other possible replies about the undesirable consequences of blowing up may be:

- "I don't like getting hassled by my parents!"
- "I don't want to have to look behind me wherever I go."
- "I don't like people thinking I am crazy and staying away from me."

At this point, without revisiting consequences, ask the teen to describe their body's physical reactions to anger. The statement "Let's explore what happens to your body when you get mad" leads the discussion in this direction. Staying away from emotions and sharing what happens to your own body when you experience anger can be a *conversational jump starter*. A young person may think, *If you are willing to share something personal with me, then I can do the same.* It may also contribute to strengthening your relationship with the teen who sees this sharing as a form of trust.

But be aware an adolescent can also respond, "You don't know anything about what happens to me!" This is a typical response when a young person is resisting an adult's suggestions. Nevertheless, as with many other approaches, describing your own physical signs of anger is worth a try.

Mention some of the physical effects their peers have described:

- "My heart beats faster."

- "My face feels hot."

- "My body shakes."

- "I cry."

- "Veins start to show in my face."

- "My muscles get tight."

- "I scream."

- "I feel my blood pressure rising."

- "I start to make a fist."

- "My breathing gets faster."

Describing other adolescent responses is often what engages a teen. Whether or not they outwardly acknowledge any of these effects, they now know the possible physical reactions to anger. At the very least, you have given the teen something to think about, and that makes this information useful.

How do we use the physical effects of anger to prevent the adolescent from "losing it"? Knowing how important control is to them provides one way of making this connection. The question "What would you think of having the power to keep your cool when someone tries to push your buttons?" makes this point. "When someone explodes, they are out of control. The person who created this reaction has shown they have more power" also emphasizes it.

Once this connection is made, explore ways the teen can calm down when they feel their anger rising. Having them recall a method they previously used is helpful. An adolescent may remark, "Everyone knows how to do that," or in some other way try to diminish the importance of this positive behavior. Reinforce that they were successful in handling their anger in the past. In other words, they knew what to do and succeeded, so they can do it again. The *power of positive reinforcement* works wonders.

If a teen's response is a shoulder shrug, an "I don't know," or dead silence, ask them to think about other people they've seen successfully calm down. They may describe a family member, friend, or teacher whom they saw get angry yet keep their cool. If so, have them describe what this person did to remain calm.

If they are still unresponsive, relate the idea to baseball players remaining calm before getting up to bat or entertainers behind the curtain before going out on stage to do a concert. Using names they would recognize, ask "What would happen if (Peter Alonso) or (Aaron Judge) came up to bat feeling uptight about a long hitting slump?" or "What would happen if (Kid Rock) started a song he'd never rehearsed?" They might respond, "They'd strike out," or "He'd sound bad." See if this approach gets some reaction.

Another way to illustrate the relationship between mind and body is by using a visual tool. This method is illustrated and explained below.

The Anger Scale and Control

The body's reactions to anger can include muscles tensing, heart beating rapidly, and face turning red. By using the anger scale, you can show a youngster the stronger their physical reactions become, the tighter their muscles get, the faster their hearts beat, and the redder their faces become. The angrier they become, the closer they are to losing control.

1_____2_____3_____4_____5_____6_____7_____8_____9_____10

Anger is under control   *Anger is out of control*

There are various ways to use this tool. These involve either having a teen describe a personal experience or choosing one of the top-ten causes of anger (chapter one) as an example. Once you've made the choice best suited for the adolescent with whom you are working, have the young person place himself or the person in the example on the anger scale.

If there is no response, illustrate the usual progression of emotions by remarking, "After being lied to, some people your age put themselves at a 6 or 7 on the anger scale. At this point, their muscles tighten up, and they start to feel angrier. As this feeling intensifies, their muscles get tighter and begin to hurt. Until they cannot hold this feeling inside any longer, and their reaction reaches a 10 on the scale. They now have lost control and start yelling or hitting the other person."

<<Sidebar—*Keep in mind teens learn in different ways. Some understand things when they hear them. These types of learners respond to discussion ideas. Others comprehend things when they see them. For a visual learner, the anger scale is helpful. Awareness of the adolescent's learning style is helpful in getting your points across.*>>

"When someone makes you angry and you hit them, who is in control—you or the other person?" was a question posed to different groups of young people in AMP. Some snickered; others said they were in control because they hurt the other person, while others saw the instigators as having gotten what they deserved. To some teens, this idea made an impression and gave them an idea that had never crossed their minds. For others, depending on their maturity level, their unwillingness to handle anger in ways different from those necessary for survival in their neighborhoods or dictated by peers and family expectations, this idea was useless. Again, you never know what is going to appeal to teens.

Anger De-escalators

Once adolescents see different ways anger can affect them and realize having the power to deal with people and situations calmly is in their best interest, finding additional tools to de-escalate the intensity of their anger becomes the next road to travel.

Some AMP participants said they kept their anger under control by:

- Counting (up or down)
- Taking deep breaths
- Writing a letter or email
- Keeping a journal
- Talking to someone (family, friend, teacher, etc.)
- Removing themselves from the situation
- Listening to music
- Playing a video game

- Engaging in physical activities (exercising, sports, running, walking, etc.)
- Going shopping

The Body Calming Down: Using the illustration shown below, we will describe the effect of being able to calm down and remain in control after being lied to by someone we thought we could trust.

1____2____3____4____5____6____7____8____9____10

You are in control of anger   Anger is in control of you

Being lied to rates a 6 or 7 on this anger scale. Now, using the same sports or entertainment figures you used above—Pete Alonso, Aaron Judge, and Kid Rock—place them on the scale and state, "If these three people are at a 6 or 7 now, and their anger keeps rising, it will definitely affect their performance."

Let that sink in for a moment. Then follow up with the question "However, if they were able to chill out enough to bring themselves down to a 2 or 3 on the scale, what would happen then?"

This gets teens thinking about ways to remain cool. "Pete Alonso and Aaron Judge would have a chance to get a hit and break out of their slump, and Kid Rock would have his audience applauding and cheering" is a possible teen response.

Now, saying, "When someone who is lied to is able to calm down, their muscles relax, and they stay in control," brings this concept back to a teen's reality.

If after a brief pause, all you get back from the teen is a weird "So what's your point?" look or raised eyebrows, the remark "There are various ways you can help yourself chill out" may give them an idea of the point you were trying to make.

Ways for calming themselves down should start flowing. If not, saying, "Many of your peers feel taking deep breaths, counting to fifty, or removing themselves from the situation are all useful approaches in calming down," or "How can knowing these ways to chill out help?" may move the conversation further along.

Using the analogy of blowing up a balloon and comparing it to the teen's muscles tightening up is another approach. Saying, "Think of a balloon being blown up. Air is being forced into it to make it larger. When you are angry, your muscles feel pressure—just as the air applies pressure to the insides of the balloon—and they start to tighten up. If there is too much air in a balloon, it bursts. If you can find a way to prevent your anger from rising—for example, by counting or breathing slowly—you will be able to stop the pressure from building up inside, and you'll remain calm rather than blow up. Does this sound like something worth doing?" takes this knowledge one step further.

<<Sidebar—Some situations call for using more than one of the anger de-escalators. This idea and others are explained in more depth later in the chapter on anger managers.>>

Feelings Related to Anger

The feelings accompanying, underlying, or contributing to anger are often those that aren't readily expressed. Fear, hurt, and disappointment fall into this category, along with frustration, anxiety, stress, and depression. These emotions can also be described as aftershocks or by-products of the situations evoking anger. These feelings were also effects of the pandemic because of:

- Breaks in routine (school, activities with friends)
- Close-quarters living
- Illness or death in families

The amount of stress caused by this phenomenon may continue to affect reactive behavior in adolescents. Some of these feelings were described earlier as causes of anger. Looking at these emotions as effects offers another perspective for understanding a teen's reactions.

Why do you need to know about these feelings? One explanation is to help adolescents become aware:

- A variety of other feelings accompany or describe anger.
- It is okay to experience these feelings. They are not weird or stupid.
- Feelings like pain and fear are not signs of weakness.

Most people who care about youngsters find this knowledge helpful in navigating their relationships with them. If people know how particular actions or comments hurt adolescents, they may refrain from continuing to use them, or at least make sure it occurs less frequently.

Finally, knowing about these feelings provides young people with another way to describe how anger affects them. The more knowledge a teen possesses about their anger, the better they will understand it and be able to control it.

Thoughts Connected to Anger

These are the final effects of anger we will be exploring. Some of the more common ideas expressed by AMP participants were:

- "I want to kill the other person."
- "I want to hurt them badly."
- "I want to see what they did to me done to them."
- "How can I hurt this person (the way they did me)?"
- "Why did I get angry over this stupid thing?"
- "How could I be dumb enough to let the other person get me mad?"

These ideas can be used as jumping-off points for discussion or as ways to give the teen more to think about.

Thoughts on Managing Anger

For adolescents, anger, like sex and drugs, falls into the *"unmentionable"* category and is considered off-limits when talking to adults. Two explanations for this were often heard while growing up: "These are things not discussed in families or by 'good' (religious) people," and "These are not things teens should know about until they are older." As a result, anger is rarely discussed, and it's a topic many people find awkward or uncomfortable.

This uneasiness is telegraphed to a youngster in different ways. Adults sometimes talk about these subjects in ways teens know aren't true. Adolescents are often made to feel guilty about bringing up their experiences and feelings in these areas.

These "unmentionables" become obstacles, or roadblocks, when working with young people. Adding to the problem is the reality that much of what teens learn about these "forbidden subjects" comes from peers, their "street professors" who are seen as cool and as experts in these areas. With these avoidance approaches and information sources, the subject of anger takes on a sort of mystique. It becomes something an adolescent feels they should handle in their own way. Needless to say, this can result in negative outcomes, as often happens with "unmentionable" topics.

Removing taboos and helping an adolescent openly express and discuss their anger grants them great freedom of spirit. Anger becomes a subject open for thought and creative solutions. A topic that can be honestly discussed with an adult, who can offer wisdom beyond that provided by "street professors." With this openness comes the opportunity for adolescents to discuss the consequences of any actions they may contemplating. Being free to openly expressing their thoughts, even about anger, gives them a means of releasing the negative energy without reacting to it.

Chapter Ten

Experiences with Anger

Past Experience → Present Situations → Future Experiences

W hen working on anger management, adolescents are asked to view past experiences, both positive and negative, to serve as the basis for handling present and future situations. This concept builds on the connections between the causes and effects of anger discussed earlier. The role of previous incidents and other influences affecting a young person will be expanded in this chapter.

Many things influence a teen—family, friends, peers, neighborhood in which they live or hang out, and schools they attend, to name a few. Many of their thoughts and actions stem from these influences. The maxim "Children learn what they live" summarizes this idea.

The Influences of Media and Technology

What young people see and hear from other sources plays a large role in their life. Two major influences are the media and technology. Through these seemingly "authoritative" sources come stories and accounts of people doing all sorts of things, both positive and negative. Heroic efforts to save lives or help others fall into one category. Unfortunately, these positive events are less frequently described, so they have limited influence on a young person.

Instead, stories involving conflicts, violence, sex, crimes, and unethical activities dominate radio and television coverage and are posted on the Internet on a daily basis. They often relate to incidents involving politicians, athletes, movie and television personalities, and music/media artists. These well-known people serve as role models to teens.

Occasionally, ordinary individuals living or working in their neighborhood or going to their schools are featured in the media. Most of these reported incidents reflect the negative ways people handle different situations. Jumping into fights with other athletes or fans, robberies, murders, and other criminal activities become "worthy" of time and space on television and radio, in magazines and newspapers, and on the Internet. Music and YouTube videos, blogs, social media, video games, and stories from friends, neighbors, classmates, and relatives add to the list of possible negative influences.

All of this exposure sends the message you are noticed when you do something violent, dramatic, or dangerous. The question is "With this barrage of negative input, how can I help a teen view and manage incidents in their lives in more positive ways?"

An adolescent's perceptions of these realities of modern life furnish a starting point. Their perceptions of the people and events they witness and the entertainment they enjoy are areas to explore. Also ask questions to gain insight into how all this exposure influences their behavior.

A young person will often remark that someone involved in a reported incident is "cool." Asking, "What makes a professional basketball player getting into a fight with a fan cool?" should elicit a response. "He didn't look soft, and he beat up the guy who yelled he sucked" illustrates one teen response.

Asking, "What happens to an athlete after he gets into a fight with a fan?" can help them begin to see that actions have consequences. Their response to this question tells you whether or not they are aware of the fines and suspensions accompanying these infractions. Inform the teen the professional basketball player's actions will result in their being benched for many games and fined a lot of money, and that's just from the athletic association.

Then ask, "How cool do you think this basketball player now thinks they were?" The teen may say, "It was worth it!" or look puzzled. Whatever the reaction, the idea some "cool" acts aren't worthwhile has been planted, and the adolescent has a new perspective to consider.

Young people receive all types of information from the Internet. They surf it for different forms of entertainment. Some websites offer boxing, wrestling, and war games aimed at destroying or hurting someone or something. Games showing combat, violence, and destruction are deemed normal.

One response to "What makes these sites so attractive?" may be "This is a way for me to let off steam. Watching things on the Internet doesn't hurt anyone." Clearly, this teen feels as if they are doing nothing wrong when they view videos and play games on the Internet.

Admittedly, some games do allow them to let off steam without bringing harm to anyone. However, some young people become so involved in Internet activity they begin to feel everything in it is permissible; they don't even think twice about that conclusion. It becomes reality.

Discussing an adolescent's thoughts about what they see and hear over the Internet, and how, in the real world, these actions can be harmful to others, or even illegal, is important. Think of an incident in which two youngsters imitate a wrestling match seen on a video or television. One of them breaks an arm, something neither witnessed on the Internet. What about viewing pornography and sex on the Internet? Thinking it's okay for an individual to force sex on an unwilling partner is certainly one negative message conveyed on social media. The pain from either of these forms of violent behavior is genuine. It is certainly not unreal or about letting off steam.

For the most part, young people believe, if it's on the Internet, it must be okay. The consequences of this belief must be discussed. Particularly in the realm of cyberbullying, where an individual can be stalked and harassed on a public site or through instant messaging (IMs), which leaves a teen at risk of constant persecution. "What do you know about cyberbullying?" starts the conversation ball rolling.

<<Sidebar—*Much information on cyberbullying can be found on the Internet and through other resources. To prevent a young person from becoming a victim of this treatment, or a perpetrator themself, it is important to learn more about this subject to understand what and how this abuse occurs. This subject is discussed in chapter five, which focuses on social media.*>>

Cyberbullying is someone threatening or gossiping about another person on the Internet. "Do you know anyone who was bullied in this manner," "What would you do if this happened to you," and "How would you feel?" are questions to start this discussion.

If your young person is resistant to divulging personal details about being victimized online, make your remarks *objective*. For example, "Suppose someone was cyberbullying your sister, brother, or someone close to you, how would you react?"

Possible answers might be "I'd go after them," "I'd be really mad," or "I'd do the same to them." Ask why they would feel this way. "My sister would be scared (embarrassed, hurt, lose sleep, cry a lot)" describes their thinking. By taking this route, you are allowing the young person to see how this cyber action affects others.

Be sure to make the point that it is NOT okay to push another person around on social media or to post personal information about another individual online or on a cell phone. This is considered cyberbullying; it is abuse, and it leaves a trail of negative emotional and psychological effects, not to mention in many cases it is illegal and carries stiff penalties. No matter your teen's reactions to what you are saying, at the very least, you have given them sobering, real information regarding Internet abuse. They can't unhear what you have said.

The influence of the "information superhighway" and other forms of modern technology can be damaging to others, especially our young. The impact these have on an adolescent's behavior and thinking is of great concern and should be addressed.

Positive Experiences in Handling Anger

Having teens remember a time when anger—either their own or that of people they observed—was managed in a positive way takes you and your adolescent in another direction. This knowledge becomes necessary and helpful for managing emotions in the future. Positively reinforcing how they successfully handled their anger in the past may allow them to manage it well again. If they observed someone managing anger in a positive way, they might apply what they witnessed to a future situation.

Some teens simply haven't had any positive experiences with anger. They have not seen others manage their anger well, and they don't remember ever handling their own anger in any way other than by reacting aggressively. If that's the case, they have no experience to draw from and may feel there is no way other than hostility to handle anger. This is one reality you may face.

There is a four-step approach I have successfully used as a guidance counselor and in AMP sessions. Each step can be either implemented using questions or just worked into your conversations with a young person.

First Step—Find out what teens want from the other person in a particular situation.

Usually, they are looking for some sign of respect, whether it's in school, on the streets, or in a public setting. Do they want an apology? Are they just looking for an acknowledgment from the other person who yelled or called them names and caused them embarrassment in front of their peers? In most cases, the cause of adolescent anger or outright hostility results from the other individual's failure to apologize or recognize their actions were hurtful or embarrassing.

Second Step—Find out what teens think might be the consequences of their reactions to situations.

Common responses include:

- "I proved I wasn't weak or soft."
- "I proved I don't take (expletive) from others."
- "I proved they can't get away with certain behavior."

Third Step—Have the teens decide whether or not their response to the situation was worthwhile.

This is probably the most crucial part of this method. At this point, follow up on the responses received in the first two steps. What was the outcome of each incident? If the situation ended and the other person left them alone, the actions were worth it, and there isn't much else to say.

However, if a teen responds they received some sort of payback from relatives or friends of the other individual, they were physically or verbally assaulted, they were ostracized by others, they were suspended from school, or they were punished by their parents, their behavior merits further discussion. The remark "It certainly seems as if what you did wasn't worth it" sums up this idea.

However, don't be surprised if your adolescent says their actions were worth the consequences. If so, leave it alone. This is often a show of bravado, a way to save face. You have still made your point, and in some unknown way, this idea may influence their thinking and future behavior.

Fourth Step—Explore what the teens could have accomplished without creating any further hassles for themselves.

Whether or not the adolescent thought their actions were worth it, this step allows them to consider alternatives. If they are resistant to this idea, ask, "If there are some other ways of dealing with situations without opening yourself up to being hassled, wouldn't it be worth exploring?"

Even after this, there still may be some resistance. If so, two choices exist. You can stop this portion of the process and inform the adolescent you will revisit this discussion at a later date. Or you can unilaterally present additional ways the situation could have been handled to prevent future problems. These suggestions may still be rejected. If so, be confident you've opened another path, and it may be taken sometime in the future.

For teens who want to continue this discussion, have them think of their own alternatives to handling situations without causing themselves grief. Remaining in control of their anger and staying calm without lashing out at others serves this purpose. Another alternative is encouraging them to evaluate a past incident objectively and answer the questions "Did they mean to embarrass me?" and "What caused the fight in the first place?"

<<Sidebar—Dealing with past incidents involves accepting the adolescent's perceptions of these situations without making any judgments. Keep this thought consistently in mind. It enables both you and a teen to continue discussing this subject.>>

Exploring Recent or Familiar Situations

The situations to explore first with adolescents are those occurring most recently. However, if they seem reluctant to use personal incidents, describe more generic ones, those common to many youngsters. We used the *objectivity method* in an earlier chapter. It takes the spotlight off the teen.

Being dissed—that is, not being respected or valued by someone else—falls into the general-situation category. The event described below illustrates one way an adolescent may experience this offense.

The Event

Someone bumps into you in the school hallway and keeps on walking without looking back or apologizing.

Before furnishing more details, ask your young person what they might do in this situation. Teens are often eager to give their opinions, something many adults don't allow. Their responses set the stage for using the process described earlier in this chapter. Whatever answers they provide are helpful. If they have no idea or shrug their shoulders, follow the steps described below.

Additional Details

You go after them and say in a loud voice in front of a crowd of their peers, "Hey, why don't you watch where you are going? What are you, blind or something?" At this point, he starts toward you, and your hands go up. Next thing you know, you are fighting.

Step One

After describing these particulars, you can start implementing the four-step method described above. Ask, "What does the teen want from the other person in that situation?" Responses from adolescent participants in AMP centered on getting an apology from the offending individual. With an apology, respect is shown, and the offended young person is able to save face in front of friends.

Step Two

Find out what your teen thinks the reaction in your example accomplished. AMP participants gave varied responses when asked the same question. The most common were:

- "The other person got what he deserved."
- "The guy who didn't take being bumped did the right thing."
- "The guy's friends would be glad he did something about being disrespected."

It is important to understand these perceptions. It is a matter of accepting—not agreeing—without judging what the teen has to say. This helps keep the discussion open for the teen to be receptive to other possibilities for managing this type of incident.

Step Three

Now, ask if there may be other ways, instead of fighting, to resolve this problem. By validating their opinions in step two, you open up another approach for managing anger, and they are more likely to give some thought to your question rather than feel they are receiving a lecture.

Some of the AMP participants replied there weren't any other ways to handle it. However, a number of them thought about other ideas. The alternatives they came up with included:

- Take the other person aside calmly and ask them if they bumped into you on purpose.

- If the other person doesn't realize what they did, take them aside, away from their peers, where they might have the opportunity to apologize. If an apology is not forthcoming, the victim of this incident can ask directly if the other individual is sorry.

- They may realize in a crowded hallway things like this just happen; it was accidental and is nothing to get upset about.

- The victim might take deep breaths or realize this incident was nothing to become stressed over.

Step Four

Looking at whether the behavior to save face was worth the consequences leads the conversation in another direction. Adolescent participants in AMP responded differently. Some stated it wasn't worth the hassle from parents, catching up on missed school, or having to watch their backs—that is, wondering if someone would take revenge. Others said, "Yeah, that kid got what he deserved," or "If he was my friend, I'd respect him for not taking being dissed."

After these consequences have been discussed, have the teen consider other ways to save face without getting into a fight. A teen may give you a disbelieving look or answer, "There *is* no other way." You may get the famous shoulder shrug, an "I don't care" with a few expletives thrown in, or just silence.

Keep in mind adolescent anger has varied causes. Teens often distrust adult motives; they have learned the less information they reveal, the lower their chances are of getting hurt again. However, they often consider these ideas in private, when they are alone, without letting an adult or their peers know. The fact that AMP participants often indicated certain ideas were valuable on an anonymous feedback survey given at the end of a workshop illustrates this point.

Alternative Methods of Handling Situations

Directing teens to discover ways to allow the victim in this hypothetical situation to save face without fighting starts this discussion. Let them know anything they say is okay, nothing is stupid, and discussing different ideas can be helpful when solving a problem in new ways. This is *brainstorming*, a way to come up with ideas without making judgments, and it is a worthwhile technique when working with adolescents.

The ideas offered by young people should be noted orally or on a SMART Board or computer. Do not discuss any suggestion until after a number of ideas have been volunteered. The more alternatives suggested, the better the chances are of finding one that's workable in this situation.

If you receive no response, there are a few ways to stimulate teen thinking. Find out if the person doing the bumping was aware this incident occurred. Ask for ideas on how to approach the perpetrator in a calm manner.

Another approach is the tried-and-true anger scale. Have the teen gauge the intensity of the victim's anger. The question "Is this situation worth getting really upset about?" can now be asked. One adolescent may see this incident as making them really angry, while another may see it as annoying, but not worth getting into a fight.

These approaches may prompt your teen to come up with their own ideas for resolving this issue peacefully. I believe restating those of some AMP participants reinforces their value:

- Letting the situation go. Being bumped really could have been an accident since the perpetrator did not look back or smirk once they moved on.

- Directly approaching the other individual and asking if they were aware of what happened. To do this without escalating the situation, use a low tone of voice, and do not get in their face.

It is also effective to tap into a young person's creativity. This can be accomplished by having them act as if they were a movie or television director putting together a YouTube video called *Bumped in the Hallway*. Challenge them to come up with a different ending. This approach also gives teens the opportunity to be in control of the outcome.

The Past-Present Connection

After exploring past experiences and discussing how they may have been handled differently, have your adolescent establish the relationship between similar recent situations and those from the past. They may or may not be willing to discuss these incidents. If they are willing to discuss them, finding out how they handled the situations is useful.

If there is a marked difference between recent and past events, discovering what happened in the intervening time is a good starting point. If the response is a shoulder shrug or an "I don't know," try the objectivity method. Using the experiences of others—either those a teen personally witnessed or characters seen on TV, in a movie, or in some other form of entertainment—can be helpful.

If the results in both incidents were negative, have the teen think of a time when anger, theirs or someone else's, was expressed in a way that neither the relationship nor the individuals were harmed, physically or emotionally. Even if a young person doesn't come up with any answers, the connection between past and present experiences has been established. At the very least, another possible tool has been added to a teen's anger management repertoire.

By focusing on other individuals' lives or situations, the adolescent is given space—that is, a chance not to feel as if they are on the hot seat. By using this method, the chances of them becoming defensive or escalating into anger are minimized or avoided.

Ways to Promote Adult Effectiveness

Repeating the mantra "Patience, persistence, determination" may be a helpful bit of self-talk or a chant to calm yourself when experiencing frustration with a teen's behavior. Keep your mind focused on the goals you want to achieve, no matter what obstacles the adolescent tries to throw in your path.

Unfortunately, there is no magic formula to foster the trust and cooperation that are essential if you want to be effective when working with an adolescent. I hope the ideas presented throughout this book will aid your endeavors.

Chapter Eleven

Anger Management Techniques

Keep in mind anger or any intense emotion, when not addressed or managed effectively, grows until the emotional pressure is too great to contain. Forceful reactions result; these include shouting, cursing, slamming doors, throwing objects, and even physical violence and death. Often our work with adolescents begins after a precipitative event. If we are to be effective, we must treat more than the single event. We must equip our youth with the techniques and tools to manage their anger and strong emotions effectively and remain in control.

To that end, I have compiled a list of anger managers that have proved effective in my work with adolescents. Using any of these techniques requires an adult to fully understand it, know how to use it effectively, and be able to share that knowledge with their teens. Some of these methods may appear similar. As always, if your gut tells you to modify one of these anger managers or create your own, go with it. You never know what will work with your adolescent.

I have separated anger managers into three categories—the first two focused primarily on adolescents, the last appropriate for adults as well:

- **Anger De-Escalators**—Focus on calming down or preventing anger from intensifying.

- **Anger Expressers**—Assist in conveying reasons for feeling anger.

- **Technique Tips for Adults**—Enhance effectiveness when working with teens.

My goal is to assist others in selecting the most appealing and suitable anger manager for the circumstance. First, a few suggestions:

- Use those methods you feel are most understandable and useful. The "whatever works" principle applies here.

- Look over the entire list of techniques. Based on previous experiences, select those you feel may be effective with your teen. (The "Information Booster" section at the end of the book has additional anger management techniques you may find helpful.)

- Select at least three techniques you *have not* attempted.

- Don't hesitate to reuse methods previously successful.

Anger De-Escalators

Physical Exertion

Explanation: Exercise of any kind (sports, walking, running, aerobics, dancing), counting (forwards or backwards), taking deep breaths, tightening and relaxing of muscles, and squeezing stress putty or a ball are all techniques that fall into this category.

Illustration: In front of classmates, a teacher puts down a teen for coming late to class. His face starts to redden, and the muscles in his arms begin to tighten.

Without using this anger manager: He explodes and yells at the teacher. As she approaches him, the student tells the teacher to get out of his face before he hits her. His behavior results in being suspended from school and receiving a long, loud lecture from his parents.

Using this anger manager: The adolescent takes several deep breaths and then feels his body calm down. After class, he explains to the teacher his mom was taken to the hospital, and he was very upset. The teacher apologizes for scolding him in front of his peers.

Depending on where an incident takes place, or with whom, a young person may avoid blowing up by walking away or becoming involved in a sport or other form of exercise to let off steam caused by the anger.

Precautions: Prior to leaving the site of an incident, it is essential to inform the other individual a "cooling-off" period is needed before dealing with the incident. The remark "I need some time to chill out, and then we can talk about this stuff" is an example of how this can be accomplished without exacerbating the situation. This behavior is also part of "Avoidance" described later in this chapter.

Repetition of a Word or Phrase

Explanation: Many of the anger managers are ways to safely channel the energy resulting from anger. In this case, repeating the name of a social media site—such as TikTok, Instagram, or Snapchat—provides the angry teen a way to diminish the intensity of their anger and "move down" the anger scale. This is a variation of the self-talk and affirmation anger managers later described. It uses a mantra or sound a young person can repeat to calm down.

Often, creating a funny-sounding name or word has the same effect. *Gobbledygook* or some other nonsense word of your teen's choosing or creation allows them to "own" this anger manager, making it all the more effective.

Illustration: A teen loses his cell phone. He is about to pull out all the drawers of his dresser, throw things on the floor, or kick his furniture. He decides instead to use this anger manager and repeats the word *gobbledygook* several times. He calms down and is able to find his cell phone.

Self-Talk and Affirmations

Explanation: Self-talk is a means of calming yourself after a situation has occurred. A teen literally talks themself down the anger scale. They may tell themselves:

- "I am calm."
- "I am in control."
- "I am not going to lose it."

Affirmations have the same goal as self-talk. They are things you say to remind yourself that you are better than your base emotions, which allows you to calm down and "take the high road." For example:

- "I am a peaceful person."
- "I am a calm person."
- "I am a problem solver."

Both of these methods are aimed at reducing the intensity of the anger teens experience.

Illustration: Darlene sees her boyfriend, Devon, with his arm around a girl outside of school. She feels her heart begin to beat faster, and her face starts to get flushed.

Without this anger manager: Darlene explodes at Devon and doesn't give him a chance to respond. He says he's had it with her short temper and doesn't want anything more to do with her. The relationship is ended.

With this anger manager: Darlene decides to wait before approaching Devon. While she takes this pause, Darlene says to herself, "I am in control. I am cool. I am a trusting person." At this point, she feels her heart slowing down, and her face does not feel as warm as it did.

She then approaches Devon calmly. He reveals the girl he was holding just found out her dad was in a bad car accident and adds, "She is someone I've known since elementary school."

The three of them walk away together, Darlene holding Devon's hand.

<<Sidebar—*Knowing this and other anger managers can prevent a teen from damaging important relationships. This needs to be repeatedly stressed. It is a way for adolescents to make sure their needs for belonging and recognition are being met. Being part of a relationship satisfies the first desire—recognition. Having a close bond with another person satisfies the second—belonging.*>>

Music—Playing an Instrument or Singing

Explanation: This method is based on the premise certain activities, such as listening to music, may calm an adolescent. Playing an instrument or singing also serve to divert the energy generated by anger into another activity, releasing it before it becomes destructive. Keep in mind there are many different activities (some listed in this section, others you've already encountered, or teen favorites) that may release your teen's spiked anger and provide them the opportunity to calm down. There is no single solution—it's a matter of finding out what works well with your particular adolescent.

Cheerful Song

Explanation: This is another way to diminish the intensity of anger. Ask your angry teen what song brings a smile to their face or what song they really like. Have them sing it or think of the words in their head.

Mirror Work—Looking at Your Angry Face in the Mirror

Explanation: An AMP participant, on the advice of her boyfriend, suggested this idea. When she looked in the mirror at her angry face, she found herself smiling at her image. After this idea was described to other teens, they all saw its value. Try it yourself and see if you laugh when you see your image.

Quiet Time—Catch a Breeze

Explanation: Have the teen go to an isolated area or their own private place where they can be alone. Have them feel, for example, the wind blowing against their face and the warmth of the sun. The young man who suggested this anger manager described his place—sitting on an abandoned car on a quiet street and experiencing whatever his senses brought to him.

Light Bulb or Buzzer Moment—"Is it worth it?"

Explanation: This idea takes into account a teen's thoughts about the consequences of their reactions to anger-provoking situations. Have an adolescent think of a light bulb or a buzzer going off in their mind as they ask themselves, "Is it worth it?"

Illustration: Another way to describe this tool is to call it the A-B-C anger manager. With this approach, explore the cause of the teen's anger and what made it escalate. If there is resistance to either of these ideas, attempt the following:

A: *Anger activator (cause of anger):* A general situation can be used. For example, an adolescent says something negative regarding a peer's family.

B: *Behavior (reaction):* Have them describe their reaction: In this case, they may say:

- "I told the person to shut up."
- "I punched the other person."
- "I walked away." (At this point in the process, this is a rare response.)

C: *Consequences (what happened):* A variety of responses may be offered. Among these:

- "The person yelled back."
- "We both kept yelling."
- "We fought."
- "We got suspended."
- "My parents grounded me for a month."

After analyzing the situation, ask the question "Was it worth it?" This is the key to this anger manager. Regardless of the consequences, an adolescent may still answer yes and believe their reaction was worth the cost. In addition, many young people do exactly the opposite of what adults think they should; that's just part of the rebelliousness of youth. However, if exposed to other approaches for managing these situations, they may consider *using this method in the future.* Who knows?

When exploring specific situations, discover the location of the incident and who observed it. If, for example, an event took place in school, peers were most likely present; therefore, saving face becomes a factor. Under these circumstances, explore ways the consequences could have been avoided without the teen "looking soft" to their friends.

The issue of control is another possible approach. AMP participants were asked, "Who is in control in a conflict? The person attempting to make you angry, or you if you avoid getting upset?" Many responded with the latter. This is often a good time to let your adolescent know the ones who start trouble are the first ones to run away from it. For a teen, this idea may make sense. They see it as a way the perpetrators save face while preventing themselves from getting into more trouble.

This anger manager can also be used as a *preventive measure.* Looking at the result of a teen's past actions and their consequences may dissuade them from repeating this behavior when a similar situation arises. Adolescent AMP participants certainly affirmed this idea.

Anger Journal

Explanation: Many young people like to write. This journal is similar to a diary; however, it deals specifically with anger-producing incidents the writer encounters. It allows a teen to deal with the situation quickly, without directly confronting the other person involved. It is also a way for an adolescent to look at the entire situation and decide how to resolve it.

This method contains three components:

1. *Describe the anger-activating incident.* Be specific and detailed—who was involved, where it took place, and how angry the teen felt. The intensity of the emotion can be described by using metaphors similar to "as mad as someone who got punched in the stomach for no reason" or by indicating a point on the anger scale. It is an analytical way to view anger and put it into perspective.

2. *Create a plan to resolve the situation.* Have the teen answer the question "What solutions can I figure out to end this problem without bringing myself additional hassles?"

3. **Describe how you will handle similar situations in the future.**

Precautions: Emphasize this is an opportunity to actually become a problem solver, not just write about their anger. Tell your adolescent to go beyond the anger and write about possible preventive measures for similar incidents in the future. Not only is this constructive, but it avoids repeatedly revisiting the cause of the anger, and prevents the possibility of dwelling on it and having it escalate again. Interestingly, when this anger manager was discussed with young people during AMP, they themselves immediately expressed the negative effects revisiting the incident could have.

Illustration: Two close friends, Sue and Beth, have an argument. Sue is really angry because Beth seems to be ignoring her and spending less time with her since she has a new boyfriend, Marty.

Without this anger manager: Sue confronts Beth and yells at her, saying she cares more about Marty and is a really [expletive] friend. Sue does this in front of Marty as well as other friends. Beth yells back and tells Sue to go to hell. The friendship ends.

With this anger manager: Sue writes in her anger journal and describes the incident:

> *I got mad at Beth because she used to spend more time with me before Marty came along. Now she almost totally ignores me. I cursed at her, and she yelled back at me. It makes me feel like I was being left on an island by myself.*

Sue develops a plan of how she can resolve the situation and make up with Beth:

> *I can call Beth on the phone or, when I see her, talk to her in private. I'll apologize for yelling and cursing in front of Marty and other friends. I'll tell her how I felt and see what she says. If Beth says she doesn't care, our friendship is over. If she is sorry, we can talk about how we can fix this problem.*

Finally, Sue tries to think about how she can prevent herself from acting and feeling the same way in the future:

Maybe, when I feel like that again, I'll try to handle it privately with Beth. At that point, we can calmly talk about how we both feel.

This method is similar to a dress rehearsal for a play. It allows a young person to read the script, play out the situation, and see how to improve their role in future performances. It also provides time to release the energy caused by anger and channel it into a constructive problem-solving.

Two-Minute Vent

Explanation: This anger manager is used for anger that is *low in intensity* or rated 1 to 4 on the anger scale. It is the point when teens are annoyed or slightly irritated. To verify this, ask them to rate themselves on the anger scale. This technique is a variation of the "just listen" anger manager found below.

There are certain boundaries adolescents must follow to utilize this technique. The following guidelines are necessary and must be made clear before you begin:

- They must not be abusive to the listener, either physically or verbally.

- They will be given two minutes to vent their anger.

- After the first minute, the listener will say or indicate with a hand signal, "Do you need more time?" If the answer is yes, allow an additional minute of venting.

- After this additional minute of venting, it's time to stop when the listener says, "I hope you were able to release some of your anger."

By setting these boundaries you are providing teens with structure and an opportunity to express their anger without hurting themselves or others. This alone may prevent the escalation of anger.

Precautions: There are two:

1. Don't interrupt; otherwise, a teen may become frustrated.
1. Don't tell the angry teen to calm down. This statement may cause them to become more upset, which will intensify their negative behavior, just as telling someone who stutters to stop results in increased stuttering.

Neutral Party—Talk It Over with Someone Not Involved in the Situation

Explanation: Adolescents can avert acting on anger if they just discuss their issues with a friend, relative, or counselor.

Precautions: The key is to speak with an *objective person*. If youngsters speak with someone who takes their side, it may result in intensifying the anger they are experiencing and prolong the hostility. For example, teens may ask particular friends or family members (those who agree with them) for their opinion about managing a situation. The typical responses may include "Let that guy know you are not someone who takes [expletive] from anyone!" or "Don't let that girl get away with that!" Bottom line, the fires of hostility are stoked and never get a chance to cool down.

Illustration: Pete's friend, John, told him Dan was spreading rumors about him and his girlfriend, Carol. Dan told others Carol has sex every day, not only with Pete, but with a few other guys behind his back.

Without this anger manager: Pete asks John for his advice. John tells him not to let Dan get away with this [expletive] and to punch his lights out. Pete is really riled up and goes looking for Dan. After their fight, both boys are bruised and get suspended. Carol starts crying and wants Pete to leave her alone; she ends the relationship.

With this anger manager: Pete goes to his guidance counselor, Mr. Dominick, and tells him what John revealed and asks what he should do. Mr. Dominick asks, "Do you know for a fact Dan actually said these things? Why would he talk about you and Carol? Is there a reason why John might tell you this stuff?" He then adds, "If it isn't true, then leaving it alone may just end it right there."

In this case, Mr. Dominick provided Pete with ideas to think about, rather than giving him the go-ahead to react to the situation. By talking to his counselor, Pete also had time to chill out and come up with some ideas on how to deal with the situation. The end result for Pete was he prevented himself from creating more hassles than this "he said/she said" situation was worth.

Visualization of Anger (Photos May Be Used)

Explanation: Ask your adolescents to describe what anger looks like—not only what they see, but also what they may feel, smell, or touch. To start young people thinking in the correct direction, use fire as an example. Have them describe its color, size, the intensity of heat coming from it, and possibly the devastation it causes when a building is ablaze. The more vivid the description, the sharper the image, and the more identifiable it becomes. This particular visualization can be used as a preventive tool.

Some of the images described by AMP participants were erupting volcanoes, exploding bombs, and boiling pots. Regardless of which image of anger they came up with, none of the participants wanted to become the anger they visualized.

Visualization of a Calm Scene (Photos May Be Used)

Explanation: In describing a calm scene, as we did earlier with anger, it is important the adolescent be as detailed as possible, and they should use as many senses as they can.

Illustration: In describing a beach, use the warmth of the sun on a person's face, the feel of the sand underfoot, and the sound of the waves softly breaking onto the beach. To complete this image, add seagulls flying overhead and the sounds they make.

Other peaceful scenes may include a place the teen enjoyed on a vacation, pictures of someone special, or images of someone with whom they shared pleasant experiences. I remember describing a photo of my oldest grandson on my office desk, which I viewed many times when I was upset; it allowed me to smile and relax.

Balloon Exercise

Explanation: Here, we are attempting to have teens divert angry energy into an unharmful visualization. Tell your adolescent to imagine blowing up a balloon, or have them actually force air out of their mouths as if they were actually inflating a balloon.

Illustration: Angie wasn't chosen as a cheerleader. She was really upset and felt she performed better than some of the other girls who had been chosen. Seeing this, the assistant cheerleading coach went over to her. She knew Angie well, so she suggested a way Angie could get past her disappointment—close her eyes and pretend she was blowing up balloons as part of her good friend's birthday celebration.

Angie smiled and said, "Thanks, Ms. Taylor, I feel a little bit calmer and am not letting this disappointment get to me."

Three-R's Method—Relax, Relate, Release

The following technique was suggested by a teacher:

1. Relax—Give the youngster an opportunity to calm down.
2. Relate—Allow the teen to describe the reason for their anger.
3. Release—Be sure the feeling has been released and its source revealed.

This allows the teen the freedom to move on from the situation, and it can serve as a means of expressing this emotion if no other method has worked.

Avoidance, Cooling-Off Period, Tuning Out —Emotionally and Physically Removing Yourself from a Situation

Explanation: This anger manager is used when a teen's anger first begins to escalate, not after they are already angry. It can involve either of two methods:

1. Chilling out: This can be demanded by the teen or the adult. Leaving the room to get a beverage or taking a short walk are other forms of cooling-off periods.
2. Tuning out or "zoning out": Tell your teen to make themselves an observer in the event, not an active

participant, and act as if they were watching the incident on television, an iPad, or in a movie.

Precautions: This anger manager is effective in that it gives teens the time to calm down. However, it is a time-out, not a solution to the problem. Stress to the teen they still must resolve their issue with the other person after this crisis-avoidance tool is used. Warn the teen, if they fail to do so, their anger toward the other person may resurface at another time, possibly with more intensity; that is the way people form long-lasting grudges. In some cases, during the interim, others become involved, take sides, and cause an even greater problem. This often occurs on social media.

Challenging Activities

Explanation: This helps divert the energy emanating from the anger to positive channels, lessening its intensity and allowing a teen the time to calm down.

Examples: Assembling a puzzle, figuring out a math problem, playing a video game, or coming up with solutions to other challenges the teen may be encountering are ways the teen's focus can be diverted from their anger.

Anger Expressers

Tell Others What Is Bothering You in a Direct, Specific, and Polite Way

Explanation: This anger manager involves the use of direct communication. It's in direct contrast to teens rolling their eyes, "staring daggers," slamming doors, mumbling under their breath, talking in a loud tone of voice, giving the silent treatment, or cursing. These indirect aggressive means of letting adults know they are angry do little else; the source of the anger and the possibility of preventing this feeling from recurring are left unaddressed. Statements such as "You should know why I am angry" or "This is something you do over and over again" don't really get into specifics; they make assumptions that are a source of frustration for both parties.

If you are on the receiving end of the anger, getting to its source becomes your objective. The how-tos of this involve calmness, sincerity, and patience. This approach will serve as an example for young people, and it becomes the means of helping them diffuse their own anger and that of their peers. By applying this method, their thoughts and feelings will be understood, and the cause of anger can be avoided in the future.

The following situation demonstrates how to use this anger manager. Two reactions are described: how this incident can escalate, and how using this tool can produce a positive result. If your teen can't—or won't—provide a response to questions regarding the consequences of their behavior, describe both approaches.

Give a young person the opportunity to judge whether they should use this anger manager with their parents or other adults. The reasons for their decision are worth discussing. This is another information-gathering process in helping to understand a teen's thinking.

The Situation: A daughter brings home her report card. Her mom tells her once again her grades are disappointing.

Without this anger manager: The daughter says, "No [expletive]! Like it's something I don't know!" She stomps out of the kitchen, goes to her room, mumbling more barely audible four-letter words, and then slams the door.

With this anger manager: The girl tells her mom, "I'm already upset with myself over these grades. When you shout at me and say I'm not doing well in school, it makes me feel ten times as bad, like being hit over the head again." This is a direct, straightforward statement not likely to be misunderstood. She adds, "Instead of just looking at my poor grades, look at the passing grades or those I have shown improvement in, and maybe then I'll be encouraged to find ways to pull up my marks." The girl is giving her mother specific suggestions on how to better communicate with her and avoid heightened emotions. The daughter expressed her needs in a calm way, without cursing or slamming doors—she was polite.

Ask the adolescent, "What did the daughter gain from acting the way she did when she didn't use this idea to handle her anger?" Possible responses may include:

- "The girl let her mother know she was mad."
- "She got her feelings out."
- "The girl didn't change anything."
- "She didn't let her mother know why she was angry."

Without making any judgments or comments, ask the same question, this time focusing on when the girl used this anger manager. Find out which way your teen thought worked best and why.

Once you've explored these ideas, ask, "Would you use this anger manager?" Depending on their reply, find out the reasons. Whatever the result, it doesn't matter. At the very least, you have provided another tool for them to use in managing their anger.

Another way to avoid escalating this situation is to say, "We need to talk about your grades. Let's decide on a time we can both discuss it." It's not only what you say, but also how you tell the adolescent about their negative behavior that makes the difference between keeping things calm or escalating them into anger. By taking this approach, an undesirable conflict is avoided, time is allowed for a teen to keep their lack of progress from getting them more upset, and the subject will be discussed, not avoided or forgotten. The timing for this discussion is a joint decision between the adult and the adolescent who, by being included, feels in control. This aids in keeping the situation calm.

Demanding, "Sit down, young lady! We are going to talk about your grades here and now!" is more likely to cause a negative reaction. Your goal is to resolve a problem, not create a bigger one.

This anger manager can accomplish a few things. It can be used as a model when dealing with an upsetting issue. We, as adults, are the models for much of what a teen learns and does. Expressed another way, if what you say and do is consistent, your credibility is certainly going to be strong.

As a person who deals with teens on a regular basis certainly knows, consistency is the key to credibility and influence. When using this anger manager, a teen may think, *My mother is not going to make me feel like I'm being attacked, so maybe things can get better.* This is the type of reaction you want from a teen. It bodes well for eliminating future hassles in your relationship.

Using this anger manager can prevent, in this case, the daughter from becoming defensive and reacting in such a way that makes this situation even harder to manage. It constructively removes a roadblock in dealing with her grades.

To say the daughter's falling grades do not have any consequence is unacceptable. This is not to say the daughter may not try to plead, "Give me one more chance to get better marks," or start her statement with "But." Patience is definitely required. After preventing this situation from escalating, the daughter should be reminded of its consequences. If the ramifications of her behavior weren't previously discussed, timing this discussion after the situation has occurred may be beneficial. In this example, her frustration has not intensified; she remains calm and ready to deal with the subject of her grades rationally.

Keep in mind there are certain predictable behaviors teens exhibit. For example, yelling back or making excuses for poor grades. These only help to escalate anger between an adolescent and a grown-up. It is worthwhile dealing with these possibilities before they occur. The remark "I know your grades are upsetting, and I feel like yelling, but if we're both calm, you won't find yourself getting more upset" can produce a positive effect.

In the case of excuses, "Let's look at what can be done about your grades, rather than blaming them on a teacher or something else. That takes a lot of energy and only takes us longer to get through this" can also help to keep this situation from escalating.

Using any and all of these tactics and understanding their effects can prevent an adolescent from reacting negatively.

Yes, this takes time! Yes, you are the older, more experienced person. And, yes, they are the children. However, isn't the ounce (maybe ten pounds) of prevention worth the pound (maybe a ton) of cure (aggravation) for all concerned? Here again, it's your choice to decide whether or not using this anger manager is worth the time and energy for both of you.

Use "I" Statements

Explanation: This anger manager is a variation of the above method. The "I" statement accomplishes two objectives:

- It is a way to take responsibility for your own feelings and tell others how you feel—for example, you say, "I feel…" instead of "You made me feel…!"

- It avoids blaming other people, which is an anger provoker. It removes the "you always/you never" accusations that ignite many conflicts. It focuses on the behavior causing the anger, not on the person.

This technique is a way for adolescents as well as adults to express their feelings without causing more hostility or harm. This idea can be used with other emotions as well (happiness, sadness, fear, pride, etc.). It is expressed in the following way:

- **The Feeling:** "I feel angry…" (any emotion can be used)

- **The Behavior:** "…when you yell at me in front of my friends…"

- **The Reason:** "…because it embarrasses me (made me feel small, etc.)."

Your statement does not have to be phrased in exactly this order. The behavior or the reason can come first—for example, "When you yell at me in front of my friends, I feel angry." Some people omit the reason in order to add more emphasis on the behavior; however, that isn't essential when using this tool.

Precautions: In my work with teens as a guidance counselor and with AMP participants, I have found many teens feel this is an effective anger manager for resolving conflicts in close relationships. It is **not** helpful, however, in situations with strangers or peers they don't know well. The remark "I couldn't care less how they feel" sums up the reaction of those who are not close to an individual.

Communicate Feelings as Soon as Possible

Explanation: If incidents are not resolved within a reasonable period of time, there tends to be an escalation in anger. There is no magic number for exactly how long a "reasonable period of time" is before irreparable damage is done to the relationship. A general rule of thumb is anywhere between a few hours and a day or two. The longer the anger goes unattended, the greater the possibility it may fester and intensify. If feelings are not expressed, both parties may become more negative, which damages their relationship further and can even result in its termination.

Precautions: Do **not** use this anger manager when teens are feeling intense anger. When they are moving toward the higher end of the anger scale, leaving the situation alone until all parties calm down is advisable. Once that happens, they can use any of the anger managers previously discussed—for example, the "I" statement—to express their anger if they are close or have an ongoing relationship.

Helpful Techniques for Adults

Use Physical Contact

Explanation: An arm around the shoulder, a pat on the back or shoulder, and a hug illustrate you are aware something is bothering the adolescent, and you are there for them.

Precautions: Be aware of how a particular teen responds to physical touch. However, without knowledge of the adolescent's background, it is wise to err on the side of caution. If you have any doubt or have never seen a particular youngster's reaction to someone being demonstrative, don't use this method. It may result in a teen taking some of their anger out on you or misunderstanding your motives. A negative reaction to touch may be the result of being the victim of abuse. Also, be aware, in some organizations, there is a strict "no touch" policy for just this reason.

Walk Alongside the Angry Person

Explanation: Young people who seem to be angry often feel alone or isolated. They have lost control, which often causes them to feel embarrassed, and they just don't want others in their way. By walking alongside, you are physically present; this should make them feel less isolated. For some teens, company, even though silent, may provide comfort during this stressful time.

Precautions: Asking, "Do you mind if I walk with you?" is important. Follow this statement with "We don't have to talk if you don't want to." This allows the adolescent the choice of accepting your company or not. It also provides them with a modicum of control and lets the teen know, straight-out, you are not there to ask questions, but you're there if they want to discuss their feelings or anything else.

Just Listen! Give a Teen a Chance to Express Themself Without Saying Anything

Explanation: This is crucial. It allows the young person to vent their thoughts and feelings in their own way, without interruptions or judgment. Some of the high school students I have worked with just needed someone to hear them out. A typical comment was "All I wanted was my (mom, dad, brother, teacher) to hear what I have to say." The importance of just listening can't be stressed enough.

Precautions: Adults too often feel they need to jump in and voice their opinion or "help" by judging a teen's actions and putting them "on the right track." This just throws up a roadblock to resolving the teen's anger. Asking, "Do you want me to just listen, or do you want my opinion?" gives you the opportunity to travel the road leading to the cause of agitation. Hopefully, this may furnish a way to help your teen effectively deal with their issue.

Use Humor or a Smile

Explanation: Many people utilize lightheartedness or other types of levity to coax a teen out of their poor mood. Turning a frown into a smile does wonders for reducing the intensity of anger, and it even takes fewer muscles.

Precautions: Attempts to use humor to reduce the anger in some teens may backfire. They may see humor as a form of being "mocked," being made fun of, or evidence of how clueless and uncaring you are about the importance of their issue. Their thinking may be "You think this situation is funny" or "You think the way I feel is a joke." If so, you can expect expletives or reactive behavior. So if you aren't sure how a teen might respond to humor, **don't** use it.

<<Sidebar—This a warning you have seen whenever tactics involving levity have been mentioned. It is important advice to keep in mind.>>

Give the Teen Space

Explanation: Some people don't want to be around others when they are angry and need to cool off. This requires time and space. In the case of a teen involved in a situation in which their emotions run high, it is important you determine if they need space. "How do I know an adolescent needs space to calm down?" and "Where is a good place for them to go?" become concerns.

The reply to the first question often comes directly from the teen, who may actually say, "I need to be by myself," or make some stronger, not-so-gentle statements, including "Get out of my face," "Stop bothering me," and "Leave me alone!" In the absence of direct statements, you have to rely on clues garnered from the teen's previous responses in similar situations.

Precautions: Personal space is another form of freedom, which is so vital to an adolescent. People typically react to having anyone standing within two feet of them, about an arm's length, particularly when they are angry. Especially then, they need breathing room and some distance from others. The need for personal space is even more vital for victims of abuse; they see people getting too physically close as a threat to safety.

Become aware of where a teen can go to "chill out." They may calm down at school, home, or where work if these offer areas for solitude. In unfamiliar territory, they may resort to restrooms, empty offices, open spaces inside or outside of a building or room. Previous discussions with a teen may have already revealed the places they like to go when the need for space arises.

In many educational facilities and social service agencies, this subject has already been addressed and plans developed for when an adolescent becomes upset. In families, however, this topic should be discussed. It could be as easy as having individuals go to their room or a bathroom, hallway, or some other empty space when this need arises.

Illustration: Sean has just come home. As he opens the door, he shouts, "That [expletive] girlfriend of mine. She can't leave her friends for a second when I want to talk to her." Then he slams the door.

Without this anger manager: When he slams the door, you approach and tell him, "You'd better watch your language and calm down right now!" He glares at you and then goes to his room and slams the door. You follow him, and he starts yelling and cursing. You wonder if he'll ever calm down, but you aren't about to put up with this nonsense, so you ground him for the next two weeks. He storms past you and out the door.

With this anger manager: You see how upset Sean is. You tell him he looks upset and ask if he needs time to calm down. He frowns and stomps to his room and slams the door. About an hour later, he comes out and says, "Darlene is so inconsiderate.

I really can't stand her sometimes." You ask what happened, so he describes why he became angry.

A teen may not approach you that day, that week, or at all to discuss a situation. However, in this scenario, Sean is aware his mother respected him enough to give him the space and time he needed to calm down.

Accentuate the Positive

Explanation: With this anger manager, you provide recognition for an accomplished task or positive behavior; this tells the teen they are being noticed and valued. A common complaint many adolescents have expressed is they are never told "when I am doing something right" and are only told about "the things I do wrong."

Precautions: Some of you may interpret this idea as ignoring the negative or assume it means there are no consequences for inappropriate behavior. **Not at all.** This anger manager is used only after consequences (both positive and negative) and expectations have been discussed.

Illustration: An adolescent has improved their grade point average from 65 to 75. Noticing this—or in fact *any improvement*—and making them aware you are interested in following their progress is a *huge plus* both for your relationship and as a motivator to continue on this path. The key point is progress has been made. Contingent on improvement may be a later curfew, the use of a car, or a new privilege.

Be Responsible for What You Say and Do

Explanation: At times, people deny having said something. "I never said that" sums up this idea. In an effort to lessen the impact of such a statement, it is usually quickly followed by "I didn't mean it that way." To the person who believes they were wronged, the damage has been done. Any attempt to "weasel out" of this situation is often met by a strong reaction. This type of denial indicates guilt. Culpability means a wrong has been committed; therefore, the guilty party is attacked.

Corny as it might sound, "Honesty is the best policy." Admitting a wrongdoing helps prevent the existing anger from intensifying and keeps the level of trust high. Taking responsibility for their words and actions is important for a teen to learn, and much of this learning comes from seeing it in those they respect.

Precautions: One means of acquiring this skill may take the form of using the "I" statement, which was explained earlier. Young people have said this anger manager is useful with their peers. Stress to your teen the importance of accountability—sometimes referred to as "manning up" (or, my term, "womaning up")—for their words or actions. Let them know this is an important way to gain respect, which is very important to an adolescent.

Be Empathetic

Explanation: This involves seeing things from another person's perspective. It can be thought of as walking in someone else's shoes or understanding where another person is coming from. It relates to how others think or feel. It is an anger manager that was mentioned when situations involving family members were analyzed.

Precautions: Be real. If you truly don't understand another person's thinking, don't make the statement "I know how you are feeling" or "I understand what you're thinking." These types of suppositions may lead to the rebuke "Don't tell me how I feel or what I think."

Instead, just give your interpretation of the feeling or thought. Such remarks begin with "What I think you are feeling…" or something similar. If you are not on target, at the very least you made an attempt to understand how the person feels or thinks.

Illustration: Suzanne found out her boyfriend, Joe, was hanging around with Joyce. She overheard Joe speaking to Joyce on his cell phone in a low tone of voice. He was in the next room, arranging to meet her after a class. Suzanne trusted Joe, but she confronted him, shouting and telling him he really hurt her, and she didn't want to see him anymore. He tried telling her Joyce was just a friend. Suzanne wasn't hearing Joe.

Later, when Suzanne was calmer, Joe spoke to her. "I think I understand why you were so angry. By me not mentioning my relationship with Joyce, it was as if I was hiding something from you. We've always been straight with each other, and this was a betrayal, screwing up all the trust we've built."

At this point, Suzanne may be more receptive to listening to what Joe has to say. Here, Joe might explain, "I was afraid if I told you I was hanging around with Joyce, you'd feel jealous."

With this anger manager: If you offer a previous situation as an example, make sure it is relevant to what is currently happening. The use of relevant parallel situations in this case may show that Joe was empathetic towards Suzanne. Joe might have said, "This was similar to a situation I once had with my best friend, Pete. He didn't tell me he wanted to hang out with other friends and stood me up. I happened to be walking home that day and saw him with other friends. It really bothered me."

Write an Email or Letter

Explanation: When people are extremely angry and moving toward a 10 on the anger scale, they may realize they need to vent their anger. At the same time, they may realize it would not be productive to express their feelings directly to those involved in the difficult situation. They may fear saying or doing something at this point that would result in losing the relationship or creating additional problems. They still have some control over their anger, but feel they might lose it quickly if it is expressed directly.

As an alternative, they communicate their feelings in written form. By taking this detour, the source of anger is expressed, and its intensity is reduced. In other words, they are indirectly venting their emotions. For some, writing is an effective way of expressing themselves and can be a useful means of managing anger. Once time has passed, the aggravated individual can then directly express their feelings calmly.

This method or using an anger journal (an anger manager previously discussed) are two ways the pressure resulting from a difficult situation can be released without negative effects.

Precautions: Be sure this expression of anger, whether written in the form of a letter or email, *IS NOT SENT!* This method of anger management allows the writer to direct their anger toward others, get it all out, and then calm down without escalating the situation. This is a way of avoiding a head-on collision between those involved in a conflict.

Ask, Don't Demand

Explanation: Stating, "I wish you would...," rather than demanding, "Do it or else!" is an effective way to avoid fueling an emotional fire. If this idea is used to correct a mistake or have a teen perform a chore, it shows respect and places the request in a nonconfrontational manner. Using this approach greatly increases the chances of the teen being compliant. The philosophy behind this anger manager is "It's not what you say; it's how you say it."

This approach can easily be explained to and understood by teens. In response to a question asked on the AMP Feedback Survey, many noted they felt this anger manager would be useful.

Precautions: As with many of these ideas, it is important for an adult to be confident in its effectiveness. In other words, if you don't believe in the product's value, don't try to sell it.

Illustration: Adult to teen: "I'd like you to lower your voice when you speak to me," rather than "You'd better show me some respect, or you'll be grounded for a month!"

Adolescent to adult: "I'd really like to be able to go to that party with my friends," rather than "I'm going to go to that party whether you like it or not!"

Accept Differences

Explanation: This anger manager reminds teens they can't control others. In other words, "Thinking differently, feeling differently, or acting differently is okay." Other than the strong beliefs previously mentioned, a teen can look at other things to learn to accept differences. These may include physical differences between people, such as height, weight, complexion, or ethnicity. These are factors adolescents usually treat with ridicule, which often turns into conflict.

The idea of acceptance can be introduced by having them see similarities between themselves and these "different" individuals. Membership on school teams, participation in the same sports and extracurricular activities, attitudes toward teachers or parents, boredom with some subjects, and irritation with rules they are made to follow illustrate some of these similarities.

Pointing out likenesses in others lessens the degree of perceived dissimilarity, which is the first step toward acceptance. This idea is the basis for this anger manager.

Precautions: Keep in mind adolescents often think in terms of absolutes. For example, how they dress, whom they associate with, and the music they listen to are usually linked to the belief of a like-minded peer group. Their way is "right," and there is no room for a differing opinion. This is the reason there are different peer groups—good-ats, anime/mangas, emo/goths, jocks, nerds, metal heads. These beliefs, like religion, are nonnegotiable. When a teen is asked to consider and understand that other beliefs are okay, they don't buy it. It's their way or no way. This is an attitude you need to be aware of and accept.

Teens look at adults' thoughts, as well as those of other adolescents who are members of other groups, as foreign and suspicious. If any person tries to discuss other ways of thinking to a member of a particular group, it becomes a war of beliefs, ending in frustration for both sides. To this way of thinking, differences set two people apart and create distance between them.

This kind of mindset may lead to heated verbal attacks or, in some cases, the use of physical force to convince the other person to see, feel, or act in one particular way. "You cannot be a part of my life, have a relationship with me, or live in my house unless you think, do, and feel the way I do" expresses this idea. It is a form of *emotional blackmail.*

Accepting youngsters' differences in thinking does not mean agreeing with them; it only means you recognize them as legitimate or okay. Finding a way to enable them to be open to a different point of view, whether yours or that of others, is the key ingredient to moving forward in your relationship with an adolescent. By accepting the differences between your thinking and theirs, and making them feel their thoughts are valued, you have built trust and created a closer bond. Regardless of what they say (which is often face-saving or bravado), becoming more connected also helps to meet their desire to be part of a relationship. It is certainly a goal worthwhile achieving with them.

Illustration: Tom, who is on the football team, sees Carl, a short, thin boy being bumped in the hallway by another student. Carl looks at the person who bumped into him but does nothing else. The other student walks on without saying anything. Tom goes over to Carl, who is also a friend of his, and asks why he didn't at least say something to the other guy; he tells his friend, "I would have stepped in."

Carl looks at Tom, and says, "Do you think someone my size could do anything to that guy? Besides, to me, something like being bumped accidentally isn't worth the hassle it can cause." Tom shakes his head and says, "I understand what you are saying, but if it were me, I'd have made that guy apologize."

<<*Sidebar — As you go through more of this list, you will see similarities between different anger managers. Often, the same idea can be expressed in many ways. Our goal is to enable young people to pick methods most appealing to them. The "whatever works" philosophy,*

again, is at work. Applied here, determining what is understandable and acceptable to a teen is the goal. Presenting variations of different anger managers often accomplishes this task.>>

Demonstrate a View of Exploding Anger

Explanation: Demonstrating or exploring what uncontrollable anger looks like is the point of this anger manager. Some young people are prone to this type of behavior. This anger manager may be used as a preventive method for teens capable of such volatile behavior. *This is where the actor/actress within has to come out if, indeed, you are so inclined.* It is a way of literally illustrating an example of explosive behavior—yelling, waving your arms around, and stomping the ground. This might bring a smile or, if your acting is really good, even applause.

After their reactions have subsided, help your teen analyze this behavior. Follow up by asking, "When some people are angry, they throw a fit by banging or kicking things, yelling, or slamming doors. This is what it looks like when I let my anger get to me. Is this how you want to show your anger or have someone else see you? If not, why wouldn't you like to show your anger this way?"

Possible responses might include "It looks dumb," "People will think I am crazy," or "Not many people want to deal with someone who acts like that." If, however, they don't care how they look or indicate their peers might think it is funny, leave it at that.

Variation: In the event you are uncomfortable acting this out, describe a young child throwing a fit, or ask if they ever saw someone displaying this type of behavior. Then undertake the same analysis as described above.

Precautions: This may "set off" your adolescent; they may think you are mocking them. Before you try this anger manager, it is important to know how they may respond, either negatively or positively. If they appreciate using humor, based on your own previous observation, try this method; it may be useful. If you are unsure of their reaction, **don't** use this anger manager.

Consider How Someone You Care about Would Handle the Situation

Explanation: Using this idea relies on teens having calmed down after an incident has occurred. In the chapter relating to experiences, adolescents were asked to describe how others successfully controlled their anger in similar situations. You may use the same examples and people with this anger manager. These individuals become the teen's role models who know the right things to do; they can be invaluable resources for the teen at a later time.

Chapter Twelve

Applying Anger Management Techniques

T his chapter focuses on applying the anger managers we've explored to situations occurring in various settings and relationships. Keep in mind these scenarios can be modified to work with individuals, groups, or classes of teens. Several of the events presented are real-life situations actually experienced by AMP participants; others are from conditions resulting from the pandemic, dealing with gun violence, and involving social media. The adolescents who described these incidents were instructed to portray situations they personally experienced or witnessed so they could see the applicability of the different anger managers to real-life situations. These events cover many important parts of teen life and include the frustration of needs, values, expectations, respect, relationships, and in the youths' eyes, injustices. Some of the incidents may sound familiar from your personal experience with adolescents, while others were chosen because they are common to this age group. The more adolescents can relate to these situations, the better the chances they will be willing to utilize anger management techniques.

First, *choose the anger managers you believe would be best suited for particular situations*. This decision is based on the knowledge of a teen's responses to approaches you've already used, ideas you think may work, or *adolescent decisions as to which of these methods they feel would work* in the incidents and relationships being described. There are several categories of situations:

- Incidents occurring in families
- Those involving peers and close relationships
- Those found in neighborhood, school, and work settings

By providing these "dry runs," you are giving teens the opportunity to test ideas for handling situations that may arise or have already taken place in their lives. This step may provide youngsters with the confidence certain methods will work in the future.

Second, *choose which of the categories to use*. This can be determined in several ways:

- Provide the list of categories to the participants and ask them to choose *incidents mimicking those they had personally witnessed or experienced*. This method was used with groups of teens in classroom settings.

- Have teens select *the environment in which they encounter the most difficulties*. This choice can be based on their need to show strength—that is, the need to prove to others they cannot be taken advantage of. These incidents can occur in their homes, schools, neighborhoods, or places where youngsters find the most difficult people to cope with. Wherever this situation is located, respect is often the hot button being pushed.

- Have teens choose a particular area based on *interest*. Conversations centering on adolescents' interests is one of the most productive ways to involve them. Two of the most popular categories with AMP participants were those dealing with intimate relationships —boyfriends or girlfriends—and those dealing with family members.

- Give your teens a *specific area* on which to focus. In AMP, we found this method more expedient with young people who were either undecided or unwilling to participate in this part of the learning experience.

- Have teens *volunteer a situation* they can describe utilizing the following three elements:

  - *The situation* causing the conflict

  - *The relationship they had with the people involved*—parent, brother/sister, friend, associate, girlfriend/boyfriend, teacher, coworker, boss, or manager

  - *The setting*—where the incident took place

Once the category selection is complete, the situations can be noted on a chart, SMART Board, or in any other way they can be displayed.

<<Sidebar—The application of anger managers to real-life situations is the primary goal here, not the formatting of the information.>>

Deciding Which Anger Management Techniques to Use with Each Situation

Look over the complete list of anger management techniques. There are two options for deciding which ones to use.

One option is:

- Read the specific situations and determine which anger management techniques *you* think are most applicable.

- Once you have listed these methods, have teens choose which *they* think is applicable to the situation being analyzed.

Another option is to expose adolescents to the entire list and *have them choose* the methods they think would be useful.

Be well-versed in all of the anger managers and be prepared to explain those that are unclear to the adolescents with whom you are working. The ones I found usually need further discussion are the anger journal, "I" statement, self-talk and affirmations, balloon exercise, and mirror work. You can prompt questions by stating, "Asking for clarifications doesn't mean someone is dumb. Smart people want information—for example, finding out what self-talk is and how it is done." However, even with this positive encouragement, some participants may choose to remain silent and uninformed. For these individuals, describing the methods listed above is helpful and warranted.

If you aren't sure how to describe some of these methods to teens, don't try to bluff. If you do, it can cause irreparable damage to their trust and throw up an unnecessary roadblock. Whatever progress has been made up to that point will come to a screeching halt. The point of this warning is to stress the importance of correctly describing each anger manager. If unsure, simply don't choose a particular method, or be honest—tell them you are unfamiliar with its meaning and find an alternative anger manager.

Noting the Settings, Relationships, and Levels of Anger in Each Situation

When dealing with the categories of situations, it is important to note the *settings* in which they occur, the *type of relationships* existing between the teens and others involved, as well as the level of anger these incidents create.

The setting and relationship provide clues as to what anger managers to apply. As an example, in a situation occurring in front of peers in a public setting—such as a school, a basketball court, a mall, or a home—face-saving needs to be taken into account. Ask yourself, *How can adolescents in these settings, with people around, find ways of handling a situation peacefully and still protect their image?* This is a common need for teens. Time and thought must go into solving this puzzle prior to working with them.

The intensity of anger can be determined by asking the teens how angry specific situations would make them feel. The anger scale can be used to gauge their reactions. The higher the intensity of the anger, the more beneficial it is to explore particular circumstances.

After you've determined the strength of the anger created by each situation, it is important to begin with those yielding the *least intense* reaction. This allows adolescents to find success more easily in applying anger managers. As their confidence grows with each success in defusing tense situations, they can work their way toward similar results with more difficult situations.

An awareness of these variables increases your chances of using this process successfully. These scenarios are enacted by the teens. The actors choose which anger managers to use in their scenarios. Then, their peers are asked to identify which tools were used in the role-plays and to suggest alternative methods for resolving the conflict. Many adolescents really enjoy participating in role-plays—a great educational tool that aids the learning process.

However, many times, young people feel too embarrassed to act out these scenes. If this is the case, incidents can be analyzed and treated the same way as they may have been if they were acted out. Identifying the situation, the people involved, and the setting are still necessary elements in this kind of exercise.

You can use the scenarios dealing with family relationships or other categories as trial balloons. They are objective means of exploring the types of situations in which teens often find themselves. These scenarios help teens understand situational dynamics and teach them how to handle incidents in positive ways.

After each of the first three incidents, explain possible approaches that could have been used. It isn't necessary to review each situation in every group. Focus on the categories and incidents you think are most relevant.

Situations Within Families

Situation 1: Samantha wants to go to a party. Her mother says no since her room is not clean, and she always comes home past her curfew. Samantha tells her mom she doesn't care about her daughter's happiness, so she makes up different [expletive] excuses preventing her from going places she enjoys. Samantha's mom says, "You can add disrespect to my list of reasons you're not going out" and walks away from Samantha.

People Involved: Mother and daughter
Setting: Inside their house

Approaches to Resolving this Situation Peacefully: One approach to use with this situation is to ask an adolescent, "What does the mother want from Samantha?" Some possible responses are:

- "She wants her to be the perfect daughter."
- "She wants Samantha to know her mom's the boss."
- "She wants her to remain a virgin."

Acceptance of these remarks is important—even if you don't agree with them. Once these explanations are presented, add, "What are some reasons her mom won't let her go to the party?"
    They may respond:

- "Samantha needs to know what needs to be done in order to go places and do the things she wants."

- "Her mother wants Samantha to show she can be responsible; she's telling Samantha ways to prove this to her."

Providing additional choices for teens to consider is helpful. Responsibility is one theme that should be considered, whether the teen brings it up or you do. Discussing its role in helping Samantha get to the party is one approach. Cleaning her room and coming home when her mom asks are ways Samantha can show she can be responsible and earn the privileges she desires.

Explore additional information that can be helpful in dealing with this situation. For example, knowing when the party is taking place can be important for Samantha. If the party is some time away, weeks or a month, she may have an opportunity to prove by her actions she can be responsible and offer her mom the chance to change her mind.

If an adolescent doesn't understand how the timing of the party is helpful to Samantha, asking, "How could knowing when the party occurs be important to Samantha in dealing with this situation?" may stimulate their thinking in this direction.

The main focus of this discussion is to teach teens to consider the full picture. This *global view takes into account the perspectives of both parties* involved. By exposing the teen to various perspectives, additional ideas for resolving the conflict may occur to them. It is a way to think beyond their own point of view. Whether it is in this example or any of the others you present, be confident you are providing teens the opportunity to gain experience and knowledge to deal with conflicts more effectively.

Before they attempt to choose an anger manger, first they must consider who is the most upset in the conflict to be resolved. Keep stressing all parties in a conflict must calm down before their issues can be resolved. With this thought in mind, have them suggest possible ways Samantha and her mom can calm down, or at least not get more upset.

If the situation is acted out, you may find some of these tools flow naturally. Depending on whether a teen viewed Samantha as being more upset, or her mother, several different anger management techniques can be used:

- Taking deep breaths
- Counting
- Giving the other person space
- Staying calm
- Listening to music
- Chanting a phrase
- Asking, "Is it worth it?"

In this example, have the teen attempt to see things from the mother's perspective. This goes beyond the idea of responsibility. The question, "How do you think the mother was feeling?" makes this point. The use of empathy—putting yourself in the other person's place—is one possibility.

It is a real mindblower when you reverse the roles of parent and child. Often, this immediately decreases the intensity of the situation. In this case, having Samantha attempt to understand the frustration her mother feels with her daughter's recurring behavior and her feelings of inadequacy since nothing she does for Samantha works. This may help the daughter understand why her mom is upset. This is not an easy thing for a teen to do, and often they don't want to; however, it's worth a try.

Next, ask, "What do you think Samantha could do with this information to help change her mom's mind?" As a rule of thumb, with close relationships, the "I" statement can be used. One way Samantha's feelings can be expressed is "I feel angry when you tell me I can't go somewhere. I am not a little girl or someone you can't trust."

At this point, a dialogue can begin as the mother describes when she lost her trust and how her daughter can earn it back. Samantha may not go to this party, but they can discuss how she can earn her mother's trust and the freedom to do other things in the future. It takes a lot of work and a willingness to let reason and understanding take a front seat, along with desire, to strengthen the relationship. It also takes persistence and a readiness to believe a relationship with parents is something many adolescents really desire, in spite of their bravado or "I don't need you!" statements.

It is uncomfortable and awkward to attempt different approaches and make changes in an existing relationship. But, remember, there is nothing to lose and a stronger relationship to gain.

Situation 2: Steven gets home late after a day with his girlfriend and hanging out with his friends. When he arrives, his father argues with him without letting Steven explain why he was late. Steven yells back, "You never want to hear what I have to say! All you want to do is yell at me!" Then he walks away muttering a bunch of expletives at his father.

People Involved: Father and son
Setting: Inside their house

Approaches to Resolving this Situation Peacefully: As with the first scenario, having a young person look at the teen's behavior from the parent's perspective can be helpful. Asking, "Why do you think the boy's dad is so pissed?" serves this purpose. You may be surprised at some of the reasons they reveal. See if any of these remarks are among the responses:

- "He has to be on his son's case about something."
- "He doesn't care about anything the boy has to say."
- "He is just an [expletive]."
- "He has a date, and that [expletive] is more important than his kid's safety."
- "When he needs to do something or go somewhere, he goes and does what he [expletive] wants. It is always more important than what his son wants to do."

Other responses from a different perspective may include:

- "He's scared something happened to his son."
- "He thinks his son just doesn't care."
- "He's worried he'll get blamed if something happens to his kid."

These types of statements provide insight into a teen's perceptions of their father (or other caretakers), as well as their ideas of how this particular situation can be resolved. Using the objectivity method, as we did with these scenarios, often has the effect of getting a teen to relate the role-play scenario to similar occurrences in their own lives. No matter their responses, watching teens in these role-play exercises provides valuable insight into how they feel or think.

<<Sidebar—Keep in mind the greater the number of perspectives brought into a particular example, the broader the understanding a teen may develop and the greater the chance they will succeed in handling future situations in positive ways.>>

De-escalation techniques are important for Steven in order to gain some control over himself before responding to his dad's behavior. These may include deep breathing, counting, or any other tools helping to de-escalate the strength of his anger. The goal is to have adolescents find ways to stay in control of their feelings and empower themselves to be regarded as responsible problem solvers. This is another way of increasing their self-esteem.

Finding the correct anger managers to help both father and son express their feelings without damaging their relationship or escalating the situation becomes the next task. Asking teens to come up with ideas on how to prevent the situation from worsening starts the conversation in this direction.

If the youngsters shrug their shoulders or use the famous "I don't know," don't be tempted to give your thoughts just yet. Use the pregnant pause—let the discomfort of silence do its job.

If there is still no response, provide some clues. One way to accomplish this is using previous situations or experiences a youngster has described. Brainstorm possibilities or have them choose anger management techniques from the list you have compiled or their own. If additional ideas arise during this discussion, try them! You never know what might work. ***Don't be afraid to go with a gut instinct.***

Knowing the father goes on and on without letting the son explain himself, ask, "What can Steven accomplish if he lets his father finish saying what he is going to say?" By doing this, you are hinting Steven can benefit by waiting. If again there is no response, ask, "Which anger manager uses this idea?" One response may be people need a chance to express their anger without speaking—in other words, ***just listen*** to what they have to say.

It is good to have responses in mind in case teens don't have any or resist giving their own. The question "How can not attempting to explain his lateness until his father is through yelling be helpful to Steven?" brings us back to the idea it is beneficial to hear his father out. If there is no response, ask, "What would happen if Steven continued explaining his actions, but his father kept going on and on and didn't want to hear anything his son had to say?" One response may be "If Steven tries to tell his father the reason for his lateness, knowing he won't be heard, he might wind up angrier and more frustrated."

Now is the time for "What question can Steven ask himself that might be helpful?" Regardless whether a teen responds, totally has no clue, or makes no attempt to answer even after a long silence, direct the conversation towards viewing the consequences of being frustrated and getting angrier. Suggesting the "Is it worth it?" technique is one idea they may find useful in this situation. Discussing how it can be helpful to Steven takes you one step further.

Two ideas may come into play:

- Finding out what's bothering his father shows Steven is trying to understand his dad's concerns.

- Listening while his father expressed his feelings would have made his father more willing to hear what Steven had to say. People who are able to express themselves without interruption are more likely to listen to others.

Some of you may not think teens are capable of understanding this idea. To make sure they do, turn the tables around and ask, "When someone hears you out and shows they understand what you are saying, what is your opinion about what they have to say?" In other words, "Do you want to listen to them?" Follow this up quickly with "Why?"

If you receive a negative response, toss this idea out and attempt to take another path. Focus on Steven again and ask, "If the father yells, but Steven does not react, how will that help Steven?" "Peace and quiet" is one possible response. If not, add, "Wouldn't having his father off his case without further hassle be worthwhile to Steven?" This statement illustrates your ability to see things through a teen's eyes, which demonstrates empathy. Although this idea may not elicit a response, it is another way to help adolescents see advantages in not reacting to particular situations.

Avoidance and "Is it worth it?" are the two anger management techniques most useful in this case. Avoidance is a temporary measure. In order to deal with an issue productively, situations sometimes require both parties to have time and space away from each other.

Discovering what a teen thinks Steven wants from his father is of great value. Possible responses are:

- "He may want his father to hear why he was late."

- "He wants his dad to give him a chance to explain himself." (need for recognition)

- "He wants to apologize." (taking responsibility)

Being direct, specific, and polite is another method to be used in this situation. The simple question "What do you want?" is an example. When it is directed toward someone who is really upset, it is an invaluable expedient tool. How this question is asked is important. Tone of voice (calm or loud, honest or sarcastic) and body language (arms folded, glaring eyes, relaxed body, face muscles loose, and soft gaze) will determine the manner in which this question is answered and whether the parties' anger escalates or dissipates.

Knowledge of nonverbal communication can greatly benefit young people. It is an important skill to learn for reading a situation correctly and defusing anger and heightened emotions before relationships are damaged. It is not easy to learn, but worthwhile to teach.

Situation 3: Tara took her sister Toni's jeans without asking. When Toni was about to go out, she wanted to wear that particular pair of jeans. She couldn't find them in her closet. The next day, she saw the jeans on Tara's bed. Toni flipped out and started yelling at Tara, calling her a thief and a selfish [expletive].

People Involved: Two sisters

Setting: The girls' bedroom

Approaches to Resolving this Situation Peacefully: Start with Tara's reason for not telling Toni she was borrowing her jeans. Many times, there is only one side an adolescent sees in a situation—their own. Some reasons for this behavior could be:

- "She was afraid her sister wouldn't give them to her."
- "Her sister is a mean and selfish [expletive]."
- "She's borrowed other things before without asking and was threatened and told if she did it again, she'd catch a beating."
- "She didn't think her sister would mind or care."
- "She thought her sister wouldn't find out."

Exploring these possibilities may also give a young person more clues on how to deal with this situation. Discussing the fact that Toni was upset when this occurred and asking a teen to give you possible reasons why starts this discussion.

This question sounds really simple on the surface, but it's not. "Because Tara took her jeans without asking" is the most obvious and probably the simplest response. However, there's more to the meaning of this behavior than meets the eye.

Asking the adolescent, "What is Toni really mad about?" or "What other reasons may be causing Toni to be really angry at Tara?" may start them thinking of more "important" issues. Privacy, trust, and honesty may be among their responses. If not, present these ideas and explore them.

<<Sidebar—Privacy, trust, and honesty are at the root of many conflicts occurring in relationships. Understanding these values may be at the heart of many situations, and using the appropriate anger managers for expressing these feelings can bring closure.>>

Empathy is one of the tools to use in order to see this situation from both sisters' points of view. Here you can have teens put themselves in either sister's place and see the situation from their point of view by developing a statement to show they understand. "Toni, by taking your jeans without asking, I wasn't acting as if I were someone close to you or someone who cares about you. It was as if I were stealing from you." This illustrates how Tara can use empathy to express Toni's point of view.

Now, let's look at it from Tara's perspective. "Tara, you thought I'd get mad at you, as I had when you wanted to wear my bracelet," or "You know I don't like to share any of my stuff with you," are two remarks Toni could make in trying to understand Tara's point of view.

In addition to using empathy, have the teens develop other ideas on how the two sisters might explain their feelings about this situation. Then, different ways of calming down before dealing with the jeans problem may also be suggested.

Asking teens whether or not they felt Toni and Tara were ready to discuss this situation is the first step. The question "When something like this happens, can people manage it if they are both upset?" opens up another avenue of exploration. Adding, "What can be helpful in getting them to calm down?" can take teens down this path.

"How else can Toni and Tara make each other aware of how they felt?" Both listening to each other without commenting represents one method. Using the "I" statement would be another way. In this case, ask, "What would each sister say?" For example, Tara may say, "When I borrowed your jeans, I was afraid to ask since you yelled at me when I asked you to lend me something last week." Or Toni may say, "I felt angry when you borrowed my jeans without asking because it was dishonest, and I have always been able to trust you before."

The Elaboration-Demonstration-Practice (EDP) Method

Now that you have been guided through an analysis of the first three situations involving family members, this last scenario will be left open for you to analyze. As a guide to accomplishing this task, a step-by-step description of the process used to explore other situations will follow. This particular process is known as the Elaboration-Demonstration-Practice (EDP) method. It will lay the groundwork for you to deal with the remaining categories and situations.

Situation 4: Jacqueline comes into her house after she had a fight with her boyfriend, slams the door, and curses. Her mother tells her not to make so much noise and to stop cursing. Jacqueline yells at her mother and remarks, "I'll slam the door if I feel like it! This is my house too, and I'll do what I feel like. What's the matter, you never heard those words?" The mother yells back, telling her daughter she'd better show some respect if she knows what's good for her.

People Involved: Mother and daughter

Setting: Living room in their house

Approaches to Resolving this Situation Peacefully: In this final situation involving family members, the *elaboration* phase takes place as elements come into play for Jacqueline and her mother. During this portion of the method, concerns and perceptions of each person's behavior are discussed. This is accomplished through questioning.

Asking, "What did the mother think of Jacqueline's behavior?" and "How did Jacqueline see her mother's behavior?" illustrate this point. When minimal or no responses are given, offer some possibilities that may be the mother's and daughter's thoughts. "Do you think the mom felt disrespected?" and "Do you think Jacqueline felt her mom didn't care what was bothering her?" describe some conversation jump starters.

Before moving to the next stage of this process, having teens look at where situations take place is especially important. The events described in the family category all took place in the privacy of the home; no other family members were present. The setting had no bearing on these particular situations.

However, if they had taken place in a more public setting, where others could witness the conflict, other factors would have come into play and would have needed to be considered. For adolescents, the idea of not appearing soft, weak, or a person others can take advantage of is a topic worth discussing. Their desires to be recognized as capable, strong, intelligent, or any number of other attributes have to be met. If a situation makes them appear weak, stupid, or feel as if they are being put down, it often causes a strong reaction. The question of how to remove someone from a situation without losing face—looking weak, dumb, or incapable of handling the attack on them—has to be answered.

Helping a youngster calm down and resolve a situation without causing damage to their image enters the picture. This should be considered as part of the *demonstration* phase of this method, which is when various anger management techniques are applied to the situation. By making EDP their choice of methods for how both Jacqueline and her mother handle their conflict, teens demonstrate their understanding of the situation and their sense of what may work to resolve the problem. Focusing on having both parties calm down, find a helpful approach to understanding each other, and then discover a way to resolve the issue assists youngsters in demonstrating their knowledge.

The final stage of this process—*practice*—involves the teens applying the information and skills they have acquired. This step occurs after they have been taught the basics of anger management. During this phase, adolescents will either demonstrate they can handle episodes in a positive way, or they will look at what went wrong and review the techniques already discussed. At this point, it's back to the drawing board. These skills take time for them to learn and try. They require patience and a willingness to Try, Try Again.

A teen may express their frustration by commenting, "I tried, it didn't work, and so what's the use?" In response, asking, "When you tried to do something new—ride a bicycle, drive a car, learn something different in school—did you quit?" can be helpful. Discuss how they finally overcame their earlier frustration.

Prior to having the teens practice their skills in this area, remind them sometimes things just don't work when first attempted. Oftentimes, an approach to a problem isn't the most effective. Teens need to know they can come to you to figure out what went wrong.

This is the method used with the first three scenarios. It can be beneficial in the remaining situations. The EDP process is used in the training of AMP facilitators, and it has proven to be an effective training strategy.

The remaining categories of relationships and situations represent areas described by teens as conflicts having occurred between themselves and others or issues causing them or their peers the most difficulty. Based on your personal knowledge of what types of relationships or situations a particular teen finds the most troublesome or preferable to discuss, determine which of the following groups and events to explore.

Peer Situations

Situation 1: Gail is upset her best friend, Doris, who now has a boyfriend, no longer spends any time with her.

People Involved: Two female friends

Setting: Outside a classroom in school

Situation 2: Two best friends, Mike and Chris, like the same girl and argue over who should pursue her. (This is a common situation for both sexes.)

People Involved: Two best male friends

Setting: School cafeteria

Situation 3: Two close friends, Pat and Chris, are hanging out with other friends who are part of the in-crowd. They are passing around a joint. (This could be any kind of situation involving peer pressure.) Chris takes the joint. Pat doesn't want to smoke pot. Chris repeatedly tries to get Pat to smoke. He keeps pushing and pushing Pat. Finally, he threatens their friendship is over if Chris doesn't smoke. At this point, Pat is really angry at Chris.

People Involved: Two best friends and a small group of peers

Setting: Schoolyard

Relationship Situations

Situation 1: Denise suspects her boyfriend, Ted, is cheating on her because one of her friends told her she saw Ted with his arm around another girl.

<<*Sidebar—"He said/she said" situations are common causes of conflict with teens.*>>

People Involved: Girlfriend and boyfriend

Setting: In a hallway at school

Situation 2: Pete is mad at his girlfriend, Renee, because she hangs around with her "backstabbing" friends who make her angry. Then she takes her anger out on him.

People Involved: Boyfriend and girlfriend

Setting: Outside of school as they are walking home

Situation 3: Patty is dancing in a club and sees her boyfriend, Eddie. She goes over to say hi. Patty notices another girl "wrapped around" her boyfriend.

People Involved: Boyfriend, girlfriend, and a third party

Setting: Inside a club

Neighborhood Situations

Situation 1: While playing basketball, John deliberately hits an opposing player, Darnell, in the face with the ball.

People Involved: John, Darnell, and six other players, one of whom is Darnell's brother

Setting: Basketball court in a neighborhood playground

Situation 2: Larry turns his bike around and accidentally hits Steve's leg with the back tire. Larry apologizes, but Steve starts cursing at him.

People Involved: Two teens

Setting: On the street

Situation 3: Janice has a party. There is a lot of noise—loud music and the raised voices of her many guests. Some of her neighbors complain, but Janice's party keeps going on with no decrease in sound.

People Involved: Janice, her friends, and neighbors

Setting: An apartment building

School Situations

Situation 1: A student yells at the teacher because she instructed him to raise his hand after he already shouted out the correct answer.

People Involved: Student, teacher, and other students in the classroom

Setting: Classroom

Situation 2: Laura, Joan, and Shannon are talking about Sherry. She overhears them and gets angry.

People Involved: Three girls in a group and Sherry

Setting: In the girls' locker room at school

Situation 3: Maria, who is normally quiet and calm, comes into class in a bad mood since her mother is in the hospital. During class, Olga says something. The teacher, Ms. Calderon, accuses Maria of talking. Maria becomes angry at Ms. Calderon's accusation and starts yelling at her.

People Involved: Two students, a teacher, and the rest of the class

Setting: Classroom

Work Situations

Situation 1: A customer in a fast-food restaurant doesn't get what he ordered. One of the food servers doesn't want to deal with the customer's problem. The customer gets really angry and throws the cheeseburger down on the counter.

People Involved: Customer, employee, and other customers and workers in the fast-food restaurant

Setting: A fast-food restaurant

Situation 2: An older coworker, Denise, gives many of her responsibilities to a younger coworker, Geri, who feels stressed and explodes.

People Involved: Two workers and other employees in the office

Setting: In an office

Situation 3: A customer comes up to a cashier. The cashier doesn't acknowledge him because she's too busy talking on a cell phone(brushing her hair, talking to a coworker). Customer explodes.

People Involved: Customer, cashier, and other employees and customers

Setting: Any type of business

The goals in presenting these scenarios are to have teens:

- Relate their perceptions of the people involved
- Look at the factors occurring
- Provide suggestions on how to resolve these situations using different anger management techniques

You have been given situations involving different relationships in a variety of settings. They can serve as a springboard for discussion with adolescents who may relate to these specific situations or similar ones they've experienced. Feel free to use any other scenarios they think are useful, or create those you think appropriate. Whatever situations are chosen, explore them with confidence.

<<Keep in mind conflicts arise in all relationships, particularly as a result of the influences of social media, the pandemic, and gun violence. These subjects are worth revealing and mentioning as sources of reactive behavior.>>

You have the knowledge you need. Before exploring situations with teens, go back to the first three situations presented, look over the list of anger management techniques, and categorize them as de-escalators or positive ways of expressing anger. This is a process both you and your teen can do together, along with considering other factors (needs, causes, and effects) affecting the way an adolescent may handle anger in these scenarios.

For parents who are reading this book, you often discover the results of this work when your child is involved in a conflict. For educators and others working with youth, this is also true. Perhaps, in the absence of any reported situations, you may think they are being handled more positively, or you would have been made aware of them. Time to follow up may not be possible with all the other things going on in your personal life or profession. Whatever your circumstances, the idea of checking on a teen proactively—that is, not waiting until something happens—is a more worthwhile and productive approach.

Chapter Thirteen

Following Up on Anger Management Training

C reating awareness of the whys of anger, providing teens with ways of understanding the effects of this feeling, and presenting ideas on resolving anger-provoking situations are all useful. However, this knowledge isn't useful in a vacuum. Having adolescents utilize this information in their everyday lives is the real test of the effectiveness of a learning experience.

So examining the how-tos of assessing the success of your efforts to teach anger management is our next step. After a period of time has elapsed—perhaps a month after presenting this information in your learning laboratory with teens—it is good to evaluate the impact of this training on their lives. However, particularly for an individual rather than a group, this evaluation interval can be significantly shorter. It might occur in a day, a few days, or even weeks after you've spent time with them in developing additional positive anger management strategies. This can certainly occur immediately after a teen has been involved in a recent conflict.

<<Sidebar—The timing is for you to decide. There is no fixed or prescribed time period.>>

An Introduction to AMP Feedback and Follow-Up Surveys

There are two evaluation tools that are used to gauge the effectiveness of the Anger Management Power Program (AMP) on its participants. First is the AMP Feedback Survey. This document is administered during the final portion of training. Second is the AMP Follow-Up Survey. It is usually administered approximately one month after the training has been completed. Both of these documents can be found in the "Information Boosters" section at the end of this book.

If you are a parent or someone working with an individual adolescent, the questions found in each document provide worthwhile ideas for you to present orally. *Writing isn't a teen's favorite thing to do.*

The AMP Feedback Survey focuses on the value of the ideas presented during anger management training. The responses to the questions on this document indicate what youngsters have learned, liked, disliked, and valued in this experience.

The AMP Follow-Up Survey is a reality check. The answers to the questions tell you whether or not, in real-life situations, teens actually used the anger management information presented during their learning experience. If they responded they didn't use this knowledge, simply ask, "What stopped you from using some of the things we talked about?" Typical responses may include:

- "I wanted to get you off my back."
- "I didn't want you to feel bad."

- "I didn't think they would work."
- "I felt like my friends would think I was soft."
- "I didn't get a chance."
- "I didn't have any problems with anyone."

Whatever the reason, patience is the order of the day. Sometimes adolescents just want to see your reaction or deliberately try to push your buttons to find out if you are going to jump on them with a resounding "Why not?" or indicate by your tone of voice or body language you expected more from them. They see this attitude as a sign you either aren't really going to listen to why they didn't use this knowledge or are judging them as incompetent in handling anger in new ways. In other words, not using the anger management techniques they were exposed to is often a test of your willingness to listen and not judge them.

Taking this thought one step further, if some negative attention is what they expect from you, they may think or feel they shouldn't try using these tools because they represent something else to be hassled about.

The bottom line in working with teens is to *keep trying*! Adolescents often act in ways that lead you to believe you will never succeed at whatever you are trying to do with them. Many of their responses are bravado or "for show." Hear them out, and then continue obtaining information from them.

Overcoming Adolescent Resistance to Using Anger Managers

There are several reasons why youngsters aren't eager to discuss their efforts to use particular anger managers. One possibility—they were not used successfully. If you suspect this is the case, remark, "Sometimes people try things, and they don't work at first," or "Things don't always turn out the way we expect them to," and wait for a response. Teens may respond by nodding, giving some other nonverbal clue, or muttering an almost-inaudible yes. You may also get a loud "Yeah, I tried it, and it didn't work. My way of handling stuff works better."

Adolescents are often resistant to change, and they fear embarrassment. After they attempt to do something differently, and it doesn't work, they go back to the ways they are used to doing things because they are easier and more comfortable. This is common behavior for not only them, but adults as well.

Acknowledge these possibilities. Make an attempt to compare anger managers to other unfamiliar things in their lives. Riding a bike or driving a car are two examples. The remark "When you learned to ride a bike or drive a car, you probably found they weren't as easy as you thought they would be" provides this connection. Saying, "When trying new things, people often experience some failures before succeeding. They may ride a bike a few feet before falling off, or drive a short distance without braking too hard or going too fast or too slow," presents ideas for them to consider. Pause to let these thoughts infiltrate their minds. Regardless of their reactions, they have been given the opportunity to add more ideas to their *mental tool kits*.

Being embarrassed about attempting a new idea that didn't work can also stop adolescents from trying to use anger managers. If you feel this might be the case, acknowledge this fear. Their response can open the way for further discussion about a recent incident.

Teens frequently look for instant results. Regardless of any setbacks, patience and encouragement are helpful in ensuring their success when using the management skills to which they were exposed in the "learning lab." This means going back to the drawing board with them. You and they have spent time discovering different ways of handling anger, so why not try finding out why something didn't work, rather than eliminating it altogether?

To accomplish this goal, ask them to describe the incident. They may remark, "That's all the time I wanted to spend trying this stuff," or offer some other form of resistance. Bring in the consequences of how the teen previously managed their anger. Explore what happened when they took care of situations in the ways they wanted. These effects may include:

- Being hassled by teachers, parents, or other adults
- Receiving payback from peers or their families or friends

If they still don't want to look at recent situations and their failed efforts to handle them, leave this discussion alone for the time being. Suggest revisiting it together sometime in the future. If they agree, this offer provides a youngster with the power to decide whether or not to bring up the subject again.

It is also worthwhile to be alert for both indirect and direct indications a teen wants to revisit a situation. They may refer to a friend's situation and how they handled it or to a conflict in which they were involved and left unresolved. Discuss the situation and how it was managed, focusing on what worked and didn't work. Consider what methods could have been used to calm things down and resolve the issues. If the teen is reticent to delve into the interaction, leave the subject alone, and wait to see if this incident is revisited at a later time.

Another approach to determining why an anger management technique didn't work is trying the *Situation Description Recorder (SDR)* described earlier as *a more objective approach.* Using this method requires examining the issue at the heart of the particular conflict, identifying those involved, and describing the setting in which it took place. If the teen doesn't supply all this information, simply ask for whatever details were missing, including the anger manager used and its result.

Using the EDP method to analyze and defuse a situation is another road to take. The how-tos of this approach were illustrated by the words and examples used in the first three family incidents explored in the last chapter.

First, have the teen *elaborate* on the details of the situation, revisiting all the factors and dynamics, including:

- The *perceptions* of both parties
- The *setting* of the incident
- The *closeness* of the teen's relationship with the other person

Then, the *demonstration* phase begins. Discuss ways the situation could have been resolved in a calm, effective manner using whatever anger managers you feel could have helped. Consider this a refresher course for the teen. Be sure they are clear on how to use anger management techniques.

The final stage is when the teen puts into *practice* the ideas discussed. Their learning is put to the test in a real-life situation.

Let's look at one handled ineffectively.

Situation: Anthony and his girlfriend, Carolyn, began arguing because he saw James with his arms around Carolyn, kissing her on the cheek. James leaves, goes down the block, and disappears. Anthony starts walking toward Carolyn at a fast pace.

People Involved: Boyfriend, girlfriend, and another male

Setting: Outside of school, just after dismissal

You (the reader) are speaking with Anthony. At this point, he tells you he took some deep breaths and slowed his pace as he moved closer to his girlfriend. As he approached Carolyn, she turned away from him and said he needed to calm down; they could talk about it later. Anthony described himself as looking at her, shaking his head, and then grabbing her arm to get her attention. Carolyn turned around and told him, "Get your [expletive] hands off of me!"

A group of their peers were nearby when Anthony and Carolyn started yelling at each other. At this point, these bystanders focused their attention on this unfolding drama to see who would win the argument.

Anthony said, "We've got to talk about you and James now!" But Carolyn pulled away from him. He tried saying to himself, *Keep calm; don't lose your cool and screw things up with Carolyn.* Then in a raised voice, he heard himself demand, "We've gotta take care of this business now!"

It was then Carolyn said, "No!" and told him to "Go [expletive] yourself!" Anthony responded by yelling, calling her a whore, and adding a few expletives. As both walked away muttering to themselves, Carolyn screamed, "I don't need a jealous man in my life!" Anthony replied, "I don't need a two-timing [expletive]!"

After this incident is described, the focus needs to be on what Anthony thought went wrong. "Where did things start to go downhill with you and Carolyn?" takes the conversation in this direction. He may react to this and say, "When I saw her all cozy with James?" Responding, "It certainly started this whole bad scene," shows Anthony you are accepting his viewpoint.

Now is the time to acknowledge what, if anything, the teen did correctly in order to provide some positive reinforcement. In this example, tell Anthony you recognized his attempts to prevent his anger from escalating. The remark "You certainly tried to calm yourself down before speaking with Carolyn... when you took deep breaths...and then later when you tried to use self-talk" teaches while providing positive feedback. Then get back to the cause of his increasing anger.

<<Sidebar—This type of acknowledgment is something many teens have said they don't receive. In their words, "My (parents, teacher) only look at what I do wrong. They don't ever look at when I do something right." This is also a way for an adolescent to see you are trying to understand their viewpoint.>>

Whether or not Anthony can see where he made the situation worse, some thoughts need to be addressed. The first involves the point when he reached out to Carolyn to talk things out. Instead, his girlfriend reacted. Anthony responded in kind, and the situation began to spiral out of control. It ended with name-calling and both walking away from each other really upset.

This reaction worsened because it also involved face-saving since the incident took place in front of peers. This is another factor that should be explored.

Finding alternative ways to prevent Anthony's anger from escalating and ideas on how to resolve this situation without harming his relationship with Carolyn are the next roads to follow. The question "What other ways can you think of to deal with this difficult situation with Carolyn?" moves the discussion in this direction.

If Anthony can't think of any ideas, stimulate his thinking, by having him:

- Think of ways he's dealt with situations involving Carolyn or other young women in the past.
- Think of some of the things that were discussed during training and determine if he now feels they might have been worthwhile attempting in this situation.

Remind him of some of the anger management techniques his peers indicated they would use—those on the list he was given or those developed on his own. Keep these ideas handy in some written form. Whatever shape this resource takes, it provides something Anthony can refer to when resolving this or future situations.

<<Sidebar—Having a teen carry a list in their phone or wallet is one possible suggestion. Asking them to consult that list, when needed, for ideas is worthwhile, especially if they can't think of any during this conversation.>>

Refocus Anthony's attention on where things worsened. Have him give reasons why this incident spiraled out of control. "When I grabbed Carolyn" or "We were in public" are two reasons the situation could have escalated. After these ideas are expressed, have Anthony try to see his responsibility in the deterioration of the incident. This is a challenging and worthwhile idea to pursue.

More often than not, a teen blames another rather than taking responsibility for having a negative role in a conflict. Keeping this idea in mind, ask, "What could you have done differently at this point?" A look that could kill or comments such as "She's the one who made me react; it's her fault," "Get off my back," and "Don't start laying a guilt trip on me!" are typical responses.

Take deep breaths, count, or think of something that can bring a smile to your face. This kind of reaction is predictable. After *you* have calmly weathered this youngster's storm with patience and acceptance, reinforce to Anthony your role is to help him find a way to resolve the situation—that is, if it is something he wants to do.

If Anthony still objects to delving into his part of the situation, ask, "Do you still want to have a close relationship with Carolyn?" If he indicates he does, then the "Is it worth it?" anger management technique comes into play. This can be addressed by saying, "So the way this situation went is not what you anticipated. It just wasn't worth what happened, was it?"

This tool has a place here, not only as a way of looking for methods to resolve this conflict, but also as something to think about when things get nasty between them again. That is a real possibility since they still need to speak to each other to resolve this issue.

If Anthony says no, but still doesn't want to deal with this situation, leave it alone. It may or may not resurface. Anthony will make this decision.

In the case of a yes response, suggest Anthony let things simmer down for a while so he and Carolyn can chill out enough to be able to calmly discuss what happened. Let Anthony know, once more, his deep breathing and self-talk did calm him down before. Suggest it could be helpful when he and Carolyn are able to speak to each other again.

Talking about when things escalated offers Anthony an opportunity to understand why things went wrong and how they could have been handled differently. Whether or not he remembers when things started to go badly, review his account of the situation. Ask, "If I remember correctly, you said you approached Carolyn and grabbed her arm. Do you think, at this point, things went wrong?"

<<Sidebar—Using an "if I remember correctly" phrase allows a teen the freedom to agree or change some of the details. It also demonstrates humility, indicating you possibly did not hear or remember correctly. This behavior is something adolescents feel adults rarely exhibit, and it will earn you points with them.>>

Whether Anthony can or cannot recall the behavior setting things off, ask, "Why do you think she got upset when you did this?" Several answers may come to mind. Among these are:

- "She thought I was going to hit her."
- "Maybe Carolyn thought I was going to turn her around and start yelling at her in front of our friends. She didn't want to be embarrassed or look like someone who would take [expletive] from her boyfriend."

If Anthony doesn't have any ideas, mention these as possible reasons for Carolyn's response.

"How else could you have obtained your girlfriend's attention?" offers another way to take this discussion. "I could have walked around, faced her, and asked her calmly and quietly if we could talk, without yelling" represents a possible response. This approach uses the "ask, don't demand" anger management technique.

Viewing things from Carolyn's perspective is another way to move this discussion forward. Once again, the use of *empathy* is helpful. When teens are able to see a situation from another person's viewpoint, it helps them understand how someone else could misinterpret their actions. Carolyn knew Anthony was really angry when he saw her with James and walked quickly toward her. This behavior suggested Anthony would be too angry to deal with the situation calmly at that moment.

When Carolyn yelled at Anthony, he could have done some deep breathing, used self-talk phrases—such as "I want to stay cool" or "I want to work this out"—or thought of a good time he had with his girlfriend. To prevent himself from looking "soft" in front of their friends (an adolescent who cares about the other person or has a higher level of maturity may add, "And make sure Carolyn also doesn't lose face or get embarrassed"), Anthony could have asked his girlfriend to go somewhere private where others could not witness their interaction.

When a discussion takes place between Carolyn and him, Anthony should use "I" statements to express his anger over Carolyn's behavior with James. It may be a method he now recognizes as useful. If not, you should suggest it. "I felt angry when I saw you acting so friendly with James since I always thought I could trust you" is a way for Anthony to express this idea.

There are other anger management techniques he could also use. This is something you can discover together. The situation between Anthony and Carolyn shows how a teen first tried to calm down before expressing his anger. He was exposed to many ideas, yet when it came to applying them, more work had to be done to help him express his anger without escalating the situation and damaging his relationship with Carolyn. In this case, Anthony needed to see what he could have done differently and learn ways to remedy the issue with Carolyn. This knowledge can also be beneficial in handling future incidents.

The AMP Feedback Survey and the AMP Follow-Up Survey

The AMP Feedback Survey and the AMP Follow-Up Survey can be used in different ways. The first is in written form. The opinions expressed by peers in these documents can help persuade a teen to attempt ideas learned during their training. Written responses are also used when there isn't enough time to get each individual participant's oral responses. The knowledge gained can be used as a jumping-off point for a group discussion at some later date.

Oral responses to the questions found in the survey represent another way of getting information from adolescents. It gives them the opportunity to express their opinions and eliminates the "I don't like to write" resistance.

The oral responses to the questions asked on the follow-up survey can be presented differently. "Of everything we talked about, what have you tried to use?" or "What situations have occurred since we spent time talking about managing anger?" are useful questions to ask. Whatever open-ended questions you feel comfortable using will serve as *stepping stones* for gathering this information.

For some teens, writing down their reactions rather than expressing them openly works best. For them, not making their opinions public to peers eliminates the possibility of looking "soft," "weak," or "vulnerable." The main focus is to have adolescents react to their experiences in positive ways, no matter what form they choose.

Teens may come to you in person and talk about an experience they had, essentially self-initiating the follow-up phase of the training. In other cases, you may choose an arbitrary time for this part of the process to take place. Mention these possibilities several times during their training.

When I (the author) facilitate this training, participants are told the reason and timing for this follow-up stage of the process. This is described to them as an evaluation of what methods were used and those that were not. The reason for the timing of this part of the process is described. If too much time elapses after the training, many of the things learned or tried may be forgotten.

A different use for the activities and knowledge gained by some participants in AMP came from their willingness to learn how to create and facilitate workshops for their peers. The opportunity to become a peer anger management workshop leader is provided at the bottom of the AMP Follow-Up Survey. The teens choosing this option decided on which activities were useful and which anger management techniques would be most effective with their peers. This topic is discussed in more depth in the next chapter. Samples of the teen-developed workshops appear in the "Information Boosters" section of this book.

<<Sidebar—*Empowering teens to provide information to their peers is one of the most effective ways of having this knowledge reach teens.*>>

The Timing of Training-Effectiveness Evaluations

Evaluating the effectiveness of the information given to teens can be useful in making adjustments to the teaching methods used to help them handle their anger. For the parents who are reading this book, providing the time and effort—and most of all having the patience—to follow up on the things you've shared with your children on this subject is important. This part of the process will be taking place continuously over a long period of time. For those of you whose profession is not practiced in one location, the possibility of multiple checkups is slightly more difficult. The likelihood for you to continue this part of the process depends on the time you can devote to it and the flexibility you have while still fulfilling your other professional obligations.

Obstacles to Evaluating Training Effectiveness and Ways to Overcome Them

Let's discuss the methodologies applicable in an educational or social services setting. Facilitating the Anger Management Power Program necessitates a great deal of effort and time on the part of both students and teachers. Both these resources may be severely limited by the need to ensure all students (K–12) from varied ethnic, economic, and social abilities and backgrounds attain a certain level of academic achievement in preparation for a college education or successful career. To assist in meeting this goal, the Every Student Succeeds Act (ESSA) was enacted in 2015 to provide states and communities additional influence over schools. Although standardized testing in reading, math, and science remain gauges of academic achievement, they are not the sole criteria determining a student's level of success in school. However, they still remain part of the achievement profile, narrowing the scope of the curriculum and requiring additional educator and student time and effort, in addition to a portion of scarce resources. As a result, funds, staff, and time for AMP training, as well as other social and emotional services, has been severely restricted of late.

<<Sidebar—*For additional information regarding the ESSA program, visit the US Department of Education at www.ed.gov and/or your state's department of education website.*[15]>>

School social workers, counselors, and psychologists find the essential time necessary for addressing the psychological and emotional needs of students is severely lacking. It has been usurped by the emphasis on student achievement and school performance. For these mental health professionals, their ability to counsel students *consistently* is limited. In addition, other duties—for example, writing reports or furnishing statistics—further limit counseling time. Students in crisis can only be seen briefly before being referred to outside agencies. Seeking help for the adolescent is often dead-ended at this point for financial reasons or due to lack of trust in other mental health practitioners.

These circumstances are frustrating for the professionals working in many educational settings, as well as those in other environments. Unfortunately, I see no change in mental health prioritization in our schools in the near future.

Overcoming Limitations

Since this is a how-to book, let's take some time and consider how to work within such constraints. The question for people in the educational setting is "Where can time be found to follow up on the work done with teens while still allowing them to meet their educational standards?" Looking back at how you were able to provide anger management training is a helpful starting point.

In many high schools, there are subjects that do not require a standardized examination. Health education is one of these areas. As part of this course, the area of mental health lends itself to discussing anger and anger management. Some high schools offer elective subjects, such as psychology and law. These classes can also provide this type of training since knowledge on how to manage anger is helpful in specific careers.

As a teacher, guidance counselor, or social worker in the educational setting, these are opportunities for exposing teens to anger management training. Upon its completion, inform adolescents there will be a follow-up about a month after their training.

How will you be able to incorporate this training and its evaluation into your limited schedule while keeping within and fulfilling your professional responsibilities? For teachers with classes in relevant subject areas or working within specialized schools and programs, anger management can be incorporated as part of their curriculum.

However, some teachers may not have the expertise in this area. A specially trained guidance counselor or social worker can bring the Anger Management Power Program to their students. If you are not the teacher of the class, the timing for this training must be carved out of their curriculum. During the initial planning session with the teacher, be sure to include time for a follow-up session.

In addition, the availability of this training needs to be publicized to staff. At the time of writing this book, there is a great awareness of the prevalence of violence in our society—gun violence, bullying, fights, and negative social media and Internet influences. An awareness of violence-prevention efforts can be made available via individual contacts with colleagues or with departmental or professional development presentations.

The Anger Management Power Program I have presented in high school settings ranged from one forty-minute period to approximately two and one-half hours per session. The length of time available to work with a particular group and educator will determine what elements of the training can be incorporated and what ideas need to be reviewed during the follow-up session.

<<Sidebar—*Variations of AMP protocols have been developed because of time limitations. To give you an idea of what to include within this constraint, look in the "Information Boosters" section of this book for the descriptions of these training formats.*>>

No matter what length of time is used for this training, the evaluation process should focus on:

- Were anger managers incorporated?

- If so, which ones?

- If not, why not?

- Were situations arising since the initial training discussed?

The answers to these questions are key to understanding the effectiveness of the training.

Obstacles to having a teen use these techniques and how to overcome them were pointed out earlier in this chapter. The more input gained from teens, the more helpful you can be to future participants in this training. The elements created by teen participants provided additional information on situations they experienced and what anger management techniques would have been most helpful. Following this lead, during your follow-up sessions, utilize the training ideas most teens found worthy.

The limited time you may have available to facilitate anger management, or any other related service as a guidance counselor or social worker, should be discussed. In either capacity, running groups usually falls within these career categories. A supervisor often dictates the number of sessions required or the time available to carry out this function. Keeping this in mind will determine the number of sessions devoted to anger management training. In the school setting, make sure this training doesn't interfere with preparation for exams or important school functions.

Another challenge you may face is justifying this type of service within the framework of your responsibilities. The idea of "advisory" is part of the New York City high school service plan for students. Under this function, staff members—including guidance counselors—have a limited number of students to follow. High school freshmen or those with a variety of challenges (academic, attendance, behavior, motivation) are provided with various forms of assistance from staff members. Among these are social skills development, which include conflict resolution and anger management training. In the state of New York, a mandated program known as SAVE (Schools Against Violence in Education) requires educators, other state employees, and students to have training in violence prevention. This policy provides validation for anger management training.

<<Sidebar—The ideas describing New York's policies and programs may be utilized in other states and communities as well.>>

Once again, finding out whether or not anger management training as a means of violence prevention is effective requires follow-up. In this case, the use of statistics on the number of incidents, suspensions, etc., both before and after the training, is often required. Not only would this method of follow-up look at statistics, which in many cases leads to funding of programs, but it can also include responses to questions relating to how effectively teens used anger management techniques.

Outside of the educational setting, agencies working with youth often look for programs providing additional funding for them and the services they provide. Anger management training may provide a vehicle to acquire *additional sources of financial support* where and when it exists.

<<Sidebar—It is an unfortunate fact that funding sources, particularly on the federal level, are becoming scarce or nonexistent. Keeping this fact in mind, while incorporating anger management training as described above without the benefit of funding, is the path to be followed.>>

Chapter Fourteen

Adolescent Reactions to Program Ideas and Ways to Take Training to the Next Level

This chapter focuses on the specific information gathered from the Anger Management Power Program's feedback and follow-up surveys, and ways to use it. The full documents are available in the "Information Boosters" section at the end of the book. To more fully understand the value of these surveys, an overview of both documents will be presented. Conclusions based on the surveys and information gained from them will furnish additional ways to better understand and influence adolescents. The generalizations you draw from these evaluations provide a foundation for working with youngsters.

There are two thoughts to bear in mind:

- Teens are unique individuals, and the lives of the ones with whom you work may differ in many respects from those of the participants in the Anger

Management Power Program (AMP). So some responses on the surveys may not apply to your teen.

- These differences can result from being raised by dissimilar families, living in varied neighborhoods, attending different schools, and working in diverse locations.

Keeping these two things in mind, do not be surprised if the adolescents with whom you are involved respond differently to situations, anger managers, and adults than the AMP participants. This individuality also applies to differences in personality. For example, some teens are more outgoing than others. This characteristic can result in their gravitating towards alternative methods of managing conflicts.

Even though teens may come from diverse backgrounds and display different personalities, all teens do share many needs and attitudes. For instance, the desire to belong to specific groups and the need to be recognized for what they think and do are important to all teens, no matter their backgrounds or personalities. Likewise, many adolescents regard adults as people who don't know what they are talking about, don't want to hear what they have to say, don't value teens' opinions, but make judgments nonetheless. Keeping these thoughts in mind, let's examine the conclusions drawn from the AMP Feedback and Follow-Up Surveys.

How to Use These Facts

Presenting the results of these evaluation tools in a meaningful way can be of great value in your work with adolescents. Before doing so, however, be sure to stress these documents were completed by your teens' peers or individuals around their age—in other words, individuals whose judgment your teens will immediately trust and respect. This alone can open their minds to the value of the thoughts and opinions expressed in these surveys. Teens are more likely to respond to ideas and comments made by peers than those offered by adults.

AMP Feedback Survey

The replies presented here are a compilation of those most frequently given on the actual surveys. The survey questions required written responses since it was used with large groups. When administering this survey to an individual or a small group, responses can be written or oral. However, written responses can furnish an adolescent with the means of organizing and thinking about their answers. Others who don't care for writing may simply respond to a questionnaire with a curt "No way!"

<<*Sidebar—Providing these questions on Google Forms so the adolescent can use their cell phone or computer might be more enthusiastically received.*>>

The questions asked and how they are presented are for you to decide. These choices are dependent on what elements of the training were stressed. Other factors include:

- The allotted time for filling out this evaluation
- The attention span of the adolescents with whom you interact
- The ability of your teens to understand different concepts

This assessment can be developed before the anger management training takes place, as part of the planning process, or after each topic is covered. For example, if you are discussing the effects of anger and ways of preventing it from controlling an adolescent's reaction, you may ask questions following this topic, rather than at the end of the training. The time, attention, and teens' ability to understand and remember the concepts are crucial factors.

After reviewing their responses, consider what ideas may or may not appeal to a teen. The conclusions reached can be used to help develop the elements you want to incorporate or eliminate from the training sessions.

Feedback Survey Responses

The **first question** focuses on whether or not adolescents felt the ideas presented were helpful. Participants felt anger managers met this goal. Their responses took two forms. The first category of thoughts was expressed in general terms:

- "Anger managers give different ways to deal with anger."
- "Knowing how to control anger better"
- "How to help and understand anger in others"
- "How to prevent anger or keep it from getting worse."

These choices can be provided as a checklist. Expressing them in this way minimizes the time and effort needed for this evaluation.

The second category pinpointed individual methods. Among the most popular were:

- Visualizing anger
- Deep breathing
- "Is it worth it?"

The **second question** focuses on what activities and ideas they liked. Their replies may hopefully become the tools you use when working with an individual adolescent or a group of teens. Many enjoy being entertained or doing things that allow them to be more interactive. Two of the more popular methods falling into this category were role-playing and using the human anger scale. Both of these involved groups of youngsters. Skits were performed, and some participants described them as entertaining or humorous. This method provides a means of viewing a particular situation objectively, allowing teens to see them more impersonally.

Variations of these activities can be used with individual adolescents or small groups (three to five young people). Showing a video—often found on the Internet under the search words *conflict* or *anger*—offers another entertaining way to explore situations.

Instead of using the human anger scale, a teen participant's idea was to use the Top-Ten Causes of Anger in Teens list or refer to their own anger activators. With both of these methods, participants are involved in the discussion and have an opportunity to voice their opinions. In the case of group experiences, they have the benefit of receiving different perspectives from their peers. These are strong selling points for both activities, and each furnishes topics for later conversations.

The **third question** asks what activities the participants disliked. As you have no doubt noted, the word *boring* is commonly used by many teens. It has been used to describe some of the training activities as well. This is not to say teens have to be constantly entertained, stimulated, or otherwise part of the perpetual movement characteristic of this age group. However, in some instances, your desire to give adolescents experiences capable of opening their minds and eyes to this kind of anger management knowledge requires some type of stimulation.

The overriding concern is to find whatever route reaches young people. Keeping this goal in mind, some modifications have been made to the AMP session since its inception. These changes resulted in the elimination of some activities and the addition of others.

It is important to note exercises involving the writing or discussing of ideas, rather than interactive experiences, are regarded negatively by many teens. Knowing what an adolescent prefers will help you determine whether or not to use particular activities. As with any program, opportunities to improve often present themselves. From the feedback given by adolescents, more effective methods of reaching their peers were found. Suggestions made by your participants can help make the anger management program you develop more successful.

<<Sidebar — Your watchful eyes, alert ears, and open mind will often lead to more effective ways to change the behavior of young people. You may get ideas from this program, use some, eliminate others, or find variations that work best. If some of the activities we eliminated work better for a teen you have concerns about, use them.>>

The **fourth question** also deals with anger management techniques, specifically which of them teens would be willing to try. Provide choices. (The full list of popular responses can be found in the "Information Boosters" section of this book.) Many of the anger management techniques described in **chapter eleven** were derived from this survey and discussions with participants.

Stress the popularity of certain methods with other teens. This may cause reluctant adolescents to choose particular methods because their peers thought they were "cool."

As you discovered from the responses provided to the first question, many teens felt various anger management techniques would be useful. The replies to the fourth question indicated five methods of managing anger, as well as those in an Other category. This aspect of the program represents the heart of this anger management training.

For specific information on the use of these tools, refer to the statistical overviews of the AMP Feedback and Follow-Up Surveys in the "Information Boosters" section. The importance of knowing the more popular anger management techniques among teens cannot be stressed enough. If it's popular with "most teens," it will be more appealing to their peers and your teens.

The **final question** focuses on rating the Anger Management Power Program (AMP). This section of the evaluation took the form of a 1-to-10 scale, with 1 being "Want Less Time" and 10 being "Want More Time." This is one way of validating the training. If participants rated your program anywhere from 1 to 6, ask for suggestions on how to improve the experience. This information provides an opportunity to fine-tune your teaching and make it more adolescent-friendly and acceptable to youngsters in the future.

The Reality of Fixed Behavior

Not all teens are willing to change their behavior. As a parent, educator, social worker, or other adult working with teens, this is a reality you must accept. Some of the participants who completed these surveys felt the information was worthless to them; some put down the entire idea of positive ways to manage anger.

However, I truly believe some of the thoughts presented still registered in all their minds. Whether they change their behavior in the present or in the future remains unknown. Some need to save face or are frightened of exhibiting new responses to situations that may result in additional pain and vulnerability—the very things they've experienced all too often in their lives. Some, like many adults, are just afraid of change. The way they typically acted had protected them. In their mind, change may take away this protection.

All we can do is attempt to expose participants to some alternatives to destructive behavior and hope it positively influences their actions, relationships, and at some point, their lives. Maturity, peers, and experiences—who knows what and when—may lead to changes in these "hardened" youngsters' lives. My hope is you and I can exert enough influence on teens to help them create a better, more peaceful life. It is a goal I feel we must strive for, no matter how many pieces of reality, challenges, or obstacles get in our way.

For parents trying to help their children, teens' reactions can be used as gauges of their ability to stay focused. For example, are they wide-eyed with enthusiasm or wearing an eyes-glazed-over, sleepy expression? If an area evokes an eager response, explore it thoroughly.

Your adolescents are continuously evaluating your efforts. Knowing what is working means staying with it and exploring subjects fully with them. It also means bringing up points in small doses and not overtalking subjects—that is, not going on and on about them—a behavior often met by looks of disgust leading to their unwillingness to continue the training they so desperately need.

Allow your teens to pick the discussion topics. In other words, helping them deal with their anger involves exploring the topics they choose to discuss. We investigated this idea in the chapters focusing on unexpressed causes, different feelings accompanying anger, and experiences relating to adolescents.

AMP Follow-Up Survey

The AMP Follow-Up Survey was administered about one month after teens completed the entire Anger Management Power Program. Its intent was to discover what parts of this learning process were actually used by them. Suffice it to say, some were able to use part of the experience, some didn't have the opportunity to attempt to use the skills, and others, who were part of the "reality" group mentioned before, totally ignored what they learned and experienced during the course of the program.

The importance of peer thinking and actions in stimulating changes in behavior should not be underestimated. We hope and pray they see the light as we look at the adolescents with whom we work and think, *Hey, kid, look at some of the ways people your age thought they could handle anger (as well as stress and anxiety) without causing further hassles for themselves. Wouldn't it be great to have some of these things working for you?* The acknowledgment of this possibility comes not only from the nodding heads we see, but in knowing how strong an influence their peers' thoughts have on them. For most teens, what their friends think and do is really important. Their need to belong, fit in, and be recognized as part of a group is very strong.

For others, what peers do or think has little meaning. These adolescents are often ostracized for being different. They feel as if they are not liked and are sometimes the victims of bullying or other kinds of abuse. They are the ones who suddenly react strongly and often fall through the cracks until they either lash out at others (Sandy Hook Elementary School shooting) or themselves (self-harm and suicide). The ideas found in the Follow-Up Survey can be viewed as thoughts for this particular group.

How to Use These Facts

The types of situations described in this survey are common to teen experiences. The way survey respondents handled these incidents may encourage other adolescents to manage their anger using the same methods. The remark "Here's how some other kids used this idea" may start a teen's thinking in this direction. Wait for some reaction, verbal or nonverbal, to decide whether or not to continue following this line of thought.

For the more independent group, choosing from a list of anger managers and applying them to recent incidents is an effective path to pursue.

Look at the specific elements of the training emphasized in this document and the reactions of adolescent participants. From these, you can get a better idea of the kinds of things that are effective and those that are not. In essence, you don't have to reinvent the wheel.

Follow-Up Survey Responses

The **first question** focuses on the **causes of anger**. Most teens responded knowing the reason for their anger was helpful in understanding how current situations may have been prevented or de-escalated. Knowing what really upsets an adolescent can help them avoid negative consequences entirely or allow them to be managed more calmly.

One situation is when teens disagreed with their parents about spending time with a particular person, someone their mom or dad didn't like. Instead of discussing it or attempting to convince their parents this friend was acceptable, they totally avoided the situation, and a hassle ensued.

Another situation impossible to avoid—and teens are aware of—occurs when they come home late, and a parent reacts. To prepare themselves for this showdown, adolescents enter the house after taking many deep breaths and deal with the fallout the best way possible. This approach may involve not answering their parent back and apologizing before the situation escalates. These are ways for young people to avoid major hassles. Describing these types of situations and the benefits of these approaches can be useful.

Incorporating the new Top-Ten Causes of Anger in Teens exercise or having them describe their own reasons for experiencing this emotion is important whether you are working with a single individual or a group of teens. It also offers the opportunity to discuss methods to diminish the intensity of their anger.

The **second question** in this survey focuses on **the effects of anger**. Adolescents responded by describing two types of reactions. The first reaction was an awareness of their own body's physical reactions and recognizing the changes in the other participant's body language. This exercise emphasized the need to de-escalate the intensity of anger in themselves and others. Once they were able to recognize these signs, they were able to chill out using some of the methods taken from their training. Deep breathing, counting, and walking away were among the tools chosen most frequently.

The second reaction involved their behavior when they let their anger take control. Visualizing the consequences of "losing it" and deciding whether it was worth it was an anger management technique we found helpful in limiting the effects of anger.

Providing a list of these types of techniques would be most helpful. Use the information in **chapter nine** as an additional resource. I feel this is an integral part of any anger management program since it provides an awareness of what can happen when emotions surface and how to control them.

The **final question** about the use of anger managers had **three components**. The **first** indicated which anger management techniques were used. The most popular methods, as evaluated by adolescent participants, were noted. This information is helpful since it provides ideas on which methods might appeal most to an adolescent. Once again, using peer appeal or a checklist is helpful.

The **next portion** asked the participant to **describe the other person involved** in the situation. Asking teens about the individual creating the most hassles for them may provide a choice of situations to use.

The **last part** of this question indicated **the result of using particular anger management methods**. Noting the replies in this portion of the survey is most effective with teens who value their peers' behavior. In other words, how peers managed incidents is often reason enough to apply the same methods in their own situations.

When using information furnished by this evaluation process, you and your teens can have the confidence that you are employing *teen-tested training methods*.

Taking Anger Management Training in Other Directions

One way to take the idea of a follow-up to another level is giving teens the chance to express their interest in receiving more training. There are two ways this process can be accomplished.

Developing Peer Workshops

This first type of training has been used with several groups of adolescents. Its objective was having them develop and facilitate an anger management workshop for peers. These teens indicated their interest in this idea by providing contact information at the bottom of the follow-up survey. For an adolescent who has shown enthusiasm during their training, simply asking, "How would you like to get more training?" will accomplish this step.

Organizing and Qualifying for Peer Workshop Presenters

With the information provided at the end of the follow-up survey, student schedules were accessed, and motivated students were contacted. The training periods were rotated as much as possible so no one subject's class would be missed too often. This process took five to six class periods, or approximately three to four hours.

In addition to their teacher's consent to attend these sessions, the students facilitating the presentations were selected by their show of commitment to this work. There are several factors to consider when judging teen dedication:

- Their belief in the ideas presented during the original training. If they have used various anger management techniques and have seen the benefits of these methods in managing conflicts, they have demonstrated their belief in this process. Putting this concept another way, if someone believes in the value of the product they are selling, they have the best chance of selling it to others.

- Youngsters' attendance and promptness in coming to the planning sessions were two other indicators of their belief and commitment to becoming peer facilitators. If more than once they forgot a meeting or the time it was to be held, provided a flimsy excuse, or didn't attend a majority of the sessions, they were ruled out as trainers. However, teens missing training meetings because of exams or other school-related responsibilities were not disqualified as peer trainers as long as they apprised us of their absence beforehand.

- Another area of commitment is evident by an individual's efforts and attitude toward the workshop planning and rehearsal sessions. Those who enthusiastically participated, shared ideas, and were supportive of their peers displayed the type of behavior and necessary qualities for becoming a peer facilitator. Those who sat back or misbehaved, often treating the training as a way to cut class, were eliminated as presenters.

The notification system found in an educational setting may be different from those in other agency or organizational environments. The qualifications for peer facilitators noted above can serve as a model for the types of behavior exhibited in teens you feel may reach this goal. They can also be modified for use in different agencies and organizations.

How and Why to Create Peer-Facilitated Workshops

- Creating this type of training provides teens with ownership of the concepts involved in anger management.

- Creating this type of training may result in an increase of peer-facilitator self-esteem since it empowers them to become leaders and "authorities" in this area.

- Peers training peers is the most effective way to reach other adolescents. It's an example of "peer power," something motivational to others also choosing this task.

Other Forms of Peer Training

Teens can also present their anger management ideas to peers in smaller groups, rather than in classes. Small-group presentations may lend themselves to uses in noneducational settings—group homes, youth organizations, religious institutions, etc. This form of peer "influencing" may also be accomplished with individual teens who are involved in peer-mentoring programs or as a means of helping family members and friends on a one-on-one basis.

The idea of being a leader and having control over peers in a positive way is an appealing thought to many young people. Earning this privilege must be tied first and foremost to their belief in the methods used in this training and their ability to uphold whatever standards are set to merit this opportunity.

Focus Groups

A focus group is another form of additional training. AMP is a work in progress; it changes as participants and colleagues suggest different ideas. Focus groups were recently recommended, and they have become an opportunity for program participants to travel another road to expanding their training. In this group activity, facilitators speak about their experiences, starting from their initial training.

One female student approached me (the author) to discuss a situation she was having in her relationship. Although not a participant in a group, her time with me represented a variation of the workshop experience.

This format allows adolescents the opportunity to discuss what worked, what didn't, and alternative ways of managing different situations. This group involvement can occur at regular intervals—for example, each month, every few months, or at a time suggested during the initial training. As with peer mediation, peer focus-group facilitators are taught how to establish group rules, maintain order, and keep participants on track. This type of leadership training is explained below; it follows the mediation model.

Teens being trained to facilitate the mediation process, a form of third-party intervention, were given information on conflict and communication skills. They were taught the mediation process, including methods for maintaining order. This knowledge enabled them to perform their duties effectively.

Mock mediations were held to hone skills and practice methods of managing possible challenges peer mediators would face while facilitating actual cases. To ensure a safe environment, an adult must be present during all mediations. In addition to acting as a safety valve, they would provide feedback on the approaches exhibited, as well as the attitudes and actions observed during this process. These comments were usually made when the mock mediation concluded, if time allowed. If not, certainly by the next day. This same process could be applied to teen-facilitated focus groups.

Offering an adolescent the opportunity to either lead or become a member of a focus group are methods for enabling them to openly discuss situations. This provides an excellent opportunity for individual teens to influence peers and increase their own self-esteem.

Chapter Fifteen

Some Parting Thoughts

We have almost reached the end of this journey together. You are about ready to "solo" with the information you have been given in this book. Before you do, I have a few final thoughts.

As a parent, educator, social worker, or youth worker, this age group represents a great personal or professional challenge, perhaps both. For some parents, dealing with an adolescent makes them proponents of the remark "I wish Sam could have been frozen from the time he was thirteen until twenty-one." However, I would feel remiss if additional thoughts weren't presented to help you develop more confidence in handling this difficult, often scary, and ever-taxing age group. Some are general views, not specifically related to anger management. I am also including quick tips for keeping peace with teens in the "Information Boosters" section as an additional resource. Check them out! Enjoy using them!

Thoughts for Parents and Other Guardians

Being a parent or guardian of a child of any age is a tough job. However, with teens, this is intensified many times over. Fears for their safety outside of the home, friends, drug use, sexual activity, education, and life goals are all reasons for us to sprout gray hair or develop ulcers. We cannot be with them twenty-four hours a day, seven days a week.

However, you have observed your young person's behavior in many situations throughout their lifetime and have a running record in your mind of how various situations were managed. These experiences provide knowledge of some of the how-tos of dealing with them. This information is a *fear breaker* when managing your teen's behavior.

There are teen behaviors, attitudes, and reactions that make dealing with adolescents a hair-pulling, teeth-grinding, and out-of-control event at times. It can be quite scary and make us feel helpless. But bad behavior should not be tolerated; this includes physically harming a family member. For this type of behavior, the tough-love approach is essential. First and foremost, teens must accept limits.

Barring a teen from the home, calling the police or other authority, and having the child removed from the home are some of the more drastic methods of behavior management. These may seem extreme, but so is the possibility of injury to themselves or others, or even death. Other teen behaviors that fall into the tough-love category include:

- Cutting classes or school entirely on a regular basis

- Coming home late repeatedly

- Engaging in criminal or destructive activities with peers or alone

Obviously, such activities demand consequences. If remedies such as grounding, loss of privileges (use of the Internet or television, having friends at the house, etc.), spending extra time in school (attending night classes or summer school) aren't effective, then tough-love decisions must be made. Seeing a child in jail, homeless, hurt, or dead aren't alternatives any parent or guardian wants to face.

Other forms of difficult behavior can be dealt with in different ways. Teen rebelliousness or stubbornness can drive a parent or guardian crazy. Often, a teen will throw a tantrum by yelling at the top of their lungs, throwing things, or cursing nonstop. Responding in unexpected ways to an adolescent's difficult behavior is useful.

If, for example, your child comes home late and demands you get their dinner immediately, long after the hour it is usually served, instead of running to prepare it (often a real temptation just to quiet them down), telling the teen to get it themself or the kitchen is closed are tactics to use. They still may demand their food. Ignore this command. If your child is hungry enough, they'll finally get their own dinner. At some time after the teen has calmed down, coolly explain, if they want dinner, they must be home on time, or they'll just have to fend for themself.

A youngster often tests a parent by exhibiting the same behavior the next day, chalking up their mom's last reaction to "temporary insanity." Consistency for children of any age is an effective way to be taken seriously. My message can't be stressed enough: Do the unexpected, and do it consistently.

When raising their voice, many teens expect you to do the same and, sooner or later, give in to their demands. In response, speak softly. This will make them listen more carefully and lower their tone of voice a few decibels. Soon, they will realize making noise is not getting them what they want. This tactic takes time, effort, and a lot of patience. However, aren't peace and quiet worth this price?

Another bone of contention between teens and parents/ guardians is being responsible at home, which includes promptly completing chores such as placing clothes in a hamper or taking care of their dirty dishes. When dealing with these issues, doing the unexpected, again, can give a resistant adolescent something to think about. For example, leaving their clothes unwashed can be an effective behavior-modification technique.

Keep in mind reacting consistently sends a clear message and can produce hassle-free results. But you must realize that no lasting change occurs overnight or after only one attempt. These changes take time and effort. The question to ask is "Will these behavior-modification exercises mean fewer hassles in the long run?" If the answer is yes, try them.

The following methods may be used to effectively handle an out-of-control teen:

- Resolving a situation with an adolescent is not impossible. Some actions just necessitate more severe measures on your part, ones you must be willing to use consistently until you are successful; if you relent, your efforts were wasted.

- Changing your response to many of your adolescent's behaviors is another effective tool. Think for a minute of someone sneaking up on you and saying, "Gotcha!" You jump! Doing the unexpected often surprises your child into behaving more appropriately.

- Asking for professional advice or speaking to other parents/guardians in similar situations can help you weather a youngster's emotional storms.

<<*Sidebar—An out-of-control teen doesn't mean* **YOU** *have to feel that way.*>>

Other techniques for approaching an adolescent's behavior are described below. These have been presented to you throughout this book.

- Learn to uncover and understand the reasons for a youngster's behavior.

- Identify a teen's needs, which may or may not be met.

- Deal with an adolescent's anger without either party becoming more upset.

- Manage the tension arising between family members. This may involve problems with peers, school, or work. In addition, other factors may be economic hard times; changes occurring because of illness, death, or divorce; the needs of an elder member of the family; or lingering aftereffects of the pandemic.

- Discover ways of modeling—or at least trying to show—positive ways of managing tough situations. Actions really do speak louder than words to your children. They provide techniques for creating a more peaceful atmosphere in your family. Children do learn what they live, the positive as well as the negative.

Putting to Work the Methods You Found Helpful

There are two ways to use the knowledge gained from this book. Think of specific ideas that may be the most helpful. Revisit particular chapters where these thoughts were presented. Jot down the page numbers, or develop some other lookup method for quick reference.

Perhaps you took notes while reading this book. There are different ways to arrange them. For example, sections of a notebook can be arranged according to topic, each one with its own anger management techniques. Another possibility is dividing the sections by anger-manager category—those used to de-escalate a situation and those to help teens express their anger effectively. Having easy access to this information will better prepare you for managing situations as they occur with your adolescent. Using iPhones, iPads, and other technology can provide easy and quick access to your reference lists.

An additional approach is to anticipate a potential conflict and prepare to manage it. Weekends are prime times for incidents to occur. Young people want to go where they want to go, stay out as late as they want, and be with whomever they care to be with—most often not family. These are the times when teens are free of school routines, and they don't want as many restrictions placed on them.

Other stressful times for adolescents and parents/guardians alike have to do with school—for example, upcoming exams, such as finals and standardized tests, report cards, and parent conferences. Participating in or attending plays, dances, or athletic events are other predictable times for conflicts to arise.

When these events do occur, it is necessary to be prepared for the expected reactions. This *hassle readiness* involves developing ways to prevent these situations from getting out of hand before they occur. This means clearly defining expectations or boundaries beforehand, communicating them clearly to your adolescent, entering the situation calmly, and remaining so during a conflict.

For parents, here is where referring to the anger managers in the "Information Boosters" section at the end of this book can be helpful. Other types of anger management techniques to learn and be prepared to use are those for keeping adolescents calm or for coping with particular sources of stress they have difficulty managing.

Another thought occurred to me as a result of a conversation with a fourteen-year-old daughter. Often, parents expect a teen to progress and develop as an older sibling did. In this case, the mother thought her daughter could do as well as her older brother did in certain subjects. The father thought his daughter was doing well in other subjects; he saw no need for her to compete with her brother. When one parent/guardian attempts to steer an adolescent in a particular direction, as this mother did, but the other parent disagrees, the result is an argument between the parents/guardians. The long-term consequence in this case was the mother's influence over her daughter greatly diminished. The teen was not being accepted for who she was and what she was capable of doing.

Accepting what an adolescent might think or do is very important. A parent/guardian's attitude often means the difference between whether or not a teen will seek their advice. The teenage years are often described as a time when adolescents need both freedom and security. The freedom to test their wings in different areas (school, career, relationships) often conflicts with their need for support and assistance from their family. This illustrates the internal struggle for the teen described above. This isn't often apparent because this age group can test adults to the ultimate limit of their patience. Nonetheless, flying solo but with a safety net is what adolescents truly need and want.

The idea is to keep the doors open. *Let them experiment as long as it isn't harmful to them or others.* You don't have to like or agree with what they are doing, but accept it. Once this happens, they will also feel the freedom to talk with you.

Thoughts for Educators

Teaching is without a doubt one of the most challenging professions. An educator is a teacher, psychologist, and parent, all rolled into one person. To say the least, there are many responsibilities, many constraints.

Among the most difficult of these duties is classroom management. In other words, the question to be answered is "With the time I have, how do I cover what is important in the curriculum and keep my students on track?"

Limiting disruptions is the key to resolving this dilemma. An unmotivated student or one with limited abilities often causes these distractions. Add to these factors increased hormones, physical attractions, and being "cool," and you know why being a teacher of teenage students is so challenging.

As an educator in New York City for over thirty years, I know the importance of classroom management cannot be emphasized enough. When I began teaching, this fact hit me square in the face when all my efforts to teach a subject went down the drain as disruptive students took charge of my time and efforts. Hindsight is a great educator.

No doubt, many education courses emphasize classroom-management techniques. The need for classroom rules cannot be underestimated. Many teachers' education programs stress having them established, written, and posted on the first day of class.

Some how-to hints for developing these guidelines can be helpful. One idea involves having students suggest ways to help keep things going smoothly in the classroom. Since they are their thoughts, teens' willingness to follow these rules is strengthened. Rather than being called "rules," students can also come up with their own name for these guidelines. Teen involvement demonstrates "ownership" and makes the rules part of "their" classroom.

Using rules can also be a means of making something *objective*, as mentioned earlier. When an adolescent calls out, puts someone else down, or curses, you can point to the rule and say, "We all agreed no one in this class would do (whatever the offense was)." It takes direct blame from the student and points out a general standard. By taking this approach, a possible conflict can be avoided, and the time spent on this infraction can be minimized.

Managing a student who is upset as they enter the classroom is worth exploring. This is not uncommon. Arguing with parents/guardians, girlfriends/boyfriends; witnessing hostility between parents/guardians; fearing the loss of a parent's job; or finding out about the sudden illness or death of a family member illustrate some emotional situations possibly affecting the student prior to their arrival in class on a particular day.

Other students may respond with "oohs" or some other disruptive behavior when a teen enters the classroom late and is in an emotional state. There are several ways to manage this situation. Among the most effective are:

- Ignoring the teen, provided they are not doing something harmful to you or the other students in the classroom

- Giving him a chance to calm down

- Keeping the class focused on an assignment while quietly approaching the adolescent to discover the reason they were upset

Keep in mind, if a teacher confronts a student in a classroom, the adolescent will react and do whatever it takes to *save face* in front of their peers. If a teen doesn't say anything, they face embarrassment and can be regarded as being "soft," someone who takes [expletive] from others—in this case, you, the teacher.

This bears repeating. One of the strongest values for a teen is respect. One way to honor this is to speak with an adolescent privately, either softly in the classroom or after class. When this is accomplished, the young person's emotions are kept from escalating.

In this and many other situations with teens, a valuable tool is to plan in advance for possible situations and ways to calmly deal with them. Role-playing can be used with colleagues and students to better prepare teachers for different eventualities within the school setting.

The hardcore student is another source of disruption in a classroom. They are:

- Often a bully, someone physically or verbally aggressive
- An individual who feels inadequate in school
- One with a limited understanding of English
- An adolescent who is in foster care, a group home setting, or a long-term truant

Any of these possibilities can be the reason for their disruptive behavior.

Often, a colleague or other staff member has some knowledge of a particularly troublesome student and can suggest ways to keep their actions to a minimum. An immediate response to their disruptive behavior is to ask the adolescent, "Do you like *respect*?" This is an attention getter that may help prevent a situation from escalating because one of an adolescent's key needs is respect. I have personally used this approach successfully with disruptive sixth graders during a workshop.

For those of you who are fairly new to teaching or working with teens, this preview of things to address and how may take away some of your anxiety. As the old saying goes, "Being forewarned is also being forearmed."

Time and the Teachable Moment

Time is a real challenge, and teachable moments arise everywhere—at school, at home, in the neighborhood, and even at church. Think of the ideas that have been presented throughout this book and couple them with the concept of the teachable moment.

The time may present itself when a particular subject causes conflict. This can occur during a particular period of history, in a social studies class, in a story or play in which two characters find they are having a problem with each other, in an English class, or as part of a news stories being discussed in a civics or government class. Discussions about student perceptions and how they used their new anger management skills can occur during a particular class; no additional time in or out of the classroom is required.

Advisories: Another Idea to Consider

The idea of advisories—found in many New York City high schools—is another path to take to institute anger management and other types of social-skills development training in young people. Schools target groups of students considered "at risk"—for example, those likely to become truants, do poorly in school, or need special classes. Small groups of these at-risk students are assigned to specific staff members. These educators keep track of the identified students' grades, attendance, and behavior, and provide them with more individualized attention. Once per week, meetings are held with the entire group, and they discuss topics relating to academics, peer pressure, and social-skills development.

This concept is a holistic approach within the educational setting. It is something I believe to be worthwhile. It can be incorporated into other educational systems, perhaps under another title.

For Social and Youth Workers

Your services cover a variety of clients and settings. Your assistance is provided to individuals, groups of adolescents, families, or school staff. You may find yourselves in schools, agencies, and homes. Throughout this book, many approaches were described to assist you in understanding anger in teens and empowering them to manage this emotion in positive ways. In this chapter, additional ideas were given to parents and educators. They may provide a menu of ideas for you as well. This information may also be helpful in developing plans for working with youth in different areas of behavior management. Even though the ideas presented below are specific in providing teens with skills in anger management, they are adaptable to other areas of concern.

Creating a Plan for Working with Teens

This method involves making several decisions:

- Knowing what ideas you feel are most appealing to the client.

- Deciding how you want to access ideas and which sources to use. With this part of the plan, using checklists is simple and efficient. It's also something adolescents willingly do since it requires a minimum of effort. These lists should include different methods and thoughts presented throughout this book; at the very least, this material can provide ideas on what elements to consider in developing a plan.

- Incorporating the Anger Management Power Program (AMP) training for teens. It can be applied to other areas as well. Initially, include the concepts you feel will work best. These tools are provided in the Program Preparation Checklist found in the "Information Boosters" section at the back of the book.

Participants in AMP provided me with some great ideas. Some became parts of this process, and they have benefited many people. My hope is we can work together to discover the most effective methods to use with adolescents. Many thoughts, techniques, and tools have been provided for you and others who have read *Peace: The Other Side of Anger*.

As you continue in your work with adolescents, different interesting and effective ideas will come to mind. Don't hesitate to use them. Working with youth requires flexibility. Feel free to share, both the ideas that work and those not as successful as you would have liked, with your fellow readers and me through my website: peacefulauthor.org.

The Importance of Following Up on the Training

The importance of following up cannot be emphasized enough. It is all well and good to provide ideas on how to manage anger. But the value of this program becomes limited if we do not follow up to discover if and how these ideas were used and if they were effective.

In chapter thirteen, the results of the surveys administered to AMP participants were evaluated. This process involved looking at what aspects of the program were used by participants. This was one means of gauging the effectiveness of some of the work done in this training modality. Besides knowing what ideas were incorporated, an essential part of this method is also discovering what appealed to the participants about the ideas they used and what didn't have an impact.

Obtaining this information can have great value in deciding to continue to use certain activities and ideas, expand on some, change others, or eliminate those not valued at all. Since AMP's inception, I have made many modifications based on participant input. The responses to these changes have been mostly positive.

The Importance of Your Feedback

Many suggestions and ideas have been presented throughout this book. What happens with this information depends on you. How and in what forms you use this information is your choice. I hope reading this book has enabled you to identify ideas helpful in your work with teens. Feel free to share your experiences with me and other readers. Whether it's positive or negative results with the training, doubts and concerns, or suggested changes or additions to the ideas presented in this book, everything is valuable. Our "conversations" will result in making this management training more effective.

Watching! Looking! Listening!

These are the keys to bringing more peace to the lives of the young people you want to help. How, when, and why they decide to put into action the techniques you've provided is up to the teens ready to implement them.

The ideas presented have been based upon my experiences with many youths as I developed, changed, and tried to improve the Anger Management Power Program (AMP). It is a work in progress, as are our teens. Hang in there with them.

Know it's okay for you to make some choices and reject others. Don't be afraid to trust your gut.

Peace: The Other Side of Anger was written for you. From it, hopefully, you've gotten ideas to use in whatever way you feel can be most helpful. Whether you focus only on anger or use this knowledge to help adolescents deal with a combination of emotions is up to you. My main goal is to provide more tools and ideas helpful in understanding young people and their anger and to assist you in empowering them to manage anger in positive ways. I sincerely hope they do.

I WISH YOU GREAT RESULTS!

Information Boosters

Additional Anger Management Techniques

Some of these methods are variations of those found in chapter eleven; others are more novel approaches. They are all additional anger managers from which to choose.

Treat Others with Respect

Explanation: Being respected by others is very important to teens. To be disrespected, or dissed, is one of the worst things for them to experience, especially in front of peers. This is the cause of many conflicts. Adolescents should be reminded of this when they speak or act. Young people often just think of respect subjectively; they forget it's a two-way street, particularly in situations with adults. This point can be made clear by the question "How do you feel when someone doesn't show you respect?" or the statement "You know how it feels not to be respected."

Illustration: John is waiting for dinner. His mom is usually home and has dinner ready when he returns around five thirty. But it is six thirty when his mother arrives, and John is really pissed and hungry.

Without this anger manager: John yells at his mother and says she is a lousy mom who doesn't care about him. Before she is able to respond, he keeps up this tirade with more insults. His mom turns away from him, tells him to make his own food, and yells, "Because of your big mouth, you can't go out this weekend!"

With this anger manager: John sees his mom come in the door, out of breath. He asks, "Hey, Mom, are you okay?" She tells him she got stuck on the subway for almost an hour and then apologizes for being late with John's supper. John says, "Don't worry. I'm not starving to death." He smiles and lets his mom settle down.

Stay Calm When Another Person Is Angry

Explanation: Many times, when people are upset, whether it is due to anger, stress, anxiety, or disappointment, others get caught up in the moment. They react with a similar feeling and get agitated. This can be described as *contact feeling*. To avoid this reaction, show teens how to deal with others who are upset. Suggest they try any of the following:

- Take slow, deep breaths.
- Relax your jaw, neck muscles, and body.
- Maintain a healthy attitude by creating a calm atmosphere. This behavior involves not being defensive. Angry people often take their anger out on those close to them. It also means being confident

about understanding the reason for the anger, without acting as if you know more than they do, are cooler, or as teens often say, are "all that."

- Don't take a person's anger personally because their judgment is impaired by the emotion they are experiencing. In this anger manager, you are providing the other person with the opportunity to vent their anger by just listening, giving them space, and providing yourself with ways to maintain your own cool. By realizing you are not the source of the anger, and you need to keep an emotional "distance," you are eliminating the possibility of adding fuel to an angry person's emotional fire.

Illustration: Doreen has a huge argument with her friend, Kathy. She is really upset. Another friend, Alba, sees how upset Doreen is and approaches her.

Without this anger manager: Alba goes over to Doreen and asks, "What happened?" Doreen starts yelling, then tells Alba, "Mind your own [expletive] business!" Alba responds, "Who do you think you are! Don't dump your [expletive] all over me!" As Doreen turns around and walks away, Alba says out loud, "No wonder you don't have very many friends." Doreen responds, "Who do you think you are, Miss Popularity?" and leaves cursing under her breath.

With this anger manager: Alba goes over to Doreen and asks, "What happened?" Doreen starts yelling, then tells Alba, "Why don't you mind your own [expletive] business!" Alba takes a couple of deep breaths and says, "Listen, sometimes, when people are angry, they need to talk about it. If you want to, I am here for you." She stands there with a smile on her face and her hands at her sides. Doreen responds, "Hey, I am sorry I told you to back off. I'm really upset. Right now, I just need some time to chill out. Maybe we can talk about this later."

Take a Bubble Bath or Shower

Explanation: With this anger manager, a teen can use the warm or cool water in a bath or shower to help relax their body, creating a feeling of calmness.

Visualize Someone or Something Special in a Teen's Life

Explanation: There are a variety of visualizations that have been used and suggested. They occur in two forms: a mental image (some find this difficult) or an actual picture of whatever/whoever can help them remain calm. These are concrete images. They may be personal photographs of special people, places, events, or pictures in magazines, on posters, or pictures they themselves have drawn. These images may help teens dissipate their angry energy.

Illustration: Mark had a big fight with his girlfriend, Jessica, over her wanting to spend more time with her friends. Nasty things were said between them, and they both walked away really upset. As Mark distanced himself from where the argument occurred, he smiled. He stopped, reached into his pocket for his wallet, and pulled out a picture of Jessica and him. They were holding each other and smiling. This is the way their relationship had been. With this image and thought, Mark decided he would call Jessica later.

Visualize the Outcome of the Behavior

Explanation: This idea is similar to envisioning the devastation that will be left by a hurricane—destroyed homes, flooded roads, and fallen trees. With this anger manager, teens create a picture of what would happen if their anger were released. It is a variation of the "Is it worth it?" method, another way for adolescents to view the consequences of their behavior. It must be used while they are still calm, before they've strongly reacted to a situation. It can also be used as a preventive measure once a situation has gone badly.

Illustration: Joey's guidance counselor, Mr. Donaldson, informed him he wasn't accepted into his first choice of colleges. Joey knew many of his friends were planning to attend that school, and now he's the only one who won't. He felt Mr. Donaldson didn't care about him or his feelings since Mr. Donaldson didn't give him an explanation or bother to ask how Joey felt. Joey's anger began to build. He decided, without holding back, he was going to let Mr. Donaldson know how lousy a counselor he was.

As this scene developed, a picture of how this situation would play out came popping into his mind. He saw himself coming into Mr. Donaldson's office, slamming the door, yelling, using whatever language came out of his mouth, and then getting right into his guidance counselor's face. At this point, he saw a security officer coming through the door, grabbing him, and dragging him to the dean's office. His mother would be called, and he wouldn't hear the end of it. He might be blowing his chance of graduating, which would get his mom even crazier.

Joey decided to approach Mr. Donaldson on another day when he was calmer, at which time his guidance counselor might have additional information.

Imagine the Anger Draining Out of Your Body

Explanation: Earlier, we discussed the physical effects anger has on a teen's body. These included facial muscles tightening, faces flushing, blood pressure rising, and hearts racing. Taking this idea one step further, let's look at the physical site of the anger as the starting point for draining this feeling out of their body.

Illustration: For this exercise, have the teen close their eyes. Instruct them to see anger as a foreign object that is leaving their body following a specific exit route. Ask them to describe the size, color, and shape of this anger object. One suggestion is to visualize a red ball the size of a handball. Describe several ways the teen can have the anger exit their body. The journey may go down through the stomach, the legs, and out through their toes. It may go up through the chest, down the arms, and leave the body through the fingers or out through their butt. It may also go up and out the top of their head or through their ears. The road taken does not matter. For some teens, their imaginations are strong and vivid. For them, this anger manager can work very well. For others, drawing a map of the path this object takes is another way to use this tool.

Visualize Pleasant Experiences

Explanation: This entails having a teen remember a time when they felt at peace or something that made them smile.

Illustration: Some of the AMP participants described swimming, riding in or driving a fast car, hugging someone special, or shopping in an unusual place, such as Paris. Have them describe the other people involved, sights, sounds, and physical sensations to make this experience really clear.

For teens who find mental imagery difficult, suggest they look at pictures from scrapbooks, photographs in which they appear, magazines, or travel brochures, videos, or posters.

Form a Caucus

Explanation: This particular anger manager involves the use of a third party—that is, someone who is not part of the situation. It is a method for teens to enlist the aid of peers to prevent situations from escalating. These helpers can be friends of those involved in the conflict or others who don't want to see a situation getting further out of hand.

Teens who served as peer mediators suggested this anger manager. A mediator's job is to help other adolescents work out their problems; they must not take sides or make judgments. This is a structured process facilitated in a particular setting, such as in an office or designated area set aside for performing this task. This type of third-party intervention can also be done in less formal ways—in stairways, hallways, empty rooms, or deserted areas of playgrounds.

This method is used, for example, if during the course of a conversation between two young people, one of them gets upset. This heightened emotion is noticeable by the teen's loud tone of voice, reddening face, clenched fists, or movement closer to the other person. Once this behavior occurs, the adolescent has to be removed from the area to chill out.

During this time, the third party accompanies the angry individual to discover the cause of their reaction. Time and space are provided for this person to calm down prior to discussing their issue. This alone time between the upset person and the third party is known as a caucus.

Illustration: Pat and Dave are arguing in the school hallway. Dave's friend, James, sees this occurring, hears Dave's voice getting louder, and sees his face turning red. James anticipates the next step is a fight. He takes Dave into a nearby stairwell to find out why he is upset.

Dave tells him Pat continues harping on and on about being a better athlete and how great he is. Dave tells James, "I had enough of his bragging. Then he started pointing at me to his friends who began to laugh. That was it. I was about to make him shut up when you stepped in." After a few minutes, Dave calms down. By that time, most of the crowd has dispersed.

Later that day, knowing Dave and Pat have been good friends for a long time, James encourages Dave to talk to Pat and let him know why he was upset. James adds, "He probably thought he was just joking and didn't realize how his remarks affected you. With others around, he knew he would have to do something if you kept yelling at him. That's the reason I wanted you to move away from them."

Wipe the Frown Off Your Face and Relax

Explanation: By replacing a frown (which uses more muscles) with a smile, a person's anger will diminish. In other words, it's hard to stay angry when you have a smile on your face.

Precautions: This anger manager should be suggested in a light-hearted manner. The tone you use may entice a smile from an angry teen, but you need to know how they respond to humor. *If you are unsure, avoid using this anger manager.*

Quit Trying to Control Others

Explanation: For many, getting others to do what they want, feel what they feel, or follow their suggestions are sources of much frustration and anger. The lesson to be learned—one person can't control how another individual acts. An adolescent attempting to convince a peer to join different groups, go particular places, or participate in certain activities often leads to alienation and frustration.

The power of peer pressure is enormous. A teen trying to resist a group's influence often becomes anxious and frustrated when the need to belong overshadows their own interests. For most, resisting the influence of friends is a tremendous hurdle to overcome. Many find themselves engaging in activities that cause them physical pain, academic stress, emotional upset, and even legal problems. Discussing alternative paths—such as sports, clubs, employment, volunteer work, music, or more positive pursuits with others—is certainly worth trying. It requires time and patience.

Lecturing an adolescent is not as effective as listening to their needs. Challenging a teen's beliefs and choice of music or friends is an exercise in frustration. This often leads to a severe reaction and may create walls between you and the teen. Listening without judging, however, can lead to discussions that forge a positive relationship.

Throw Yourself into Your Job or Special Interest

Explanation: This tool helps divert energy from feeling angry into something productive rather than destructive. It helps to diminish the intensity of anger and provides the means of diverting this feeling into positive channels. These diversionary tasks may include focusing on a project at work, a school assignment, hobbies, a form of physical exercise, shopping, or an undertaking that may have been avoided.

Recognize Another Person Is Angry Before Dealing with Them

Explanation: Earlier in this book, the physical effects of anger were explored. The bodily signs discussed were reddened face, glaring eyes, tightened facial muscles, and clenched fists. Other teen reactions include curt answers to questions, loud tone of voice, slamming doors, or noisy footsteps. Once these behaviors are observed, preventing an adolescent from letting anger take control of their actions is important.

When people are angry, they often feel isolated and alone. Once you have noticed your teen's anger, let them know you are aware of what they *might* be feeling. This brings about the realization someone is trying to understand how they feel.

Precautions: As with other situations previously discussed, the way you communicate your observation will determine how willing the teen is to discuss their feelings. If, for example, based on your observation, you ask, "Why are you angry?" The response may be "Don't tell me how I feel" or "How do you know how I feel?" This is a common complaint by adolescents—they want adults to recognize they are capable of expressing themselves, rather than having others speak for them.

Illustration: How an adult describes what they observed is very important. For example, using expressions such as "You look (sound) as if something is bothering you" and then being silent can be very effective. An alternative might be describing the behavior by saying, "Slamming the door and throwing down your books makes me think something is wrong." Then patiently wait for a response. The teen may remark, "Not really," "It's nothing," "I don't want to talk about it," "Not now," or express an emphatic "NO."

Whether or not the discussion goes any further doesn't matter. What you have done is open the door; the teen knows someone cares enough to notice something is wrong. This eliminates the common teen complaint "(So-and-so) doesn't bother to notice when something annoys me." In the absence of an outright no, the responses "Not really" and "Not now" are a teen's signal to ask more about the reason for their anger. These remarks are invitations to explore their feelings, but at a later time.

With a "Not really" response, ask "What is (annoying) you?" The words aren't important. At this point, a youngster may just shrug it off with an "It's not worth it" or begin talking about the anger-activating situation. If not, you have shown them you were paying attention to what was being said and are leaving the door open for further discussion.

It is worth noting this path may be opened hours, days, or even weeks later in a matter-of-fact way. A "You know the other day when you noticed…" remark exemplifies this indirect discussion opener. Be alert to it. It will enhance your relationship with the teen and your role as a good listener.

With a "Not now" response, you might say, "It sounds as if you want to talk about the situation bothering you, but not right now. Let me know when you feel like discussing it." Here, too, the "when" may take place sometime later. Your patience is required. It will pay a tremendous dividend to your relationship with the teen.

Listen to and Respect Others' Suggestions/Opinions, Regardless of Their Relationship

Explanation: This anger manager relates to young people receiving respect for their opinions, thoughts, and ideas, as well as their openness to others with whom they have relationships— parents, older siblings, friends, teachers, administrators, agency staff members, and individuals in their work environment.

Young people often feel as though what they have to say is not valued. In their role as a son/daughter, employee, or athlete, they may think their views are not considered important to the adults with whom they interact. In these instances, a teen's need for recognition is frustrated, so they may react negatively to what others have to say.

Bottom line: Listen to what teens are saying. If they feel you are genuinely listening to and considering their opinions, they will be more inclined to offer you the same courtesy.

Understand Different Perspectives

Explanation: Many conflicts arise because of differences in perception. In other words, each party sees the same situation differently. This anger manager acknowledges that fact.

Illustration: Use a real-life example of a person, place, etc. both you and your teen have witnessed, or choose one of the situations reviewed during an AMP session. Follow up by asking, "What aroused the teen's strong feelings in this situation?" and "Could another person see this incident differently?" If you receive an "I don't know" or shoulder-shrug response, explore additional scenarios. You can refer back to the events described in the "Experiences with Anger" chapter to assist you in accomplishing this task, or furnish your own examples.

Leave the Situation Alone After Saying, "We Can Talk About This Later"

Explanation: This anger manager is a variation of avoidance. In this case, you allow yourself to cool off by informing the other involved person you would like to speak about the upsetting situation "later when you are both more calm."

Precautions: It is important to actually say this, not just think it. If these words are not spoken, the other person may feel as though the relationship isn't important to you or they are being ignored. If so, their anger may intensify, resulting in damaging or destroying the relationship.

Give Out Positive Karma

Explanation: In dealing with an angry teen, it is best to use a soft tone of voice that is in no way accusatory. The point is to make sure they don't feel blamed for the incident in which they were involved. In addition, a teen should be given physical space (usually at least two feet—a good arm's length) between the two of you. In other words, you are not in their face, which usually is considered confrontational posture.

Your voice and posture convey your willingness to hear the cause of the anger without making the other party feel attacked. It provides a comfort zone in which an adolescent feels you are there to help deal with their anger, not intensity it.

Precautions: As with other anger managers, asking a teen if they want to talk about the cause of the anger is helpful. If you see a reddened face, clenched fists, piercing eyes, other nonverbal signals, or hear an "I don't want to go there" or "I need space," leave them alone. At this point, suggest a place for the adolescent to chill out.

Offer to Have Something to Eat or Drink with the Angry Teen

Explanation: This anger manager was recommended by a high school student participating in AMP. Food and drink have a comforting effect, similar to holding a person around the shoulders or walking alongside them. Removing the agitated person from the location of the conflict and guiding them to a place where they can have something to eat or drink will likely have a calming effect.

Use the Power of Silence and Just Wait

Explanation: When dealing with a manipulative silent person—one who uses silence as their method of expressing anger—you might say, "You seem angry and not willing to talk. What is bothering you?" Then, just wait. If they respond, "I don't know," or give some nonverbal cue, ask, "If you could guess, what would your answer be?" Again, wait.

An alternative is to ask open-ended questions. Using the above exchange, you might say, "You seem angry and not willing to talk," and leave it at that. Then, again, just wait.

Precautions: When the teen begins to speak, only interrupt if they become physically or verbally abusive. Then, just wait again.

Focus on the Issue, Not the Behavior

Explanation: Some behavioral signs of anger are noted below:

- Using sarcasm

- Using personal attacks
- Using the words *always* or *never*
- Acting out physically

Investigating the reasons for these behaviors should be the focal point of your discussion with the teen.

Illustration: An adolescent is late for class. As he enters the room, the teacher stops the lesson, and all eyes are focused on the teen. He sits down forcefully and slams his books on the floor. The teacher resumes the lesson. A little while later, he goes over to the student and asks to see him after class. After the class ends and the other students have exited the classroom, the teacher sits next to the teen and asks, "What's going on?"

Map an Escape Route (Allowing an Angry Teen to Save Face)

Explanation: This anger manager involves moving an angry teen to a private place where they can calm down without witnesses. This allows a teen to save face and maintain their image in front of peers, which is hugely important to them.

Illustration: Quietly move the teen from a public place to where none of their peers are around to hear what the two of you are discussing. This can be done using a soft tone of voice, a nod, even a slight smile, while saying, "Let's talk about this situation in my office (stairwell or any quiet place) undisturbed."

Guided Problem Solving

Explanation: This anger manager involves guiding the angry adolescent through an analysis of the situation that is causing their anger. The goal is to help them calm down, evaluate the situation using the objectivity method previously discussed, and come up with nonconfrontational solutions to repair their relationship with the other party.

Illustration: After hearing the angry teen's version of the situation that spiked their anger, guide them through a calm, objective analysis of events in order to come up with a solution. To do this:

1. Give limited options.

   - "If you could have a great solution, what would it be?"

   - "What are the pros and cons of this solution?"

   - "What would be the best-case scenario?"

   - "What would be the worst-case scenario?"

   - "What is most important aspect of this situation to be resolved?"

2. Help them choose from the options suggested.

3. Commit to the plan developed by the teen.

Don't Personalize the Situation (It's Not About You)

Explanation: In simple language, "Don't take the other person's anger personally." Look at it as just another element of the situation. In other words, avoid getting "sucked into" another person's feelings. The effort it takes to objectively analyze the situation is well worth it if it results in maintaining a relationship and avoiding the escalation of anger.

Precautions: Here's where you do NOT react to the anger as if you were responsible for it. For certain, this is difficult for anyone.

Do Something Unexpected—Laugh at Some Behavior Intended to be Upsetting

Explanation: This particular anger manager was provided by a teacher. Its intent is to let an incident bounce off the individual, rather than upset them. Occasionally, teens enjoy trying to upset another individual. If the victim does not respond as expected, the game is over. For adolescents who are the focus of taunting, bullying, or other forms of intimidation, this strategy *may* be helpful.

Illustration: As a teacher is writing on the board, her back to her students, a rolled-up piece of paper is tossed at her. It hits her back. Instead of becoming defensive, demanding to know who did it, or perhaps lecturing on respect, she simply smiles and remarks, "It's very nice to know you care enough about me to want my attention."

Question the Source of Anger and Whether It Is Within or Beyond the Teen's Control

Explanation: With this anger manager, the angry person must be able to think rationally. They must be calm, in control, and somewhere between 1 and 5 on the anger scale.

Illustration: Two questions to be asked are:

1. What is the source of the anger? In other words, what caused the person's anger? The possibilities may include:

   • Frustration of a need

   • Tasks not attempted or completed

   • Lack of respect for property, opinions, and family

- Unfairness

- Any of the many anger activators previously mentioned in this book

2. Is it within the person's control or beyond it? In other words, looking at one of the causes listed above, is it a matter of feeling frustrated, disrespected, or something else? Or does it come from a source outside the individual that needs to be remedied?

Once these questions are answered, a plan to resolve the teen's anger can be developed. This is similar to what we described in the anger journal section under "Anger Management Techniques" earlier in this book.

In some instances, the teen may conclude nothing can be done to alleviate their anger and that of the others involved in a particular situation. Just accepting this reality may go a long way towards reducing the intensity of the teen's anger about something they perceive as unfair or wrong.

<<Sidebar — *This is a reality many of us face in our society. Remember the famous serenity prayer. "Know what you can control, know what you cannot, and know the difference."*>>

Ask a Teen Who Has Hurt Another, "How Do You Think It Made the Other Person Feel?"

Explanation: You may use this method if the teen has harmed you or another person. You are teaching the concept of empathy, which is putting them in the other person's shoes.

Precautions: This suggestion requires the adolescent be at a certain level of maturity or sensitivity. "I don't really care," sometimes expressed in more colorful language, may be their reaction. At this point, the only thing you can do is have the teen consider the individual they harmed and the possibility their actions may have jeopardized that relationship.

Tips for Adults

S ome of the methods found on the Anger Management Techniques list are beneficial for adults. It is not always easy to deal with young people—they know your hot buttons! Try some of these tips before the teen you deal with "gets your goat."

1. Using physical outlets
   - Deep breathing
   - Exercising, any kind
     - Running
     - Walking
     - Weights
     - Dancing
     - Counting
2. Using avoidance: cooling-off period, tuning out (emotionally distancing yourself)
3. Chanting or repeating a word or phrase
4. Using visualization (imagined or with actual pictures)
   - An image of anger

- A calm scene (beach, forest)
- A special person

5. Throwing yourself into your job or something you are interested in

6. "Catching a breeze"
   - Going to an isolated area where there is no one else around. Sitting down, letting the wind blow against your face, and feeling the warmth of the sun.

7. Using stress putty
   - Squeezing or manipulating something in your hand

8. Taking a bubble bath or shower

9. Writing in an anger journal
   - Indicating an anger activator: What made me angry?
   - Writing: How do I resolve the situation?
   - Noting: How do I prevent it from happening again?

10. Talking it over with someone who is not involved

11. Listening to music, playing an instrument, or singing

12. Not trying to control others

13. Accepting differences

14. De-personalizing the situation or person: It is not about you.

15. Focusing on the angry person's issues, not their actions (signs)
    - Acting out of or showing signs of anger
    - Using sarcasm
    - Using personal attacks

- Using *always* or *never*
- Physically acting out

16. Making your muscles tense, then relaxing them

17. Imagining the anger draining out of you

18. Visualizing a pleasant experience or doing something or going somewhere you would really enjoy
    - Swimming
    - Riding in a fast car on an open road
    - Hugging someone special
    - Shopping in Paris
    - Getting a massage or some sort of pampering

19. Asking someone who has done something negative to you, "How do you think that makes me feel?"

20. Singing a cheerful song in your head

21. Doing something challenging
    - Puzzle
    - Sudoku
    - Solution to something bothering you)

22. Questioning the anger
    - What is its source?
    - Is it within you or beyond your control?

The Anger Management Power Program (AMP)

Feedback Survey

The following is provided as a model. Participants were asked to fill out a form. For many youngsters, using Google Forms, cell phones, or computers to furnish this information may be more enticing.

[Male/Female] [Age] [Setting]

1. Did you get any ideas from this workshop that you feel will help you?

   [Yes/No]

2. If so, what were they?

3. Which part(s) did you like the best and why?

   __a) Visualizing Anger
   __b) Human Anger Scale
   __c) Group Work
   __d) Role-Plays
   __e) Giving Your Ideas

__f) Talking About Your Experiences

__g) Discussions

__h) Other

4. Which part(s) did you like the least and why?

__a) Visualizing Anger

__b) Human Anger Scale

__c) Group Work

__d) Role-Plays

__e) Giving Your Ideas

__f) Talking About Your Experiences

__g) Discussions

__h) Other

5. Which of these ways of handling anger do you feel you would try?

__a) "Is it worth it?"

__b) Self-Talk

__c) Chanting or Saying a Word or Phrase

__d) Physical Coping (Deep Breathing, Counting, etc.)

__e) Picturing Anger and Getting Rid of It

__f) Other

6. How would you rate this experience? (Put a circle around the number.)

1   2   3   4   5   6   7   8   9   10

(Want less time)   (Want more time)

The Anger Management Power Program (AMP)

Follow-Up Survey

The following is also provided as a sample. Participants were asked to fill out a form. For many youngsters, using Google Forms, cell phones, or computers to furnish this information may be more enticing.

[Male/Female]   [Age]   [Setting]

As a participant in the Anger Management Power Program (AMP) given at [Place] on [Date(s)], you engaged in various activities, received materials, and discussed aspects of anger and anger management. In order to assess the impact of this training, you are being asked to complete this survey. Please do so and return it as soon as you can. Thanks for your time and effort.

1. Has knowing the causes of anger helped you deal more positively with the anger of others or your own?

[Yes/No]

If yes, how has it helped you? (Give situation, circumstance, outcome)

2. Has knowing the effects (physical, mental, emotional) of anger helped you deal with the anger of others or your own? [Yes/No]

If yes, how has it helped you? (Give situation, circumstance, outcome)

3. Have you been able to utilize any anger managers?

[Yes/No]

If yes:

a) Which one(s)?
b) What was (were) the situation(s)?
c) What was (were) the result(s)?

If you are interested in additional training or becoming a trainer, please provide the following:

[Name] [Telephone number] [Email]

Survey Overviews

Statistical Overview of the AMP Feedback Surveys

As of this writing, AMP has been presented to a diverse group of approximately 1,000 teens and 600 adults—undergraduate and graduate students, parents, and professionals—for the purpose of:

- Gaining insight into teen thinking and providing them tools for managing their anger

- Gaining confidence in using the tools and ideas presented in this book.

An Overview of the Information Gathered from the Surveys

Adolescents participating in this program were primarily seventeen- to eighteen-year-old high school upperclassmen. Allow for age-related differences in responses if your participants are not in this age group.

Survey Results

The results in these surveys are based on the responses we received most frequently or the ones that represent what the majority of all participants felt. Based on this information and my decades of experience working with adolescents, this book was written after choosing the *most* effective anger management techniques for teens.

Question 1: Did you get any ideas from this workshop that you feel will be helpful?

Results: Three-quarters of the respondents answered yes. They gave different reasons for feeling their exposure to AMP was useful. Many of these thoughts centered around specific anger management techniques. Among the most frequent and most relevant responses falling into this category are:

- Anger management techniques give different ways to deal with anger
- Talk to myself
- "Is it worth it?"
- Visualize anger
- Visualize a calm scene
- Breathe deeply
- Stay calm and relax
- Walk away and calm down

Other ideas noted, most often specifically by adolescents, include:

- Know how to control my anger better
- Different ways to control anger toward myself and others
- How to help and understand anger in others
- Channel or express your anger in positive ways

- How to express anger without hurting others

- Prevent anger or preventing it from getting worse

Question 2: What parts (of AMP) did you like best?

Results: The top choices and the reasons most often given were:

- Role-plays—They were funny/entertaining.

- Better visuals

The basic conclusion drawn from the teen participants' ratings indicates a majority felt AMP had value to them. The reasons they cited include:

- Real-life experiences

- Group work

- Shared ideas

- Talked and listened to each other

- An opportunity to learn how others deal with situations

- Giving your ideas (discussions)

- Opened my mind to others' thoughts

- Like to express myself

- People can hear me out

From these responses, we concluded young people:

- Like to be entertained and often learn from such experiences.

- Respond to objective material (role-play situations) rather than focusing on individuals directly

- Seek recognition for their opinions—this shows they are valued by their peers

- Like to hear what their peers have to say and what they have done

- Like to be helpful to others—this makes them feel more valued, which is another form of recognition

These conclusions may provide ways to reach their peers in both a timely and efficient manner. Now, let's focus our attention on the flip side of this coin.

Question 3: What did you like *least* about this experience?

Results: The top choices and the reasons most often given were:

- Survey
- Don't like writing
- Prefer talking
- Group work
- Boring
- Don't like it
- Some members of the group did nothing

As you have no doubt noted, the word *boring* is a common expression among many youths. It can be found in this program's activities, as well as in other types of situations. This is not to say teens have to be constantly entertained, stimulated, or otherwise part of the perpetual movement characteristic of this age group. However, opening their minds and eyes to anger management techniques they can incorporate into their daily lives requires some sort of stimulation.

The overriding concern is finding whatever route will lead to their understanding these ideas and learning these techniques. Keeping this goal in mind, after looking at these surveys, some modifications were made to the Anger Management Power Program.

That said, let's move on to what I believe is the heart and soul of this program.

Question 4: Which ways of managing anger are you willing to try?

Results: The survey listed five anger management techniques, along with an Other category. The following are the most popular methods chosen by participants (keep in mind many can be used with younger children as well):

- Physical coping (deep breathing, counting, sports, exercise)
- Visualizing a calm scene (beach, forest), a person you love, or a situation that made you feel good and helped you relax
- "Is it worth it?"
- Picturing anger and getting rid of it
- Learning to use *wishing/wanting* rather than *should/demand*

The following responses were in the Other category; they are listed in order from the most popular to the least:
- Self-talk
- Listening to music
- Ignoring the other person

- Chanting a word or phrase

- Talking to people

- Anger journal

Here again, knowing what appeals to peers may be helpful in giving teens ideas that might work for them or those they may be willing to try. It certainly can narrow down the list for both of you.

The final question, relates to rating the Anger Management Power Program (AMP).

Question 5: How would you rate this program?

Results: Here, respondents were given a scale ranging from 0 ("Let me out of here, a waste of time") to 10 ("I want more training"). This is how AMP scored:

- 6 to 10 = 55% of participants

- 5 (Middle) = 21% of participants

- 0 to 4 = 18% of participants

- No Rating = 6% of participants

Statistical Overview of the AMP Follow-Up Survey

Total number of high school participants: 421
Ages:

- 14–15 years old = 25%

- 16 years old = 24%

- 17 years old = 36%

- 18 years old = 15%

Grades:

- 12th graders = 31%
- 11th graders = 8%
- 10th graders = 9%
- 9th graders = 52%

Information Gathered from Survey

Even though the number of teens involved in this assessment is less than those participating in the AMP Feedback Survey, its results are helpful. This disparity is due to time constraints.

Survey Results

The responses below are those received most frequently. They may be effective in directing the work with other participants.

Question 1: Has knowing the causes of anger been helpful?

Results: These responses focused on specific anger management techniques:

- I think about the situation before acting.
- I know when I am faced with a situation, when it occurs, I hold anger in and let it pass.
- When my mom and I disagree, I leave, take deep breaths, and discuss it later.
- At home, I ignore my mom when she nags me.
- It made me think about different situations and what the consequences would be.

The second category of responses related directly to general as well as specific reasons for anger. These included:

- I realized what gets me angry and try to avoid it.

- Whenever I wanted to get or do something and heard the word *no,* I would really get annoyed. Now I calm down and deal with it better.

- I was very upset with situations in my family, and instead of withholding my thoughts, I revealed them.

- Knowing the causes of your anger helps you to deal with anger in a positive way rather than overreacting.

- By knowing how I react to certain things, I try to stay away from people who give me the wrong feeling and get me angry.

Question 2: Was knowing the effects of anger useful?

Results: Responses often included the use of anger management techniques. The following are among them:

- Think about the problem. Ask yourself, "Is it worth having a negative reaction?" The example given: "A person pushes you. You're not having a good day. Think if it is worth fighting because you can hurt them or get hurt yourself."

- I was mad at my best friend for something she had done. I thought of all the good times we had and just let it go.

- I knew when I get mad, I turn red. I try to remind myself to calm down and breathe.

- Anger can lead you to make many mistakes as well as hurt others. When I'm angry, I think of the effects of anger.

- I understand why we get mad and what physical effects, thoughts, and feelings I have, so I think before I do something.

The other group of responses to this part of the evaluation dealt with the general and specific effects of anger. These included:

- I might not want that negative outcome, so I avoid the situation.

- When I see my friend is quiet, I know he's upset about something.

- It makes me try not to get angry.

- When I get mad, I get hot and irritated and don't like the feeling. I try not to get upset. I start thinking mean thoughts, so I try to avoid anger.

- When I am angry, I am stressed out and lose weight. Now I try to think positively to prevent it from happening.

- Based on their physical appearance, I can tell if something is bothering another person.

- It made me realize all the danger people may face, based on how they act.

Question 3: Have you been able to use any of the anger management techniques?

This question had three parts: The first indicated which methods were used. The next identifies the other person involved in the situation. The last part indicated the result of using the particular tools. A list of the top-ten anger management techniques was provided, as well as a list of multiple methods used in tandem. Some of the young people indicated responses to all three parts, while others only noted the anger management techniques they used.

Top-ten anger management methods:

- "Is it worth it?" (also known as the light bulb/ buzzer anger management technique)
- Deep breathing
- Counting
- Walk away while saying something such as, "I need to calm down, and then we can talk."
- Think before acting or speaking
- Listening to music
- Writing (letter, poetry, anger journal)
- Talking to someone (close, who is not involved)
- Exercising (sports, walking, etc.)
- Staying calm (not yelling)

Techniques Used in Tandem

- Remain calm/"Is it worth it?"/Walk out/Slow, deep breathing/Counting
- Chant, "Ticktock"/Take a walk/Breathe
- Exercise (walk)/Deep breaths

These lists provide some of the most common methods adolescents used. Some of these tools will be repeated throughout the surveys.

The Nature of the Situations Described

There are two types of incidents to be described: The first category lists situations involving different relationships. The next grouping relates to more general types of events. All these will appear under the headings of specific anger management techniques.

Method: Deep breathing

Situation: Argument with my mom
Result: I calmed down.

Situation: Argument with siblings
Result: I was able to calm down.

Situation: Brother gets me angry.
Result: I was able to talk to him.

Situation: I was going to fight someone.
Result: I cooled down and walked in circles.

Situation: Arguments with my girl
Result: I got angrier. (Sometimes it doesn't work.)

Situation: My brother got on my nerves.
Result: I didn't get angry like I normally would.

Method: "Is it worth it?" (light bulb/buzzer)

Situation: Fight with brother
Result: I calmed down.
Thought: Now I bite my tongue more often and do my best not to do or say anything harmful I don't mean.
Result: I didn't yell at anyone.
Result: Everything discussed was done calmly and collectively.

Situation: Verbal fight with a friend
Result: I realized, after tensing, having a fight wasn't worth it.
Method: Walking away

Situation: I started an argument with my mom.
Result: I left, and later we spoke about the situation.

Situation: My friend and I had an argument.
Result: I walked away and let her calm down.

Situation: Argument with my boyfriend—I was mad and tried to explain, but it wasn't working.
Result: I calmed down and told him later that day everything was okay.

Situation: Argument with my mother
Result: This helped me.

Situation: Argument with a friend
Result: I felt better and apologized.

Situation: I was mad at my mom.
Result: Went to my aunt's house

Situation: I was arguing with my sister.
Result: Walked away and ignored her
Method: Talk it over with someone who is not involved

Situation: Fight with mom. Went to aunt's house.
Result: She calmed me down.
Situation: Boyfriend problems. Talked to my best friend.
Result: She calmed my anger down.
Method: Talking it out

Situation: Argument with sister
Result: Resolved anger

Situation: Fighting with parents/peers
Result: No one was hurt.

The participants' responses make these anger management techniques credible to peers. The situations described in this survey are common to teens. The way survey respondents managed these incidents may encourage others to use the same methods. The remark "Here's how other kids used this idea" may start the response ball rolling.

At this point, let them decide. Wait for a reaction, verbal or nonverbal, to decide whether or not to continue in this direction.

Varied Formats for Facilitating AMP

S ession differences are dictated by the length of time available and audience demographics.

Main Training Components

1. A greater understanding of the concept of anger
   management

2. The causes of anger (obvious and less apparent)

3. The effects of anger (physical, emotional, and psychological)

4. The anger management techniques used to de-escalate
   anger and those used to express it

5. The application of anger management techniques in
   anger-producing situations

6. A summary of the entire experience (feedback surveys)

Interactive Workshop Options

- Four-session workshops given to students in their subject classes

- Single-session, peer-facilitated seminars

- One-hour presentation to adult audiences

- Two (one and one-quarter hours) sessions to college students as part of a conflict-resolution course

- Two-hour workshop for college students

Program Preparation Checklist

When planning to use the Anger Management Power Program (AMP) concepts found in this book, it's important to create a plan. First, consider the presentation as a whole without getting into a specific agenda:

1. Write a list of chapters/pages on which you found the ideas, concepts, and anger management techniques you may use.

2. Make an outline of these key points.

3. Make further notes on how to best use this information.

4. Consider using a combination of anger management techniques to resolve conflicts.

The remaining plans deal with the specific presentation format, approaches to be used, and methods of gauging the effectiveness of the training.

The following represents the type of analysis needed to decide on how to appeal to your target audience—in this case teens—in the most effective way.

Will you deal with teens as a group?
- Small (2 to 10)

- Medium (11 or more)

- Unsure at this point

If you plan to work with individuals, how will you manage this?
- One-on-one

- Several individuals over a period of time.

Will you elect to work with a larger group during a set period of time?
- Lecture/seminar

- Discussion

- Part of another program—if so, decide which one(s)

- Combination of these

What tools or documents will be used during your presentation, and how will they be presented?

1. Anger scale
   - Chart (to be displayed in your facility or office)

   - Handout

   - Power Point presentation, whiteboard, or SMART Board.

<<Sidebar—*These may be used with the following tools as well.*>>

2. Visualization of anger (pictures, written descriptions)
   - Displayed in a particular room in the facility

   - Displayed in your office

- Other

3. Situation description recorder (similar to a suggestion box)—must include _what_ occurred, _who_ was involved, and _where_ it took place

   - Create situations to be discussed

   - Record the personal situations

   - Other

4. A list of most effective anger management techniques (minimize number)

   - Specific methods

   ◊ Hang in particular place(s) or office(s)

   ◊ Hand out

   - General list

   ◊ Hang in particular place(s) or office(s)

   ◊ Hand out

5. Other ideas not covered in this book

Based on the above particulars, now the overall design, flow, and evaluation of your specific presentation must be determined. Things to consider:

- Method of gauging the effectiveness of this training.

- Format of discussions to take place

- Individual participants

◊ Result of personal experiences or those witnessed

◊ Something revealed during a conversation

◊ Time to be allocated during the anger management training experience

- Group participants

◊ Result of member experiences or as witnesses of a conflict

◊ Time to be allocated during the anger management training experience

- Situations to be used as examples

◊ Visual: personally witnessed

◊ Auditory: heard from individuals involved or from witnesses

- Role-plays created for spontaneous follow-up

- Combination: (If so, which ones? Be specific.)

- Other ideas

The Anger Management Power Program (AMP)

Peer Workshops

Peer Workshop I

If a group of teens expresses an interest in developing a peer workshop, it is important to note the activities chosen by the adolescents who originally developed this format.

The time available for presenting this workshop must be considered when choosing the activities.

<<Sidebar — The information for each activity can be noted using a SMART Board, whiteboard, or chart paper.>>

1. What do you want to learn from AMP?

2. What does anger management mean? Here, teens can list two or three responses, or they can give the program's definition, which is "expressing anger without hurting yourself or others."

3. Anger scale is placed on the board. (Facilitators can choose the terms to be used for describing both extremes and briefly explain them.)

| 1 | 2 | 3 | 4 | 5 | 6 | 7 | 8 | 9 | 10 |

Anger is under control   *Anger is out of control*

4. What gets you angry? (Facilitators can use the top-ten causes of anger in teens list and the human anger scale exercise, both found in chapter one, for this portion of the program.)

5. Responses to question 4 are noted and placed on the anger scale.

6. What was the effect? A situation is described using any of the causes, and the "Is it worth it?" anger management technique is described using the A-B-C format below:

A—Anger Activator: The cause of the behavior
B—Behavior: A person's reaction when they became angry
C—Consequence: What happened after they reacted

7. From the causes placed on the anger scale, choose one to describe a situation. Adolescents can use the Situation Description Recorder (SDR) and outline it on a SMART Board.

8. Distribute an abbreviated list of methods the facilitators chose to present.

9. Explain the anger management techniques most often misunderstood—for example, the "I" statement, self-talk, anger journal, and look at yourself in the mirror methods.

10. Have audience members choose three techniques to use.

11. Choose two or three situations, from either the anger scale or the SDR, to either role-play or discuss. Have participants describe the techniques they would use in their particular situation.

12. What did you learn from this workshop?

Peer Workshop II

The following description of the workshop was written by teens exactly as it appears below.

1. One or more members of the team will display the following: "What do you want from this workshop?"

   Note the word *aim*. (*Goal* may be substituted in noneducational settings.)

   Indicate the term *anger managers*.

2. Introduce yourself and the peer-trainer team members.

3. "We are here to do a workshop with you on anger management as part of a program known as the Anger Management Power Program or AMP."

4. "What do you want to learn from this workshop?"

   Note two or three responses and indicate on SMART Board or chart.

5. "What is anger management?"

   Indicate two or three responses. Use whatever words exemplify to "express anger without hurting others or yourself."

6. "What do you think our goal is for today?"

   Note it as the "aim" and center it.

7. "What goes through your mind when you are angry?"

   If no response, pause then ask, "What thoughts or feelings do you have when you get angry?"

8. "What happens to your body when you get angry?"

   Note three or four responses.

9. "What can you do to relax yourself when your body reacts this way?"

10. "These are several anger management techniques." (chosen by the facilitators and noted)

11. Display the anger scale and explain its purpose.

1	2	3	4	5	6	7	8	9	10

Anger is under control   *Anger is out of control*

12. "What makes you really angry, and where would you put it (the cause) on the scale?"

Note three or four responses for each question.

13. Select one response and illustrate the A-B-C method.

    A = Anger Activator
    B = Behavior
    C = Consequence

14. "What is A in this situation?" Then "B?" Then "C?" (Note all responses.)

15. "What is the most important part of this anger management technique?"

C should be encouraged.

16. "What question might come to mind when using the A-B-C method?"

If not already indicated, add "Is it worth it?" to the list of techniques indicated by the facilitators.

17. Distribute or post a list of approximately 10–12 techniques chosen by the facilitators. From this list, ask the participants if any of these methods needed explanation. If no response, the following often require clarification: the "I" statement, self-talk and affirmations, anger journal, and look at yourself in the mirror.

18. "Choose three of these you are willing to try."

19. Role-play. (If no volunteers, try the alternative method.)

With volunteers, ask for a situation showing individuals getting angry, or have participants use the Situation Description Recorder (SDR) and describe a situation. Ask for volunteers to act it out. Direct actors to reach the point where they raise their voices (nothing physical).

Ask observers, "How could either one have managed their anger without the situation getting out of hand?" or "What techniques could have been used to calm this incident?"

Without volunteers, ask for a situation—for example, "What could be done to prevent both parties from allowing their angry to escalate?"

20. Summary: "What have you learned from this AMP workshop?"

Additional Resources for Parents/Guardians, Educators, Social Workers and Youth Workers

E ach state has its own resources. Generally, on the Internet, search for, *domestic violence, child abuse, suicide prevention,* and *substance abuse.* You can also refer to state agencies' and mental health associations' websites. In the case of someone in imminent or immediate danger, dial 911!

The following resources are helpful:

Child Abuse Prevention Network

National Child Abuse Hotline

National Domestic Violence Hotline

Suicide and Crisis Hotline

Substance Abuse and Addiction Hotline

Quick Tips for Keeping the Peace with Teens

1. **Speaking first makes things worse.**
   Hearing a teen out before responding prevents the reaction "You don't want to hear what I have to say; you only want to tell me what I did wrong."
2. **Raised voices mean fewer choices.**
   When an adult reacts to a teen's yelling by doing the same, it shuts down any chance of discovering the source of the problem and makes finding ways to resolve the situation impossible.
3. **Embarrassment leads to harassment.**
   When you embarrass a young person, you can bet on being verbally assaulted. If a criticism needs to be made, do it in private and without making a teen feel dumb.
4. **Ask and you shall accomplish a task; demand and things can get out of hand.**
   Frame what you want from a teen as a request rather than a demand or threat; then you'll have a better chance of getting a positive response.

5. **Helping a teen fulfill a need draws them closer to you and the deed.**

   For example, when a young person has a need for recognition, and you accept or ask for their opinion, they will see you as someone worth listening to and will be more likely to work with you.

6. **A compliment works like relationship cement.**

   Most teens are used to being told what they did wrong. Complimenting them takes their view of you and their relationship with you to a different level. "What? Someone actually sees when I do something right?" makes this point.

7. **Considering a teen's perception can give you a better reception.**

   "Wow, someone really listens to what I have to say!" sums up this point. It clears the way for you to be heard.

8. **Asking about a teen's desires will help prevent emotional fires.**

   When you enter into a conversation with an adolescent, ask what they want. Doing so prevents incorrect assumptions from being made and avoids the comment "How do you know what I want!" By not telling them how they think or feel, you provide them with the freedom to express what they want and the knowledge you respect them.

9. **Listen and ask to accomplish a major task.**

   This idea was illustrated during a conversation with a teen. Asking an adolescent if they want you to *just* listen to what they have to say, or offer your opinion, goes a long way. Adults often jump into a discussion with their view, while all the teen really needed was a chance to get something off their chest.

10. **It's not a teen's personality or physical description that should be prominent; it's how they act that should be dominant.**

When you deal with a teen, it's their behavior, not their looks or the type of person they are, that should be your focus. "You acted without thinking when you cut Mr. Brown's class" should be the comment, rather than saying "You're a sloppy dresser!" or "You are stupid."

11. **Speak to, not at, a teen, and they'll be more willing to chat.**

No one likes to feel as if they are being put down. When having a conversation, discussing their behavior, rather than judging it, encourages them to listen more attentively, rather than shut you out.

12. **Give a teen a chance to explain; chances are, your words won't be in vain.**

First, hear what a teen has to say. Then, they will be more open to listening to your thoughts.

13. **When a teen is misbehaving, provide them with an emotional safe haven.**

When a teen is upset, sometimes they need to go somewhere they feel they won't be scolded or judged. This is often in a counselor's or social worker's office, or even just their own bedroom.

Acknowledgments

First and foremost, I'd like to extend my gratitude to the teenagers, college students, parents, and professionals who participated in the Anger Management Power Program (AMP). Without their responses and suggestions, this program would not have evolved and become the inspiration for Peace: The Other Side of Anger.

I'd like to thank my life partner, Betty Litto, for her thoughts and suggestions, which made the second edition of this book more understandable and reader friendly. My gratitude also goes to Steve Levine, who has an MS in school and community psychology; his ideas in obtaining teen responses to the surveys and comments on their results were invaluable. In addition, I'd like to extend my sincere appreciation to our granddaughter, Isabele Lieber, for developing a simple way of providing youngsters access to and a method for completing the surveys that are an important part of this book. My sincere gratitude extends to the teens who took the time and expended the effort to respond to my questionnaires, providing their perceptions on the effects these topics have had on their lives.

Finally, my tremendous thanks also go to the members of my family, friends, colleagues, and students for their thoughts and support, which have so greatly influenced the writing of this version of *Peace: The Other Side of Anger.*

Endnotes

1 Report, *The Washington Post*, December 6, 2023.

2 News Conference, *ABC World News*, December 2022.

3 "Statistics on Gun Violence," Gun Violence Archive, https://www.gunviolencearchive.org.

4 "Youth Attitudes on Guns," Everytown for Gun Safety, Southern Poverty Law Center (SPLC), American University's Polarization and Extremism Research and Innovation Lab (PERIL), August 8, 2023.

5 Garbarino, J. et al., "Mitigating the Effects of Gun Violence on Children and Youth," *The Future of Children*, vol. 12.

6 Garbarino, J., "Perspective: The War-Zone Mentality—Mental Effects of Gun Violence in US Children and Adolescents," *The New England Journal of Medicine*, vol. 387, pp. 1149–1151, September 29, 2022.

7 McCarthy, C., "Gun Violence: A Long-Lasting Toll on Children and Teens," blog, http://www.health.harvard.edu, June 28, 2022.

[8] Black, B., "Anger and Social Media," https://www.mental-help.net/internet/social media-anger, December 28, 2022.

[9] Mayo Clinic, "Teens and Social Media Use: What's the Impact?" Healthy Lifestyle—Tween and Teen Health, February 26, 2022.

[10] Winans, J. et al., Childhood 2.0: The Living Experiment, https://ww.childhood2movie.com, 2020.

[11] Murthy, V., "US Surgeon General Social Media Advisory," 1440 News, May 24, 2023.

[12] Abenes, M., "Teens in America: How the COVID-19 Pandemic is Shaping the Next Generation," https://www.psychiatric-times.com, November 12, 2021.

[13] Allegrante, J. P., "What You Need to Know About the Pandemic's Lasting Effects on Adolescent Mental Health," https://www.tc.columbia.edu, April 11, 2023.

[14] Hussong, A., "The Impact of COVID-19 on Adolescents' Mental Health," an interview by Kim Spurr, College of Arts and Sciences, University of North Carolina, https://college.unc.edu, November 8, 2021.

[15] "ESSA," The US Department of Education, https://www.ed.gov/laws-and-policy/laws-preschool-grade-12-education/every-student-succeeds-act-essa, and/or your state's department of education website.

About the Author

Dave Wolffe earned his bachelor of arts degree and master's degree in education from Queens College. He has been an educator for over thirty-five years. He taught grades one through nine for most of his tenure with the New York City Board of Education and was a high school guidance counselor for the last thirteen years of his career. He served as an adjunct lecturer at John Jay College of Criminal Justice in New York City for thirteen years and taught a sociology of conflict course in the Dispute Resolution Program there.

    Dave Wolffe was certified as a peer mediation specialist from the International Center for Conflict Resolution of Columbia University Teachers College. While working as a high school counselor, this training enabled him to teach high school students to facilitate peer mediation sessions with other students. During this experience, he and many of these young people helped to establish, facilitate, and participate in schoolwide and boroughwide violence-prevention programs. In addition, he is a certified mediator; Westchester Mediation of Cluster, located in Yonkers, New York, granted him this credential. He is also a fellow in the National Anger Management Association (NAMA).

In addition, he developed an anger management program known as the Anger Management Power Program (AMP), on which this book is based. Dave has facilitated this training experience with over 1,000 high school students and well over 600 parents, educators, and other individuals who are concerned with youth in this area. He also established and has presented violence-prevention workshops based on this program for the New York City area's teacher education college programs, has worked with mediators in this area, and has created a facilitator-training method for this program.

Dave currently resides in Connecticut with his life partner.

Connect with Dave

Email: peacefulyouth422@yahoo.com

Website: peacefulauthor.org

Facebook: Dave Wolffe-Author

Instagram: peacemeister0618

LinkedIn: Dave Wolffe